PHILLIP'S CRUSADE

THE TRUE STORY OF THE CHILDRENS CRUSADE

CHARLIE BELL

SONSHIP
PRESS

Visit our web-site at: 21stcenturypress.com
                           and 21centurybooks.com

For childrens books visit: sonshippress.com
                           and sonshipbooks.com

2131 W. REPUBLIC RD.
PMB 41
SPRINGFIELD, MO 65807

DEDICATION

I would like to dedicate this book to my daughter Mary. I would get busy doing other projects for long periods of time but she would always push me to write more on the book. She often stood over my shoulder as I typed and watched as every word was being written. She laughed out loud; she cried; she even slugged me in the shoulder if she didn't like what I was writing.

Thank you, Mary, you were and are a great inspiration to me.

TABLE OF CONTENTS

Introduction 7

Chapter 1:   Children's Crusade 9

Chapter 2:   Lord William 21

Chapter 3:   Be Normal 39

Chapter 4:   The Boy Prophet 51

Chapter 5:   The Message 57

Chapter 6:   Madoc 71

Chapter 7:   Last Preparations 75

Chapter 8:   On the March 81

Chapter 9:   Troubles/No Troubles 91

Chapter 10: Cedric 99

Chapter 11 Finding a Way 109

Chapter 12: Finding Friends 119

Chapter 13: Mademoiselle Michelle 131

Chapter 14: Of Knights and Ladies 145

Chapter 15: Sir John 161

Chapter 16: Bitter Waters 177

Chapter 17: River Bend 189

Chapter 18: To the Sea 197

Chapter 19: Marseilles 203

Chapter 20: Moment of Truth 211

Chapter 21: Partings 229

Chapter 22: The Sea 239

Chapter 23: Storm 249

Chapter 24: Rescued for What? 259

Chapter 25: The Saracens 263

Chapter 26: To What End? 269

Chapter 27: Major Adjustments 281

Chapter 28: A New Master 289

Chapter 29: Any Justice? 297

Chapter 30: For the Sake of Christ 305

Epilogue: 315

Appendix: 317

INTRODUCTION

"It really is quite amazing," said my history teacher. My interest had already been peaked by the topic of the Crusades that we were studying at the time. What could be more amazing and yet disheartening than the misguided pride of the Crusades of the Middle Ages. Men from most parts of Europe had left their families and homes in order to follow the leaders of the Catholic Church and of the different countries in order to "take back the Holy Land" from the Moslems.

Many different crusades were attempted by the "Christian" Europeans and every one of them ended up leaving real Christianity with a spiritual "black eye." Not only did the Christians of the time misunderstand God's intentions for reaching the world with the "Good News" of the Bible but from then on, until now, the Moslems would misunderstand also. That misunderstanding has cost the lives .... and souls of countless thousands over the centuries.

"Let's look at the Children's Crusades," the teacher continued.

"Sounds interesting," I said to myself. Over the next hour I listened in unbelief as the teacher talked about the events that lead up to the Children's Crusades and then as he talked about the incredible events of the Crusades themselves.

After that day I determined to do more research on the Children's Crusades but was disappointed to find out that very little had ever been written on the subject. How could such a strange "quirk" in the history of man be so forgotten?

"Someone should write a book about this," I thought to myself. As is often the case, that is the first step in a person taking on the task for themselves. "Phillip's Crusade" is the final result of much research and thought about what "might" have happened during this extraordinary event.

The book tries to stay honest to the historical record as well as the time period. The Medieval times were a very interesting period of European history. The feudal system, the developing cities, and the growing trade between countries and continents made normal life more exciting. The roles of kings, knights, noblemen, and the working class were very well defined. The Pope and other religious leaders like bishops and priests held an amazing amount of influence over the people of Europe.

The final question that I had, while reading about the stories of the Children's Crusades, was a spiritual one. "What part did God actually have in all of this; if any?"

Though written history during the Middle Ages is very sparse, we know that Christ has been working through his people continually over the past 2000 years. We know that Christ can take strange and difficult events and still work in the hearts of individuals even when it seems impossible.

"Phillip's Crusade" will introduce you to characters that have wishes, desires, and needs just like ours. It will give you insight into how Christ works in the hearts and lives of individuals like us in all places of the world and in all times of history. Our journeys may take us down different paths. Our paths may be difficult and the roads ahead may be rough, but our God who, "is not willing that any should perish," will ultimately lead us "home," if we will follow Him.

1

PHILLIP'S CRUSADE

Phillip didn't sleep well that night. He was full of anticipation for the morrow and every little sound roused him slightly, keeping him from enjoying a deep sleep. Finally, the lone small window in his dormitory showed that the morning sky was turning slightly lighter.

It was time. If he didn't depart undiscovered now, he would never hear the end of it from John, Louis, and the other boys who served with him at the great Cathedral of St. Denis.[1] His humble attire would invite their ridicule.

He and his friends had often poked fun at the pathetic looking peasants and he wanted desperately to not have that same vain awareness cast his way. Still, he was looking forward to the adventure and thought it would be fun to get away from the humdrum chores and studies at the cathedral.

He felt odd stepping outside the church compound wearing unfamiliar simple serf's clothes.[2] He had gotten so used to his nicely woven one piece altar robe that he was horrified at the thought of being seen

---

1. The reconstruction of the Cathedral of St. Denis was the dream of Abbot Sugar, a Benedictine Monk. It was originally built from 486-751, rebuilt in 775 during the Carolingian era, and its final reconstruction dated from 1137-1144 AD and was built in the Gothic Style.
2. The serf occupied the lowest rung on the social ladder in the feudal system.

in the oddly sewn rags that his mother had dropped off for him a few weeks ago in anticipation of his return home.

An early start on his journey would also assure him of getting to his parent's home a good bit before dusk. It would be a full morning's walk to Paris and then it would take the afternoon hours to travel still further south to the Lands of Lord William.

Phillip took it all in as the streets of Paris were beginning to come alive with the sights and sounds of the day. Humble wooden wagons rattled along as serfs brought their goods to sell in one of the many open-air markets. There was an unusual air of hope in their manner. Maybe this year they could sell enough to not only pay what their lords required of them, but also buy a little more freedom.

Some servants were actually buying their freedom from the lords and able to focus completely on their own lands and crafts. Others serfs were able to own their own businesses and live as independents.

Two major events were happening to the feudal system that were causing nobles to find ways to raise money. Until this time they had just been paid in labor or perishable items their tenants were raising on their lots of land. Acquiring money for trade was enabling them to participate in the wars and crusades[1] by purchasing new and improved weapons and buying the services of professional mercenaries to fight with them.

Money also helped the nobles satisfy their developing taste for material goods that were being made by the different guilds as well as being imported from all parts of the world.

This was why it was so important for Phillip to get home and help his family with their harvest. A good year of crops meant that they would need all of the help they could get. After working the mandatory three days on the lands of Lord William they could turn their efforts

---

1. The word Crusade actually means "for the cross." The crusades themselves were a series of "holy wars" in which Europeans tried to recapture Jerusalem and the land of Jesus' earthly ministry from the Moslem Turks. The first Crusade was called by Pope Urban II to help the eastern Christians defend themselves against the Turks. The crusaders set out in 1095 and did succeed in recapturing Jerusalem. There followed at least seven other crusades, continuing into the thirteenth century, but the crusaders were never strong enough to maintain a lasting presence in the Holy Land.

to their own crops.

Down the dusty crowded streets the serfs plodded, wagons full of goods and heads full of dreams.

It was the year 1211 and Paris, France was one of the greatest commercial and cultural cities in all Europe. King Phillip Augustus had reigned supreme over France for over thirty years and the country was enjoying a measure of stability and prosperity unlike any in its history.

Pope Innocent III[1] had been the Pontifus Maximus[2] for 13 years and had proven himself to be extremely zealous and ambitious. He not only pushed for another crusade to be formed in order to take back the "Holy City"[3] from the heathen Saracens,[4] but he also implemented sweeping religious campaigns aimed at purifying France from the Albigensians and other independent Christian churches.

France itself was slowly beginning to break out of the rigid feudal system where the nobility ruled with an iron fist and the peasant masses were practically slaves to them.

Trade with other parts of the world was in full bloom and therefore industry was vital. Guilds were begun in order to protect the new middle class of journeymen who specialized in jewelry making, weaving, currying, embroidery, entertainment, and other trades.

Because of "business" there were many more transactions between

---

[1] Pope Innocent III was also known as Lotario di Segnior Lotario de' Conti. He was born Italian nobility; his family were the counts of Segni, Italy. Related to Pope Gregory IX and Pope Alexander IV. Nephew of Pope Clement III. Received his basic education in Rome, Italy, theological education in Paris, France, legal training in Bologna, Italy. Cardinal in 1190. Innocent brought the doctrine that since the spirit take preeminence over the body, and since the Church rules the spirit and earthly monarchs rule the body, earthly monarchs must be subject to the pope. Immediately upon election, he set out to make the pope an ecclesiastical ruler of the world with secular political power.

[2] Pontifus Maximus is Latin for High Priest and was a designation used for Roman Emperors and later for Catholic Popes

[3] Jerusalem

[4] One of the names for the Moslems of Northern Africa.

[5] The bourgeoisie were the middle class merchants of the day.

the nobles, petty nobility, guildsmen (bourgeoisie),[5] military, Church, and even peasants. Paris, like few other places in the world felt the impact of this new and exciting age.

On either side of the street, Phillip watched as the bourgeoisie opened up their merchant shops. What a sight they were! Even though he saw them often, Phillip could not help but pause along the way to look at the treasures from "all over the world" as many of the stores boasted.

Across the street at MONSIEUR HENRY'S, Phillip noticed a small mob of people gathering, so he shifted his sack of belongings to his right shoulder and trotted over to see what the commotion was about. He squeezed in behind a very short but stout middle-aged woman. Looking over her slightly knotted brown hair he read a freshly marked sign that said, "NEWLY ARRIVED MATERIAL AND CLOTHING FROM THE EAST."

What does it say?" asked one of the peasant bystanders.

"I don't know," said another, "but I'll bet that cloth and those clothes being displayed aren't from around here anywhere."

"No," said Phillip, "it says that it is material from the East."

The stout lady in front of Phillip turned and loudly muttered, "We'll probably have to wait till the richies model it around the city before the likes of any of us will see that material again." There was a muffled chuckle.

"That's the truth," another lady said. "Oh well, stuff like that isn't of any practical use anyway."

The people stared for a little while longer. "It sure is pretty though," the lady standing in front of Phillip said a little wistfully. Everyone nodded in agreement. Then the crowd slowly began to dissolve back into the busy streets.

Phillip waited until the crowd was gone and entered the shop. He walked over to the beautifully colored material and without touching it his eyes caressed the beautiful blues, reds, and purples. They were exotic colors and creative patterns. It was a far cry from the usual drab colors and coarse material that the commoners wore.

"Hey, what are you doing?!" yelled the young clerk from across the room. "Don't touch that!" As Phillip turned his head, the young clerk stopped. "Phillip?! What are you doing, dressed up like you just got off of a . . . a . . . ?"

"A barley wagon?" Phillip finished with a grin.

"Yes...what's the big idea?"

"Well Timothy," Phillip began grudgingly, "it's a short and simple story. You know my family works as indentured servants on Sir William's land, right?"

"Yes, but I thought they'd dumped you off on the Church a long time ago."

"Not exactly," Phillip said, leaning against a display stand. "Back then my family couldn't afford another mouth to feed. Rent was high and the year's crop didn't produce. 'Not enough rain,' they say. My father brought me here to Brother Andrew and asked if they would see if I was religious material. I don't know what all was said and done, but I guess Brother Andrew saw something he liked. Later he told me that many boys like me were turned away."

From a little room off of the main store a low raspy voice called out, "Timothy, Timothy! You need to finish bringing the furniture and trinkets from the store room." Phillip recognized the voice of Henry, Timothy's father.

"Just a minute father, I have to straighten out these two corner shelves that were knocked into this morning." Turning back to Phillip the slightly older Timothy whispered, "That will buy me a few more minutes. Now, go on."

"Well," continued Phillip, lowering his voice and drawing closer, "I see my father, mother, four brothers, and little sister every year when they come to the city to set up their stand at the open market. Once, about five years ago, I even went to their house."

"I get it," Timothy said knowingly, "it's family reunion time again."

"More than that. My father came by St. Denis about two weeks ago and asked Brother Andrew if I could spend the whole harvest season helping the family work. I think he even gave the Church a little money as a gift."

"A gift, you say?" Timothy winked mischievously, "I'll bet that 'gift' went right into Brother Andrew's pocket." His chubby face produced a half-cocked grin.

"Don't say such things," Phillip snapped back. "Brother Andrew is a good honest man. He is a man of the Church."

"Right, and the Barbarians are only poor misguided souls who 'accidentally' stumble cross the French border from time to time. Come on Phillip, everyone knows that the priests at St. Denis' take a little extra now and then so that their vows of poverty aren't so discouraging. I'm not saying that there is anything wrong with getting something for your services," Timothy added with a countenance of fake naiveté.

Phillip knew that what his friend was telling him was true. He had been around long enough to see it first hand. It didn't seem all that wrong though. People did offer it freely to the individual priests, but it wasn't supposed to happen, nonetheless.

"I've heard that it happens, but only a few bad ones do it. I'm sure, however, that Brother Andrew would not be one." Phillip said calmly. "The Church is trying to find out who the individuals are and put a stop to it promptly." He almost felt justified in saying it for the "Church's" sake.

"Timothy, give me a hand with this table," the raspy voice in the back said as it moved closer. "Phillip," the seasoned merchant said. "What in the world are you doing in that outfit?" Henry looked Phillip over curiously. "Well, never you mind," Henry said before Phillip had a chance to respond, "I'm glad you're here. Do me a favor and tell Brother Thomas that I'll be at Mass tomorrow morning and that I'd like to have a word with him about helping us finance the next shipment that comes in."

"I would, Monsieur, but I'm headed out of town and will be gone for a while," Phillip answered.

"That's all right boy, I'll just have Timothy run over there a little later, I'm sure he needs the exercise," the older man said looking at his over weight son.

Timothy ignored the slight and beamed, because the errand would afford him the chance to drop by Aragon's shop and see his daughter. "I'd be glad to father, and maybe while I'm out I can drop in and look around Aragon's to see if our prices are staying competitive," Timothy added.

Phillip threw his sack back over his shoulder and began to leave, "Say a prayer for me, if you have the time, Phillip," the senior shop-keeper said. "I can sure use a blessing today."

Back out on the street the dust was really beginning to kick up as Phillip headed for the northern gate of the city. A few people Phillip knew looked twice at him as he walked by. With a questioning look, they would wave a greeting at him. "I should have gotten out earlier," thought Phillip.

One more break before leaving town. He would stop by and have a quick visit with the widow Madam Christina. Phillip's stomach felt nervous as he arrived at the door.

"Why do you feel this way when you come here?" he asked himself. "I don't have anything to worry about," he told himself. He said a quick prayer, "Lord, help me feel the way I should."

The door opened and the butterflies jumped back into his stom-ach. "I thought that it was you standing out here Phillip," the beautiful Madam Christina said with a smile. "Please won't you come in?"

Without looking daunted at all, Phillip crossed the threshold and entered into the modest home. "Thank you very much. I just came to tell you that I won't be coming by for a while," he said trying to avoid a direct gaze into the widow's eyes. A tall majestic looking woman, the widow's kindness shown in her dark brown eyes and made her face glow with a beauty that was more than anything physical. Phillip could-n't help but be drawn to this lady who was twice his sixteen years.

It was only four months ago that Christina's husband had fallen ill and did not recover. A few months before his death, John and Christina were invited into the textile guild. Both of them were very skilled at their trade and investors were eager to put capital into the future of this young couple with so much potential. With John's death, everything was lost. Not only were their dreams crushed, but also the creditors demanded immediate payment of debts. Christina tried to keep her credit and hold on to the investments, but the guild was a little hesitant about standing fully behind a new member, and a widowed woman at that. All she had left were her house, her tools, and her daughter Anna.

Christina and John had been very faithful to the Church all of their lives. Their marriage was held there, their daughter was baptized there, they went to Mass at least once a week, and they gave on a consistent basis. Christina had told Phillip once that her husband had even wanted to become a priest but that his parents were set against it.

The priests at St. Denis' felt strongly about helping Christina in every way possible during her recovery from the loss of her husband and her business. Phillip had started visiting the widow's house since right after John's death, bringing food, money, or helping in whatever manner he could. His intelligence and common sense proved to be useful in helping with general things around the house and with their business. With the reputation and support of the cathedral behind Christina it would only be a matter of time before she got a new foothold in business.

As Phillip sat down, Christina asked, "Why are you dressed in those clothes, Phillip, if you don't mind me asking?"

"No, no, I don't mind you asking," Phillip said, shifting in his chair to a more comfortable position. He then began to recount the chain of events that were leading him out of town for the harvest season.

Anna sat by her window watching the sun's rays peek through the wooden slats as they randomly highlighted different parts of her room. She had always loved mornings. They seemed to wash away all of the past day's troubles. Lately, however, those once magical mornings had only brought days of grief for her and her mother.

"Father, father, father, today's my special day." The words came out painfully. "You promised me last year on my fourteenth birthday that this year would be special. You were going to make me the 'prettiest dress in the land.' You were going to take me to the fair and to all of the shops in town in order to show the nobles, 'the fairest princess in the Empire.' Father I love you. You know that I adore you. No, no, I hate you," Anna said, her face changing from an expression of sadness to one of anger. "You lied. Why did you lie? You hated liars." She buried her face in her hands and quietly wept.

"Lord, please help me make it through this day. I don't think I have the strength to see anyone. I don't want to see a smile or hear a laugh. I can't be happy. I just want to hide." With that simple prayer Anna remained quiet, her heart calming and breath slowing, "Amen."

Anna washed her face and began readying herself for the day. Outside in the hallway, she could hear her mother hurriedly walking around preparing for breakfast and probably getting her material and loom laid out for the day's work

"Anna."

"Coming Mother, I'll be ready as soon as I get my dress on."

"Don't bother," came her mother's reply.

Puzzled, Anna poked her head out of the door, "What did you ..." Anna's chin dropped. There stood her mother holding a beautiful light blue dress up to her own shoulders with a smile. "Mother," Anna said knowingly. "It's beautiful."

It was beautiful. The material was colorful but ordinary. However, the lace, stitching, and design transformed it into a work of art.

"Mother, but how could you have paid for it?" Anna said, reaching for the dress.

"Well, first of all, we've owned the material and lace for quite a while. Secondly, the dress was over halfway completed before I ever touched it. I worked on sewing up the hems and putting the finishing touches on it when you weren't around. Here, Anna, with love from your father and I. I hope you like it."

"Like it? It's wonderful! It's gorgeous!"

"Your father loved you so much, Anna. I'm sure that he is watching right now with anticipation. Now, go. Put it on for him.....and for me."

Anna threw her arms around her mother for a quick hug and then darted into her bedroom clutching the precious gift.

"By the way," Christina said to the closed door in front of her, "you might as well spend a few minutes and make yourself up a bit. You wouldn't want to be seen at the fair looking like you just got out of bed."

In her room Anna closed her eyes and whispered, "Lord, you are wonderful to me. Forgive my doubts. Oh, and please tell Father thank you for me. The dress is beautiful and I do love him."

A few minutes after Anna began putting her dress on, she thought she heard her mother talking to someone in the front room. "A man's voice," she thought. "Phillip," her heart leaped. It has to be him. Lord, this is indeed a perfect day.

Anna hurried to finish readying herself. She ran a comb through her hair, winked at herself in the mirror, opened the door, and walked out with grace.

"My, my," said the male voice, "is this little Anna? Young mademoiselle you are as radiant and beautiful as your mother, and your dress . . . " he said eyeing it carefully. "Your dress is masterfully done."

"Thank you kind monsieur," Anna said to the smartly dressed gentleman.

"Anna, I would like you to meet Mr. Geno. The man stood, took her hand, and nodded politely. "Mr. Geno is Lord William's head of household affairs, and an old acquaintance of your father."

"Yes, indeed," the older gentleman said through a smile. Then turning to Christina, he said, "I'll have the money for the material to you by Thursday. I'm sure his lordship will want to see your work as soon as possible. I'm sorry I can not take you up on your offer for breakfast, but I have much to do today here in town."

"Yes, of course," Christina said politely. Have a nice day." Mr. Geno gracefully stepped out of the door and walked to his waiting buggy.

"Mother, what did Mr. Geno want here?"

"Very good news. Very, very good news. The recent replacement for Lord William's tailor has not pleased him. Mr. Geno is in Paris to find another, and we are going to be given an opportunity to win the contract." Christine was bubbling. "Finally a chance." She stopped as if snapping out of a trance. "What are we doing wasting precious time? I'll tell you the details on the way to the fair. If you'll put your shoes on and get my things, I'll put our breakfast in a bag to take along with us."

Anna rushed into her room, put her shoes on, and then spent a few more minutes at the mirror. She then went into her mother's room and began collecting a few things. She picked out a broach that her mother liked and that would go nicely with her dress. "What else?" she thought, "Oh yes. That off white shawl would go nicely also.

Mother only wore it on special occasions and this was special. Anna searched the dressers and all through the closet but could not find it. Then the thought struck her. "Madame Josephine always liked that shawl. I wonder. . . ?" "Mother," Anna called walking towards the front room. "Your shawl, did you sell your shawl?"

Phillip was almost finished telling Christina about his departure when Anna came walking in. Phillip stood to greet her out of habit, and then he really saw her. "Anna," Phillip said, searching his mind for the right words to say. "You look very . . . . nice." It was far from adequate but it was all that came out. Without meaning to, his eyes quickly scanned Anna's figure. The dress made her look very mature.

Anna stood with flushed cheeks. She tried to regain her composure a bit. "And you," she said looking into Phillip's face and trying to return the compliment, "you look nice too."

Christina looked over at Anna. Then Anna took a good look at the ill-fitting rags that hung on Phillip's lanky body. Christina chuckled but Anna covered her face with her hands in embarrassment.

"I'm sorry," Christina tried to say while still laughing.

"That's quite all right," Phillip laughed along.

Anna wanted to cry out of embarrassment but a muffled laughter came out instead. The awkwardness of the situation soon vanished.

"Happy Birthday, Anna," Phillip said. "From what your mother has said, it is a good thing I came by early, otherwise I would have missed you." Anna smiled her thanks.

"Do you think you could spare a few hours to escort a couple of lonely unprotected damsels around the fair, Phillip?" Christina asked.

"Oh, yes that would be nice, Phillip," Anna added enthusiastically. Phillip was already shaking his head.

"I wouldn't dream of appearing with the two of you dressed like this unless I was carrying your things and walking ten feet behind you. Besides, if I don't get going now, I won't get to my parents house until after dark. I'll tell you what, though," Phillip said smiling, "I did intend to leave a blessing with you. Come and let us pray." Phillip raised his hands placing them close to the forehead of Christina and Anna.

"Precious Mary, mother of our God, please hear our prayers and intercede for us before the Father. Bless Madame Christina and Anna during their time of need, and bring customers here in order for them to rebuild their business. Especially bless Anna today on her birthday. Let her enjoy it in your protection and love. Amen."

2

LORD WILLIAM

The afternoon sun was beating down upon Phillip's head when he spotted a small clump of trees up ahead and to the right of the road about 150 yards. The day was hot and dry and a fine powdery dust covered him from head to toe. "A quick dip in that pond sure would be refreshing," he thought. By the time he got right up on the pond he had convinced himself that the cool pond water would be just what he needed to be refreshed and ready for the rest of the trip.

Phillip took a thorough look around to make sure that no one was in sight and then he shed his clothes and laid them on a rock next to the pond. The high bushes would shield him from being seen by anyone. Dipping his left foot into the water he jerked it out quickly and shivered. "Oh well, here goes nothing," he muttered under his breath. He leaped as far out as he could. "Splash!" He rose to the surface and sucked in air. It was cold but perfect.

After a few minutes of swimming around, Phillip found a rock that he could stand on and still be up to his neck in water. He stood there, slowly moving his arms so as to keep his balance. He let his mind wander back to the late night swims he and his friends often took in the man-made ponds at the cathedral. A smile grew on his face.

"Are you crazy, Louis? They'll hear us for sure."

"Trust me. I've done it dozens of times. Follow me and we'll be able to get through the halls and out the side door without raising so much as an eyebrow." Louis was right. That night's swimming lesson went without a hitch, and in the years that passed, Phillip found the late night "lessons", as they became called, to be therapeutic. Somehow the physical exertion along with the slight deception involved was a release from the strict daily routine the priests imposed upon him at the cathedral.

This swim in the country pond was having the same relaxing effect. Snap. Phillip jerked his head around only in time to see the bushes behind him moving. "Hey, who's there?" he asked. About that time Phillip noticed that his clothes and bag were gone. "Come on. Bring my things back. I don't have anything that's worth putting your soul in jeopardy for." No response.

Convinced that the thief had slipped away, Phillip slowly waded toward the shoreline, wondering what he was going to do. "Maybe the thief will have looked through his belongings and discarded them after finding nothing." It was his only hope. Phillip climbed out of the water and began to search through the bushes where he had heard the rustling.

Just as Phillip was about to reach into the bush in front of him, a sudden noise came from behind. Before he could turn around, CRACK! Everything went dark.

"I still say we should not have gotten involved, Thad. We don't even know this boy or have any idea who he belongs to," said the young lady sitting on the passenger side of the wagon bench.

"Whoever he is, we couldn't have just left him floating in that pond. Surely he deserves a Christian burial," said the young man beside her as they bumped along in an ox driven cart.

"How do you know that? He's probably a common thief or something worse," said the young woman as she tried to calm her crying baby. "We know everybody from around here, and this boy is definitely not from one of Lord William's." The wagon bumped on.

"Do you think he is nobility?" asked Thad.

"Why would you say that?" his wife asked.

"Well, Mara, the boy looks healthy and strong enough but his skin is almost white and his hands don't have any calluses. I'll bet he's not worked a day in the fields in his life."

"Now that you mention it," said Mara, "he just might be nobility."

A burst of coughing and hacking came from the back of the wagon. The young man tugged on the reins until the ox came to a halt. He and his wife turned in their seats and watched, speechless, as the blanket they had laid over the back of the wagon moved in quick convulsive motions. Thomas jumped off of the buckboard and rushed around to the back. Flipping the covers back half way, he uncovered a half naked boy unconsciously twisting and turning as water was spewing out of his mouth with every cough.

"Quick Mara, come back here and help me. It looks like the Good Lord might want to spare the boy."

A few minutes passed, the coughing subsided and the boy lay half conscious shivering in the hot sun. "Thad, I don't think he is going to snap out of it. Let's take him up to the Castle Velva and see what Lord William wants done with him." The young couple climbed back up onto the backboard and headed their cart to the East.

The fair was not very far from Christina and Anna's house, but they wasted no time in getting there. Anna felt like everyone was looking at her and, in truth, they were. She and her mother were pretty women but the fine workmanship with which their clothes were created, made them look anything but common. Christina used to feel odd about wearing nicer clothes than other common people, but her husband assured her that the clothes were good advertisement. It didn't bother her any more that people watched them. In fact it made her feel special.

"Mother, look at all of the merchandise." Anna was wide eyed as she stopped and looked down the broad street that housed the tables of goods that people were selling. As far as the eye could see, there were merchants and people weaving in and out of tables and carts. Christina reached over and put her hand into Anna's. Together they walked right into the middle of the chaos.

"Come quickly. I think he's coming out of it," were the first words Phillip heard. He opened and closed his eyes rapidly trying to bring the contents of the room into focus. There was a dull throbbing in his head that turned into a sharp pain when he tried to sit up. Phillip was disoriented and afraid.

A strong hand wrapped itself around Phillip's left wrist restraining him. Immediately Phillip remembered the swimming hole and the rustle in the bushes behind him. He tried to jerk his arm away but found that the grip of his keeper was unyielding.

"Hold it, Boy. I'm not going to hurt you." Phillip was then pinned back onto the bed. "Look at me. Stop struggling and just look at me."

Phillip really didn't have a choice, so he stopped, and focused his eyes on the person leaning over him. He was a big, rough looking, middle-aged man. His beard was full and burly. It would have been a frightening sight if a big grin hadn't been on the man's face. "That's better," the man said.

"Who are you, and where am I?" Phillip asked.

"Who am I?" the man said, "The question is. Who are you? Boy, you've been lying in that bed for the better part of three days now, just moaning and groaning. You have the whole place shook up."

"Three days! Oh no! I've got to go!" Phillip exclaimed trying to get up. As soon as he started to rise, the pain came pounding back to his head. "Ouch!" He exclaimed as he dropped back on the bed.

"I don't think you'll be going anywhere for a few days. Besides I think Lord William will be coming to see you pretty soon."

"Lord William? Why would he want to come and see me?"

"After all this is his castle, you know." The burly man said with a grin. "It was his idea to keep you here until we found out to whom you belonged."

"Lord William," Phillip mumbled in disbelief. "And who might you be, Monsieur?" he asked the man.

"I am the keeper of the house."

"So you're up, Boy. Well I'm glad to see it," interrupted a man just stepping into the room. "Joseph, go get the doctor and tell him that the boy is awake. Ask him to come as soon as possible," the newly arrived man said to the keeper of the house.

"Right away, my Lord," Joseph replied respectfully. Joseph lumbered out the door and vanished down the hall.

Phillip recognized the man who had just come in as Lord William. He had seen him many times in Paris, but only from a distance. Even though his clothes were a bit worn and dusty, they were made with nice material and in a fashion that was only reserved for people of great importance.

"Boy, who in heaven's name are you, and what were you doing in this part of the country? We've asked every serf and noble that has come through here in the past three days, but no one has had a clue."

"Well, sir . . . . ," started Phillip.

"Now don't think that I really care boy. It's just that I feel a little responsible for those who come into my land," Lord William interrupted.

By this time a young pretty girl slipped into the back of the room and was listening to the conversation.

Phillip hardly had time to notice because he was busy trying to tell Lord William who he was. "Well sir, I really don't live around here but . . . "

"I knew it." Lord William piped in again. "I told Joseph that if you were from around here I'd know who you were." He leaned close to Phillip, squinted one eye, and asked roughly, "Are you one of those roving bandits? Tell the truth now, Boy. I'll find out anyway."

"Yes sir, I mean no sir. If you'll just give me a minute I'll try to explain."

"You'd better have a good explanation son. After all, you have a lot of . . . . "

"Father." The girl in the back of the room interrupted. "I imagine if you'd just give him half a chance, he'd be more than glad to tell you his story. Besides, he doesn't look like the criminal type to me," she said, looking Phillip over and smiling.

For the first time Phillip realized that he was laying there half naked. He covered himself with the blanket on the bed and returned his attention to Lord William, "Yes sir, that is my intention."

Lord William pulled a nearby chair up and sat in it. "All right boy, this mystery has gone on long enough. Give it to me straight, and don't leave out any details. I like a good story as much as the next man. Maybe more."

Phillip started from the beginning. "My family is from here, Sir, but I live in Paris. You see, many years ago . . ." Phillip told his story all the way up to the point of walking to the pond because many people felt that swimming was a bad omen. He said that he was wading in the pond when he was attacked from behind. "...and after that, everything that I remember is like a nightmare."

"A nightmare?" Lord William said leaning over as if to hear a secret told by a special informant. "What do you mean boy?" Lord William was extremely superstitious. Dreams and nightmares were of special interest to him.

"Well sir, I don't mean real nightmares. I mean that the few memories that I had were very confusing and accompanied by a lot of pain."

"Never you mind then," the lord said straightening up. "I think that this mystery is pretty clear now," he said disappointedly. "Young man, you will stay here and rest until you are able to leave. The chancellor will make sure that you are taken care of." Then he spoke as if to himself, "Why do I do this for the son of common laeti[1]?" He pondered the question as he arose slowly. "Ha!" he belted out with a chuckle, "what the heck! The world is changing after all."

As he turned to leave, Phillip said, "Sir, if you don't mind?"

"Yes, Boy, what is it?"

"My parents, Sir, they must be wondering where I am."

"Of course. They will be told. I'll send someone to inform them." William left the room with his daughter trailing behind.

When the room had finally cleared and Phillip was left alone, he collapsed back onto his pillow. What a headache.

The nightmare came back to Phillip's conscience. He shuttered. "Maybe that's what it would be like to die," he thought. The pain and fear were so real. He tried to push it out of his mind. He didn't want to die.

---

[1] The laeti were those landworkers that we might think of as "tenant farmers ." They were allowed to live and work the land in exchange for their loyalty and tributes.

"Thank you very much. This is more than adequate Sir." Phillip was sitting before the servants table with a large, highly decorated stone plate filled with food. It was obvious that this year's crops had fared well, but Phillip was a little confused as to the meaning of the special treatment.

Lord William was sitting nearby in a chair against the wall watching as Phillip timidly began to eat. "I'm sure you are wondering what in heaven's name is going on," Lord William said with a curios grin.

"Well Sir, I do sort of feel like a calf being fattened up for the slaughter," Phillip said with half a grin as he dipped down with his fork for another stab at the pheasant on the plate. Over the last week, he learned that the general attitude of the castle was one of levity and very little formalities.

"Harrumph," William laughed deeply. "Joseph, the boy has a sense of humor. I think he will do quite well."

"Yes sir," the husky chancellor said.

"Eat Boy. I never like to talk business to a man who has an empty stomach. Can't think right." With that, Lord William got up and exited the room through a highly arched doorway that led to the main dining room. The Chancellor stayed with Phillip but didn't say anything.

Phillip slowed his eating pace a little and glanced around the room in order to keep his eyes busy while his mind had a chance to guess at what Lord William was scheming. This room was not different than any other room in the castle, as far as basic design went. The walls were made out of large stone blocks that kept the rooms cool and a bit dim. The large outside windows made the place breezy when the heavy wooden shudders were pulled aside. On the bottom floor, hardened clay covered most of the floors, while especially made clay bricks covered the floors of the most important rooms. Straw along with a smattering of flower pedals and herbs were strung across all floors in order to keep the place clean and smelling fresh.

Every room had its own decor and furnishing. This particular room was very plain as far as decor went. Phillip noticed a large crack in the stone wall above the window. With his eyes now transfixed on a single object, his mind went to work.

"Business?" Phillip thought. "What kind of business could Lord William possibly have with me?" Then it hit him, "The Church, of course! That's it. They have some sort of business with the Church." Having figured it out, Phillip ate the remainder of his meal with a renewed vigor.

"Boy, I mean Phillip," Lord William began when he returned, "I am a man that is very plain about what he wants. This business that I want to discuss with you, well . . . .well," he paused.

"Yes sir, about that business. I owe you so much. I am willing to do what you ask, but I should have been at my parent's house over a week ago. If I go all the way back to St. Denis I will most certainly be another two or three days tardy. Truly sir, if you wish me to take your message back to the Church, I am compelled to, but surely there would be somebody else that is going that way," Phillip rattled off.

Lord William sat there for a minute with a puzzled look on his face before bellowing out, "What in blue blazes are you talking about?! I don't want you to be an errand boy, I want you to stay on with me for a while here and help with my bookkeeping during the harvest. I've inquired about you at St. Denis's and they have informed me that you are a good-tempered lad with the talent of numbers as well as other things. I think that the pay we will give you would be considered generous for a boy of your age." With that Lord William stared hard at Phillip.

"Well sir, I, I . . . . "

"You what? You'll take it and be glad of it, that's what," William said.

"Yes sir, I will. But . . . . . what about my father's crops, Sir? It will make him short of help," Phillip said apologetically.

"What does it matter to you if they are short or not? From what I understand, you don't even really know your father very well. I do, and let me tell you, he does not deserve your loyalties. I know my people, and I know that your father is just plain lazy. I suspect that he has sent for you because he realizes that he might actually have to do some hard work in order to get those crops in. Are you listening to me? You will only be used and sent back when your work is done." With that Lord

William stopped, sighed, and looking at the distraught look on Phillips face concluded, "I guess I have given you a choice though, haven't I?"

"Yes sir," Phillip mumbled knowing in his heart what his answer must be. As he was about to answer, he perked up as if just given good news and answered, "Sir, I will indeed work with you here, but my wages will go towards my family's credit. That is if you agree, of course."

"Hmm," Lord William began. "It will be as you propose. Joseph, make note."

"Yes sir," Joseph replied.

"Phillip, you may leave the room now. Go to Geno and he will make arrangements for your stay."

"Yes Sir, thank you, Sir," Phillip said as he got up and walked crisply out of the room.

"Joseph, I like the boy. Why is that?" Lord William asked, turning to his chancellor.

"Yes Sir. There is something about him, isn't there." Joseph replied gazing at the door.

"He has loyalty. A little confused, but he does have loyalty. There is more too."

"It's been a long day Phillip. Close the books up and do be quick about it."

"Right away Mr. Bernard," Phillip replied, making a last notation and putting his pen down next to the book. Phillip then busily straightened up without talking. Mr. Bernard did not like people to talk while they were working. That was all right with Phillip though, because he didn't feel very comfortable around Mr. Bernard anyway.

Mr. Bernard was Jewish, and this alone made Phillip nervous, not to mention the fact that he also was very cooly professional. Phillip had worked for him for over a month now and no conversation, other than business talk, had passed between them.

Phillip paused a little while he was tidying up and looked over at the handsome, middle-aged man that made him feel so uneasy. He didn't look any different than anybody else, on the outside. "I believe we're set Mr. Bernard."

Giving the place the once over, Mr. Bernard simply replied, "Bright and early young man."

It was only a few minutes walk to Phillip's room. He stayed in the servant's quarters that were right across a thin alley from the main castle. As Phillip approached his abode, he spotted a hooded figure standing in the shadows across the alley from his room. "Mademoiselle Michelle?" Phillip half whispered, "Is that you?"

"Yes," the figure whispered back, "Come with me," and then she briskly walked through the alley. Phillip followed. Coming to a small door at the west end of the castle, the figure opened the unlocked door and walked in. Again, Phillip followed without hesitation.

Inside, a lamp had already been lit, giving the small room its only light. A quick glance around revealed a small room with no windows and no other doors.

"Phillip, I had to talk to you alone," the figure said, pulling its hood down. There stood the very attractive daughter of Lord William clothed in a full-length robe.

"Mademoiselle Michelle, I can't be here alone with you."

" I understand your concern, but this is so very important, and I felt that you care in matters such as this."

"Matters such as what, Mademoiselle?" Phillip asked politely, "and how could I possibly help more than your father's own priest?"

"I need an objective voice, and Father Archer would never say anything that my Father might not agree with. I already know what he would say," Michelle said moving closer to Phillip.

"Can we not talk about this in a more public area?" Phillip suggested as he took a half step back.

"No," Michelle said in a whisper, "Father would not like me talking to someone as yourself about such matters, and in the few times that we have spoken, I could tell that you would understand my feelings." As she finished the sentence, she picked up Phillips left hand and cupped it in both of hers.

Phillip's heart raced with confusion and emotion. "All right, this situation that you are facing, what exactly is it?" he asked with as much of a businesslike tone as he could muster.

Still holding Phillip's hand, Michelle sat on the armrest of a large chair and began. "It is really quite simple, Phillip. My father and Lord Jacques have never really gotten along. I believe it started with their fathers. Anyway, they have been cooking up some sort of business deal to increase their profits off of their lands. Actually, I know nothing of land deals or household affairs, but I do know this. Somehow, during their dealings I became part of the bargain." With an intense look into Phillip's eyes she continued, "In two months, on my seventeenth birthday, I am to be wed to Lord Jacques." Phillip did not respond, but took a minute to think. This was not shocking news. Many people knew of the situation including him. This sort of arranged marriage took place all of the time in order to not only keep royalty in the bloodline but also to make a bond between two royal families. Finally, Phillip responded. "I am sorry, but I do no quite understand the problem."

"The problem is," Michelle began as she stood back up, putting her face only a foot from Phillip's, "I do not want to be given to some crusty old man who has not spoken two words to me since I was a child." Emotion was welling in her and her whispers were more intense with every word. "Phillip, I want a man to caress me with love, not maul me with the hands of a beast." When she had finished, her moist brown eyes stared passionately into Phillip's.

Phillip could say nothing and knew that he did not have to. No sensible thoughts came to rest in his mind and yet it seemed that a thousand thoughts passed through in a second of time. Finally, he whispered the words back to Michelle, "What can I do?"

Michelle said nothing but slowly lifted Phillip's hand up to her face and stroked her cheek with the backside of his hand. Phillip took a half step forward completely closing the gap between him and Michelle and then gently ran his hand across Michelle's cheek. Michelle closed her eyes and moved her lips toward Phillip's. He couldn't resist. He didn't want to.

A minute later, or two, or maybe ten, Phillip lifted his head up and looked at the ceiling. While taking a few deep breaths, he embraced

Michelle tightly.

Then, for the first time, a clear thought came to Phillip. "What am I doing?" This newly found presence of mind shook him back into reality.

Putting his hands on Michelle's shoulders he again put space between his body and hers. Michelle looked up at Phillip with a puzzled look. "Mademoiselle Michelle, I must leave now. Obviously, I am of no use to you in this matter." Phillip took his trembling hands off of Michelle and reached for the door.

As he began to swing the door open, he stopped and looked back into the dim room. Michelle appeared more irresistible than before. Phillip thought that he would surely leap back into the room and take her back in his arms more vigorously than ever. However, he found himself instead, outside walking briskly through the evening air towards his lodging place.

During the next couple of days, Bernard noticed an intense internal struggle going on inside of Phillip. His work had slowed and his usually cheerful countenance had been traded for constant look of concern. Also, when he would turn and look, Phillip would be muttering to himself as if in an argument. Finally, Bernard could not stand it any longer. "Young man, may I speak with you for a moment after work today."

Looking surprised, Phillip looked up and replied, "Yes, of course Mr. Bernard." At this, Phillip looked more worried than before.

Mr. Bernard stopped what he was doing and said, "Young Phillip, things are beginning to slow a bit. Why don't we quit a little early? Come over here and be seated please." As soon as Phillip was sitting down, Mr. Bernard also sat down.

"I have seven children, young Phillip, and I have learned to recognize when they are bothered by something. You are obviously wrestling with a matter." Phillip looked down at the floor. "Not that I should be overly concerned with your problems, but you are a good worker and your work output has been dropping off the past couple of days," he added.

Phillip looked back up at his boss. "I am so very sorry," he said. "I promise that I will do better. If you allow me to finish out my term, I will work harder than ever."

"Hold on there young Phillip. I don't want to get rid of you. I want . . . . . well, from what I understand, you have never really had a father, have you?"

"No, I have been raised by the priests of St. Denis most of my life."

"As you know, Phillip, I am not one to pry into another man's affairs, but I will make an exception in this case. Young men of your age run into situations that require the advice of a father. Phillip, I am offering my fatherly advise to you. If you don't want it, just tell me, and I will not bring it up again."

"But Mr. Bernard, how could you help me? I mean . . . well . . . you know, we're different."

"Don't worry young man, I was young once myself."

"Yes, but I mean . . . well . . . you are Jewish," Phillip finally spit out.

"Oh, I understand, this is of a religious matter then."

"Not directly, it's more about a girl, but we still think differently, don't we?"

"Not so different, I think," Mr. Bernard said finally realizing Phillip's real problem with opening up to him. "Phillip, I want you to go home now but think on this. Was this Jesus that you call Christ raised in a good home? What about most of the other leaders of your religion written about in your New Testament? Before you answer, just remember that they were all raised in Jewish homes. I will not bring this up again." With this Mr. Bernard got up and finished putting things away.

Phillip also got up and finished organizing things for the next days work. When he left work, he had more to think about than when he came.

It was dusk as he reached the door of his abode. The walk from work did not give him the time he wanted to think, so instead of entering in, he continued to walk down the alley. Before he realized it, he was right upon the little room that Michelle had led him to three nights before. It surprised him as if the room had sneaked up on him. He stood there with his heart racing. Some of the same emotions he had felt came rushing back, but before he stood there long he heard the handle of the door jiggle as if someone were about to open it from the inside.

Phillip jotted into the shadow of a corner and stood still, holding his breath. Phillip thought to himself, "What am I doing? What am I hiding for?" He still didn't move.

He watched as the door opened and a handsome young man stepped out. Phillip recognized him as one of Lord William's permanent guards. However, he was not in uniform now. The young soldier then quickly disappeared down the dark alley.

Phillip was about to turn and walk home when he heard the door handle of the heavy little door begin to jiggle again. Again Phillip remained in the shadows.

He was dumbstruck when a small hooded figure stepped over the threshold carefully closing the door behind it.

"Mademoiselle," Phillip gasped appearing from the shadows.

As soon as her name was mentioned, Michelle whirled around and looked astonished at Phillip. "Phillip, what are you doing here?"

Regaining a little of his composure, Phillip answered, "I was just walking and thinking."

"Do you always walk in the shadows?" Michelle said, as if she was thinking out loud. Phillip didn't say anything. As he watched, Michelle suddenly straightened up her shoulders and stared right through him. "Phillip, you were spying on me for my father, weren't you?"

"Of course I wasn't, I would never . . ."

"Oh, Phillip, how could you?" Michelle said as tears welled up in her eyes.

"No Mademoiselle," Phillip began, but before he could say more, Michelle turned and began to run away. Phillip began to follow and almost called out loud but he caught himself. It would be foolish to draw attention to the situation. Phillip stopped and watched as Michelle disappeared around a nearby corner.

The next day at work Phillip didn't wait until time to stop work before he struck up a conversation with Bernard. "Bernard," Phillip began as he looked up from his books, "may I talk with you a bit as we work? I promise that I will not get behind."

Bernard smiled. "I was wondering when it would come out boy. You look more troubled today than yesterday. Then, go on with it."

Phillip had been thinking of how he would word his questions without bringing up Michelle's name. "It's about a girl here in the area."

"A girl? Here you are only in the area for a short time and you already have girl problems?" As soon as Bernard noticed Phillip turn a little red, he go a serious look on his face and said, "I'm sorry, go on. I do know a bit about the many and varied problems that come along with a female."

"There is a young mademoiselle here that led on like she really cared for me. She warmed up to me very quickly, and expressed her care for me while we were in a private place. I was taken back by her openness, and I fled," Phillip said with his head down avoiding the eyes of Bernard. After saying this he paused as if he had more to say but did not know how to say it.

"Stop work for a moment and sit over here," Bernard said realizing how much this troubled Phillip. "We are ahead of schedule anyway so lets take a break." As soon as Phillip sat down, Bernard pulled a small three- legged stool up next to Phillip's chair and replied, "You don't have to tell me all that is happening young Phillip. Tell me what you wish and I will help if I can."

Phillip put his elbows on his knees and looked up at Bernard. "I don't think I should say more."

"That is fine, but may I ask you a few questions?" Bernard asked.

"Of course," Phillip said straightening up.

"Did you know this young mademoiselle from before?"

"No, not really."

"Don't you feel that she expressed her feelings for you a little boldly?"

"That's exactly how I felt," Phillip said intently.

"But you are not as bothered by her feelings for you as you are about your own feelings," Bernard said calmly.

"That was the case, but now its more complicated than that."

"More complicated?" Bernard asked more as a comment than a question.

Forgetting what he said about not saying more, Phillip continued, "Yes. I came to the conclusion that I had left at the right time, but it did not mean that I didn't care for her. I had decided to talk to the young mademoiselle again but in a less threatening place, but that very day I found her to be with another young man. Why would she do this?"

Bernard's eyebrows went up. "Young man, it sounds to me like it is this young mademoiselle that has a problem, not you. I'd say that there are two good possible answers to her problem. As you grow you will find that some ladies are in love with the idea of romance and love, and if you fall in love with one like this you will of all men be most miserable. The other possibility is that this young mademoiselle is running from something or everything and you are her escape."

Phillip slowly looked up into Bernard's eyes and without saying a word acknowledged his perceptiveness. "Thank you," he said still thinking about what was said. Both of them went back to work and the matter was never brought up again.

During the last three days that Phillip worked with Bernard they carried on an ongoing conversation about many things. They even talked for hours about Jesus, the one the Christians claimed to be the Messiah. Phillip was surprised that Bernard was so open about the topic, but was excited about being able to give a witness. Bernard was very knowledgeable about the Old Testament and obviously a pretty religious man himself. When their last day was done and the books were closed, Phillip was a little disappointed that Bernard seemed to be as adamant against Jesus as the Christ as when they had first talked about it. Maybe someday he would have another chance to talk to his friend of this matter.

"Well young Phillip," Bernard began, "you have done well here and learned quickly. I have given a good report to Sir William about your services, and maybe in the future you will come again. Here take this," Bernard said handing a small pouch.

Hearing the coins rattle as it was handed to him, Phillip put up his hands and said, "It was to be understood that all of my wages were to go to my family."

"It was understood, but Sir William wanted you to have this gift. I think you amused him."

Phillip accepted the gift, with wide eyes. He had never really had any money of his own. Even though it wasn't a great deal of money, Phillip's mind began to dream up all of the things that he could buy with it.

Home? The church was Phillip's home. He knew that the church would never be the same to him now that he had spent this time away and learned so much about the world outside of the cathedral walls.

Phillip road back to Paris with a young serf named Leo who was in the service of Lord William as a supplier. Even though Phillip usually enjoyed meeting and talking to new people, he didn't talk much to Leo, instead he studied everything around him as they bounced along. The trees had almost shed all of their leaves and the grass looked cold and hard. The ponds and lakes didn't look as inviting as they did back when Phillip was first coming into the area.

It was the people that they passed that he was really interested in. There was no hope in their eyes as they and their wagons were mostly empty. Phillip felt for these people. "These poor hopeless people." Their clothes seemed a little more ragged and their mules and oxen appeared older and more worn. Then he wondered, "Am I like this? Is this me?" He felt his heart ache. He felt lonely.

A few miles from the city, the cart that Phillip was riding in approached a lone figure slumbering along the same way that they were going. It was the strong figure of a young man. Phillip did not make any special note until they were passing. It was the young guard that he had seen with Michelle. Phillip tried not to stare but the contrast in the young man was very noticeable. Instead of a nice uniform, he now wore regular serf's clothes. His handsome face was a bit disfigured by a swollen upper cheek and partial black eye on the right side. The most noticeable difference was not physical. The proud dangerous look in his eyes was replaced by a look of fear and defeat. He was a guard no longer. Just another hopeless serf and Phillip felt sorry for him.

3

BE NORMAL

Phillip, John, Louis, and a few other students were sitting around a large table that they used to study on. There were a handful of large books spread around the table so that everyone could share them. John looked up from his writing for a moment and glanced over at Phillip. "You had better get to work Phillip," he said, "Father Thomas will be checking in on us soon."

Phillip was sitting there staring at a blank piece of paper. "Yes, thank you," he replied without looking up. He picked up his plume, pulled a book close to himself and slowly began writing. Phillip's writing got slower and slower until it stopped all together.

"What are you doing?" John whispered loudly at Philip. This caused the others to stop, look over at Phillip and wait for an answer. Phillip had been noticeably different ever since he returned from his stay at Lord William's. It wasn't that Phillip was doing anything "wrong" but just that he was different. Everyone had noticed it and was talking about it; including the priests.

Phillip looked up and scanned around the table looking into the eyes of his fellow students and friends. "It's just not this simple anymore," he said closing the book closest to him and pushing it half way across the table. "Its just not this simple." The others were still staring as if that answer was not complete. "I guess I've seen too much. The questions that I have don't fit into this nicely packaged theology that we're fed." Realizing that his friends weren't understanding what he was talking about, Phillip reached over, picked up a book, and began writing again. The others began writing again also.

The new attitude of Phillip was making everyone a little uncomfortable. Phillip had always been the perfect student and usually the favorite of the priests, but now he seemed to be developing a rebellious attitude.

When Phillip's errands took him near to the West bank area of Paris he would visit his former boss, Bernard, in the Jewish quarter. Of course he never told anyone that he had gone. Not even Louis or John could be trusted with such a secret.

Phillip would only stay as long as he thought it was prudent. Though he loved talking with Bernard, he couldn't even imagine what would happen to him if Father Timothy found out about it. Bernard never tried to push his religion on Phillip but they did talk a lot about things of the Old Testament. Phillip learned as much about the Old Testament from Bernard in the few times that they had talked than all of the many hours of study that he had spent with the Priests.

"I guess I should go now," Phillip said. "Thanks again for talking with me Mr. Bernard."

"My pleasure Phillip," Bernard responded. "I never thought that I would enjoy talking to a son of the gentiles. No offense," he said.

Phillip smiled, "None taken."

"Ever have any more girl problems?" Bernard asked.

Phillip flushed a little with embarrassment as he remembered all that had taken place a few months earlier. "No, no more girl problems," he assured Bernard. "The truth is that I can't remember the last time that I even had a conversation with a girl."

"Hummm," Bernard said rubbing his beard, "that sounds like a problem in itself."

"Not to me, its not," Phillip responded. "A lot less problems this way."

"I guess so," Bernard said still rubbing his beard. "However, there are some problems worth having." He smiled. "Now go boy."

Bernard opened the door for Phillip to leave but there standing right outside was a priest. Phillip was startled. Phillip expected to see anger in the priest's eyes but instead he also seemed startled at seeing

Phillip.

The two stood staring at each other for a moment before Bernard put his hand on Phillip's shoulder. Phillip turned to look at him. "Go on boy," Bernard said, "it's nothing. Father Gerard is an . . . . ." the priest outside gave Bernard a look as to say 'don't say anything'. Bernard finished his sentence, ". . . an acquaintance of mine."

Phillip looked at Bernard in puzzlement. Bernard smiled and said again, "It's nothing. No go on."

Phillip began to pass the priest but Father Gerard grabbed Phillip's arm tightly. It was as if he wanted to say something but he couldn't. However, Phillip got the unspoken message. The Priest didn't want anyone to know that he had been there either.

A couple of days later Phillip was sitting in Father Timothy's personal study. He had spent the passed few days sweating about the incident at Bernard's house over in the Jewish quarter. Then it came; the summons to see Father Timothy. He was sure that Father Gerard had informed his superiors about his unscheduled visit.

"Phillip, I've been hearing things that I can hardly believe." Phillip braced for the worst. Then Father Timothy continued, "Some of your teachers say that you are asking threatening questions in class and that your assignments have not had appropriate conclusions. What is your response to this?"

"Father, I don't want to be rebellious and I apologize if that is the impression that my teachers have of me," Phillip said with respect. "I don't mean to threaten anybody. I just ask questions that come to my mind. As far as my written assignments are concerned, I put more thought and study time into them now than I ever did before."

"Study and thought are important to all of us Phillip but unrestrained thought can easily land you in the devil's traps," said Father Timothy. "More than one of the other priests has informed me that you not only question foundational Church doctrine in some of your written assignments but that you have even raised these doubts in open discussion in front of other students. Phillip can't you see the danger in this?" Father Timothy looked long and hard at the young man in front of him.

Father Timothy leaned back and sighed. "How old are you Phillip, eighteen?" he asked.

"Seventeen," Phillip replied looking down at the floor.

"Young man, most of those priests were ordained before you were even born. They are well studied and have taught many students, like yourself, who have gone out to be very respectable servants of the Church. The greatest theologians in recent history wrote the books that you study from. If the conclusions that you are coming up with as you study are different from these great men, don't you think that there is a good possibility you have come up with a wrong conclusion?"

Phillip kept his gaze on the stone floor beneath them. "I don't know Father. As I read from the Bible and other theology books I seem to run into conflicts. I try to search out the Scripture in order to discover where I might have gone wrong in my studies. Sometimes I find our theologians to be validated and sometimes I just can't find validation."

Father Timothy couldn't help but be a little impressed by the obvious thought processing that Phillip had been putting into his studies. However, he had seen other "would-be" servants of the Church fall away from the true faith at crucial times in their development. He liked Phillip and would do what he could to bring him back into "right" thinking.

"Phillip," Father Timothy began carefully, "do you understand the doctrine of the 'elect' and the 'non-elect'?"

"Of course, Father," Phillip began. "The doctrine of the elect states that God has chosen to entrust true understanding and true interpretation of Scripture to a few elect individuals who then have the responsibility to explain it to the non-elect who can not correctly interpret Scripture for themselves."

"Phillip, maybe you do not understand that you, as a student, are not yet one of the elect. The very fact that you are coming up with a divergent understanding of doctrine in your own studies only proves this fact." Phillip looked up at Father Timothy with one eyebrow raised. Father Timothy knew that he had finally hit on something that was making sense to Phillip.

"Phillip," he continued, "if God finally extends to you the office of the elect, you will then understand more fully of what I speak. Until then, it is your duty to study as much as is possible about the established truths passed down by our elect forefathers and then accept, support, and teach those truths. If your mind begins to deceive you into thinking differently from those established doctrines you must learn to put down your contrary thoughts and just accept by faith what the elect have already established."

Phillip pondered what Father Timothy had just said. It made sense. "Yes Father, you are right. I have been foolish." Phillip even chuckled a little at himself for having been so ridiculous. Again he said, "You are so very right."

Father Timothy stood up and immediately Phillip arose also. "Of course I'm right," he said with a fatherly smile on his face. "Now go back to your duties, and learn what you're supposed to."

Suddenly Phillip remembered about Father Gerard. "Father," Phillip began, "is that all you wanted to see me about?"

Father Timothy raised an eyebrow, "Of course," he said, "I trust that there is nothing else that we need to discuss."

Phillip thought for a split second and then responded, "No Father, there is nothing else."

This conversation with the senior priest had made a lot of sense to Phillip and he went back to his duties and studies with a great weight off of his shoulders. No longer did he draw different or varied conclusions from his theology books and neither did he ask questions of the teachers that were "threatening." But that did not stop the questions from coming to his mind.

After Phillip proved that he was back to his old self, the priests allowed him to go back to many of his old duties for the Church. One duty that was noticeably missing was that of visiting Madame Christina and Anna. When Phillip asked about it, he found out that Christina had gotten the contract for Lord William and didn't need the same assistance that the Church had given before. Phillip was sorry that he was not able to go and see them.

Everything went well for Phillip for a couple of months. He was able to keep his contrary thoughts in check and was becoming more dedicated to the Church and its doctrines than ever. For the first time in his life he was visualizing himself as a priest or even a monk. Though he had been going to schooling for a long time and focusing on theology he had never really visualized himself being in this ministry like now. There was no question in his mind that theology was indeed the "Queen" of studies and he could visualize himself as a clergy in an influential place. It seemed closer. It seemed real.

Phillip enjoyed helping the priests with mass and running errands for the Church. On Tuesdays the Church would set up a large cart in front of the steps of the Church and hand out old bread that had been donated to the poor. Phillip used to look at most of these people with disdain as they slithered by and picked up an armload of free bread. Their clothes were very worn and the smell was oftentimes so pungent that sometimes Phillip would step back from the cart in order to escape the stench. Little dirty faced, scantily clothed children clung to their mothers as they swarmed the cart. This scene of humanity never moved Phillip before now. He now saw these people as victims of the work of the devil and he wanted to help them.

Easter was coming soon and the whole city seemed be talking more about it. Each day brought more and more excitement and everyone in St. Denis felt it. As Passion Week began, there was a mass everyday and each service was filled with weeping praying people. Everyone was making sure that they were caught up on their confessions as Sunday approached. Father Timothy came up with a very good idea for a climax to the Easter week. Now that the Notre Dame Cathedral was getting closer to completion, the archbishop and others felt a little pressure to compete for the patronage of the people. The boys at St. Denis would put on a short play showing the crucifixion of Christ before they had communion. All of this would have to be done in the streets of Paris because of the masses of people.

That morning as people gathered outside nobody talked about regular everyday things. From the beginning there was an air of expectation. As people arrived they prayed, talked in low tones about "spiritual" things, or said nothing at all. Everyone was there somewhere. The poor, the wealthy, many of the elite, and King Phillip himself would surely be right up front during the whole thing.

Christina and Anna were slowly walking toward the designated area for the Easter events in a quiet and reverent state of mind. Everyone else seemed to be in the same mind frame. It was a crisp Easter afternoon but the air was clear and the streets, houses, and shops were cleaned up for the events to come. No business was transpiring this holy day and it seemed more special than any other time that Anna could remember. Hand in hand Christina and Anna walked along not talking to anyone but only nodding in acknowledgement of their friends as they passed by.

Anna's pretty dress looked as fresh and clean as the first day she wore it on her birthday some months past. She and her mother were a sight to see. Although not as tall as her mother, Anna had many of the same facial features that made her mother the envy of many of the local women. Some men had already made it clear that they were interested in Christina, even though there had not been a proper amount of time for mourning.

"I feel like I am looked at as a piece of property by some of these men," she had told Anna, "or just a good investment." She was referring to the fact that she had indeed won a good contract from Lord William a few months ago. "I am not ready for anyone else in my life. I have you; Anna, and I still have the fresh memories of your father right at the front of my mind. Yet, each time I go out those men start being overly kind and gentile. No, there may never be another. With you Anna, I am very happy. Your skills in sewing are coming along quite nicely, and together we will be just fine."

Anna wondered how long it would be before she could consider being interested in any young man. "It will be a while," she thought, "mother needs me." The thought of waiting a little longer than most young ladies did not really bother her. She enjoyed her mother now more than ever and felt that she was becoming more like a good friend than mother. Also, she had seen plenty of young women get married and lose all independence, all personality, and all joy because of an overbearing husband.

The crowd was getting more and more dense as they neared the open area. The relative quietness of the great mass of humanity was almost eerie, but there was some talking in hushed tones, sounding like a very low dull hum hovering above the people like an invisible cloud. When Christina and Anna finally found a spot to stand, they were about 100 yards from the front, yet they had no problems hearing the songs, prayers, and message.

Everything was so wonderfully done that Anna was entranced during the whole event. There were thousands of people all around her and yet she felt like she was the only one. The feeling was the same all the way up until the passion play began to be acted out. As the procession began with the bleeding Savior carrying his cross, people began to agitate. At first Anna thought it was just because people were trying to shift around a little in order to see, but as people in the crowd began to weep and cry out, Anna became startled.

"Come quickly Anna," Christina whispered loudly. "We must leave now."

"But mother, it is not over yet. The play is going very well, and..." Anna began.

"Let's go, now!" Christina said louder grabbing Anna's arm and starting to turn.

Anna looked at her mother a little startled, but followed obediently. As they finally weaved their way out of the crowd, they both glanced back at the crowd without stopping. The crowd was pushing in on itself and more and more people were crying and screaming. All of the reverence and quietness had evaporated. "Mother, what is happening?" asked Anna with her eyes wide opened.

"Keep walking quickly Anna and I will try to explain. About twelve years ago your father and I went to Tours to look into a business deal. We left you at your grandmother's house. While we were there, we heard a ruckus in the streets. Your father asked the shop owner what was happening and he explained that the new Cathedral had just been completed and it was being dedicated that very week. Almost all of the laypeople of this city and surrounding cities had helped in the construction at one time or another, and now were gathering to dedicate it as a finished work to God."

Slowing down a little and letting go of Anna's arm, Christina continued talking while she looked straight ahead. "We walked outside to
watch what was going on that special day. We thought we might see a
truly glorious day of praising God, but instead we found ourselves
being unwillingly pushed toward the Cathedral steps by a frenzied
mob. People were crying and screaming prayers toward the new building. People started crawling toward the steps on their knees and some
on their bellies. It got more and more crazy until people were tearing
their clothes, beating, and scratching themselves in penance. Finally
your father pulled me close to himself with one arm, put his shoulder
down and started bulling himself out. We were both bruised and
scratched, but felt lucky to escape with such few injuries."

"Do you think these people would get like that?" asked Anna looking back to see if she could still see the crowd. "Besides, could it not be
a moving of the Spirit that is going on? Did you not feel moved by the
service and the play?"

"Yes, I felt moved, but I don't think the Spirit would move people
to harm themselves or others."

Phillip had also thought the day started splendidly. Though he was
very involved in the ministry lately he couldn't remember when he had
"felt" so excited about his Christian faith.

As the priests moved out into the front, the crowd moved closer
and became perfectly silent. Father Timothy stepped forward and
began the service. The Latin readings and monotone singing began to
have a hypnotic effect on the already wired crowd. As Father Timothy
came to an obvious decrescendo, he paused, raised his hands and said,
"Please turn to the side as the boys of the church will reconstruct the
final events of the Passion Week.

With that cue the boys began the precession. Some played the part
of the Roman centurions with others playing the part of the crowd.
Louis played the part of Jesus carrying the cross through the other boys.
With the sight of the pretend Christ, the crowd of people began to get
agitated. The boys that were playing the part of the crowd that Jesus
was going through began jeering "Crucify Him! Crucify Him!" The

masses of people that were watching began to cry out and pray as they watched the reenactment of Christ's crucifixion. Even though this was nothing like what the actors guild could put on, the common people were greatly moved and one could tell something was going to happen.

Someone yelled out. "Those filthy Jews! Look what they did! They crucified Him! They killed our Lord!" Things got quickly out of hand. No longer did the people sit by and watch the pretend drama. Many people started yelling out curses about the Jews. Phillip, playing out his role of a centurion suddenly stopped and looked out at the crowd. The people themselves became the more interesting attraction to watch. People started to fall on their knees and faces and crawl on the ground and repeat prayers of penance. The boys stopped their play as they realized what was happening. Many of the people in the crowd were chanting, "They crucified our Lord! They crucified our Lord!"

Phillip got caught up in the incredible moment and found himself shouting along with the people. "They crucified our Lord!" He began to feel hate inside of himself. "They crucified our Lord!"

After what seemed like only a short time to Phillip, a small group of men came running into the middle of the crowd, dragging two other men in between them. This disrupted what everyone was doing and attention turned to this new event. One of the men in the group yelled out angrily, "These men are Jewish dogs." He didn't have to say anymore. The crowd instantly exploded in anger. The crowd became a mob and the mob moved in on these men, screaming and cursing. Phillip had also moved in closer to be a part of what was going on.

People started hitting the Jewish men with anything they could get their hands on. The crowd was screaming, "They crucified our Lord!" and were whipping the Jews with ropes and with their hands and kicking them as they lay on the ground trying to cover their faces. As Phillip moved in closer he could see the men being beaten, and he found himself wanting to also strike these "God haters." For a moment the people stopped hitting the men and just cursed at them.

One of the men lying on the ground ventured a look up at the crowd. Phillip froze. He felt sick all of a sudden and almost passed out. Bernard! Phillip did not know what to do. His feelings of passionate hate were gone immediately and feelings of shame took their place. While Phillip stood still the crowd began to push him out of the center until he found himself on the outside of the vicious circle. Phillip looked around and noticed that most other people were standing around neither taking part of the activity nor doing anything to stop it.

Phillip glanced back at the men beating Bernard and the other Jew and realized that the two men might be killed, but he felt helpless to do anything about it. He turned to where Father Timothy was and noticed that neither he nor any of the other priests moved to help the dying Jews. King Phillip also did nothing nor did he offer the assistance of any of his personal guard.

Phillip looked back at the now distant crowd and knew that his prayer wanting Bernard to come to know Jesus as the Messiah was not ever to be. Phillip was ashamed of his people, ashamed of the priests, ashamed of the Church, and most of all he was ashamed of himself. Condemnation was upon them all. In heaven, God himself would be disgusted at them; not pleased.

Stumbling against a building of some sort, Phillip leaned up against it with his back and slowly slid down to his seat with his face cupped in his hands weeping.

4

THE BOY PROPHET

The young priest replied, "But your majesty, the boy is very persistent and very convincing. He also has with him many people from his home city of Cloyes and two priests from Orleans who are also convinced by the boys words,"

With the news that the boy had a small following with him, King Phillip II looked at the priest through his one good eye, raised an eyebrow, and sighed long and pronounced. "Show the boy in and the priests, but leave the rest outside."

As the priest left to summon the guests, the King's chancellor leaned over close to the King's ear and whispered a question. "Do you feel that this boy and his vision may actually be a sign from God?"

"Not for a minute," came the cool reply of the king. "I don't believe in all of that religious vision stuff, but I do know that others do. I am king of the land and, in general, people respect my power and authority, but there is one authority that people respect above me. The authority of God in the eyes of the people is held above my power."

"The Pope is the mouthpiece for God and not even he would go against your authority right now. He needs you too much," whispered back the chancellor. "How can a mere boy with stories of visions and letters from God be any kind of threat to your power?"

"My dear chancellor, with over 20 years being king, I have learned that I can control lords, cardinals, kings, and even the Pope by threats, money, deceit, and blackmail, but religious fanatics cannot be bought.

Not even twelve-year-old ones. I will see this boy, hear his story, pat him on the head, and send him home."

As the boy entered the great chamber, he did not even stop to stare at the fantastic marble walls nor the artistic treasures that hung upon them. The King watched as the young peasant boy walked briskly toward him, with two priests on his heels. The boy was dressed in peasant's clothes but the king felt that he walked with the confidence of royalty; shoulders squared and chin up. The lad's eyes met the king's solemn gaze as he first walked in and refused to release it until he reached a respectful distance from where the king was sitting. He bowed in respect.

"Stephen of Cloyes your majesty," announced an official that stood to one side of the boy and priests.

"Young man, you come to me with some quite outstanding claims," started King Phillip. "I, myself am inclined to dismiss you to your home immediately, but as you have no small following, I feel it wise to hear your story and judge the matter firsthand." The king sat up very straight in his chair and looked down his nose at the boy who stood below the platform where he was seated. "Please recount all of the details of your claim at this time."

For a moment Stephen seemed not to be able to speak, but then found his words. "Your majesty, just two months ago I was near my house working in the fields, when the midday heat caused me to seek a tree for shade and rest. As I lay there away from my brothers, I heard a voice call my name. I turned to respond, but was met only by a light which shone so brightly, I was forced to bury my head in my hands. 'Stephen, I am your Lord and I require your service.' I looked up and noticed that the light did not move. I felt that I was indeed being called by a supernatural being. 'Who are you?' I asked.

'I am your Lord Jesus Christ,' responded the light, and began to transform itself into the shape of an angel. It was most definitely something beautiful beyond words—a white robe flowing, fair skin, and white flowing hair. I had no choice but to bow and respond as Paul did in the days of the Bible, 'Lord, what would you have me to do?'"

The king listened intently as the boy continued to speak boldly and confidently. He was not awed by the boy's story though, as many others in the room obviously were. The king had a look of agitation and worry. In his high-pitched voice the boy continued on with his story, speaking with words of a learned man and using gestures with this hands to express himself more vividly.

"The Lord then told me that he wished to send a crusade to the Holy Land to recapture it from the infidels. I remarked, humbly, to him that I was just a boy, not even able to hold a sword.

'I do not need swords and soldiers,' said the Lord, 'I will show the world that I am God by using the weak things of this world in order to retake the Promised Land. I will indeed send an army, an army of children.'"

With this Stephen paused and let the words sink in. Murmuring began in the great chamber, but no one chuckled nor laughed, for the king was very solemn. King Phillip stared straight at the lad and then at the priests with him and then back at the boy. A smile then came to his face. The smile quickly turned to a muffled chuckle and abruptly to a boisterous bellowing laughter. Soon many in the chamber joined the king in laughter. As the king finally regained his breath, he spoke demeaningly to the lad, "An army of children? That is indeed very funny. Four great armies of the finest fighting men in the world have had only limited success in winning battles against those devilish Moslems, and you propose that an army of children can do what these men have not been able to accomplish?"

At this the two priests with Stephen were noticeably shaken. They hung their heads and did not look at the angry king, but Stephen stood firm and replied fearlessly, "Not what I propose, but what God proposes. The Lord told me that people would not believe." With that he reached into his purse that hung by a simple leather strap from his shoulder to his hip. At this gesture people around the room began to crane their necks in order to see what the boy was taking from his purse.

Stephen quickly produced a rolled up piece of parchment and handed it to the king's secretary. "Your majesty, this is my proof. After the Lord spoke to me that first time he told me that he would, in front of many witnesses, help me write a letter; this letter. He told me that in three days I was to find a certain priest named David in the city of Orleans who would be my witness, and he would then send me a 'helping spirit' in order that by my hand this letter could be written.

Your Majesty, I can neither read nor write. On the appointed day, I indeed found Father David waiting for me. With he as my witness, along with a few others, I called for the 'helping spirit' to come to me and do as the Lord had commanded. Quickly, I was filled by a supernatural force and took plume in hand. This letter that you now have is the result."

The king looked over to his secretary who held the letter and nodded. On cue, the secretary unrolled the parchment and began to read. "I, the true Lord of the heavens and earth send this boy Stephen to bare witness of my will. I will that the Christian world reclaim the land that I have promised to all those who would be my children. This crusade shall not be by force of might, but by the faith of children, so that the world may know that I am God. I, the Lord will be their guide, I, the Lord will be their sustenance, and I, the Lord will divide the great Mediterranean Sea so that my children may walk across on dry ground." Finished, the secretary handed the letter to the king himself.

King Phillip opened the letter and looked it over silently. When he had finished, he looked up at the boy and priests who were looking back at him silently. "Which one of you is Father David?"

From Stephen's right side a small, slightly built priest took one step forward and replied humbly in a cracking voice, "I am, your Majesty."

"Do you bare witness that all that the boy says is true?" asked the king.

"I do, your Majesty," not looking directly into the king's eye.

Looking over at his chancellor, King Phillip spoke, "We will look into this matter. Dismiss our guests but ask them not to leave the area for two weeks. At the end of two weeks summons them to come before me again." With that the king rose and exited the chamber through a door in the back.

Soon the Archbishop, a few of the king's counselors, and King

Phillip were seated around a rectangular table in a small room behind the main hall. The serious look on the king's face had not disappeared, and the rest of the men sat silently. "How is it that this 'boy' speaks like a seasoned statesman instead of a simple son of laity?"

"It is remarkable, your Majesty. His very manner is captivating," remarked one of the counselors.

"Yes, captivating. So captivating that I fear he will captivate the hearts of this simple but religious people. I expected the nonsense of a farm boy but instead I am confronted by this." The king said, motioning his hand towards the door that leads to the great hall.

"Your Majesty, is it at all possible that what the boy has experienced is real?" spoke a young counselor two chairs to the left of the king. Many of the others were thinking the same thing but did not dare announce publicly their thoughts on the matter.

The others expected the king to fly into a rage at this announcement but quite to the contrary, he fixed his gaze at the table in front of him, "I, too, for a moment had to ask myself that question. The confidence and manner of the boy made me think also that at least he believed what he was saying." Raising his voice and standing, the king still fixed his eye on the table but said, "The boy is proposing a crusade. A crusade of children! How can I for one second think about sending children off to certain death? It is absolutely preposterous. It would rip the heart out of the people of France and I would be responsible. I tell you the boy is a lunatic. No matter how he appears, no matter his story, I say he is a lunatic and this story of Christ appearing has been carefully thought out to feed his lunacy. With this announcement he slowly looked over the faces in the room until his gaze rested on the Arch Bishop. "Archbishop, how do you feel about this whole thing?" the king said recognizing the Archbishop for the first time.

Aged and dressed in splendid robe, the Archbishop stood to his feet and breathed in deep and long. "I, too, am impressed by the boy and his story. I hear the testimony of the priests with him and I see this letter as evidence and must confess its intrigue. My conclusions however, are very doubtful as concerning any real revelation by God in the matter. In France, I myself am the spiritual leader of the people and voice for God.

I received no revelation from God nor any hint that he would be sending a boy in order to tell me his will. God would not set up an order in the Church and then circumvent it by speaking to a lowly peasant instead of his appointed servants." With this the Arch Bishop paused to see how his words were being received. The looks of the others in the room were bright with agreement, except for the king who was looking out of a nearby window.

"The only human position above mine is that of the Pope, and I have heard nothing about a 'children's crusade' from his Holiness," the Archbishop continued, but as soon as he spoke those words, the king whirled around so suddenly, that the Arch Bishop stopped immediately.

To his secretary the king spoke directly, "Send a messenger to the Pope immediately. I would have testimony of him that he knows nothing of this "appearing of Christ" and therefore it cannot be from God. The people might be interested in the ravings of a twelve-year-old boy, but one word of contempt from the papacy will clear up this mess in a day." With this the king's mood changed to one of relief and light-heartedness. Looking to his chamberlain, he said, "Find the boy and his people and send them home. There is no need for them to stay another day. As soon as we have word from the Pope that all is nonsense, we will need no more evidence."

The chamberlain's messenger did not need to look very hard in order to find Stephen. The boy was in Paris outside of the large square that was St. Genevieve's courtyard. He was standing on the back of a cart waving his letter in the air and giving his testimony. About two thousand people surrounded the cart in a tight semi-circle, listening intently to the message of the peasant boy.

5

THE MESSAGE

"Very nice," Christina said as she held up a man's shirt in order to examine the stitching in the hems. "Anna, you are getting better each day. Your lines are straighter and your stitches are evenly spaced." With that, Christina lowered the shirt and looked at Anna sitting down smiling in front of her.

"May I go a bit faster now mother?" Anna said in response. "Now that I am doing more work, I feel more confident."

"Your work is good, sweetheart, but I want you to go slowly for a while yet. Quality is everything. As women, our work must always be better than that of men if we are to compete," Christina said matter-of-factly. "Right now, concentrate on every cut and every stitch. Speed will come in time without you even realizing it."

The rest of the afternoon, Anna watched her mother work. She was working on something extraordinary and beautiful, a once-in-a-lifetime opportunity—the wedding dress of nobility.

Christina had not only won the contract of Lord William, but had also won the favor of his wife. The dresses that Christina had made for the lord's wife were received very well. Madam cared very much about appearance and the detail and craftsmanship stitched into every dress that Christina made gained the Madam's approval immediately. When the special contract was put out for Michelle's wedding dress, Madam would not even consider another person.

After a few hours of tirelessly watching her mother's nimble hands glide through her work, Anna announced that she was going to the market to buy food for supper. Anna had taken over most of the household duties when her mother's work had taken precedence over her time, but she didn't mind. She liked to go out of the house and do the shopping. Paris was interesting with all of its new stores popping up everywhere. Many times Anna would shop at places quite a distance from her house just to see more of the city. Her mother never complained about her being gone to long but she was careful not to take advantage of her mother's good nature. Anna didn't mind the cooking either, but cleaning was tedious and never ending. Cleaning took a lot time every day, because now that they made fine, clothes the house needed to be kept spotless. Every piece of furniture, the walls, the floors, and especially her hands had to always be clean.

"Good-bye mother, I'll return shortly," announced Anna as she walked out the door. Christina was concentrating on the task before her and didn't even acknowledge her daughter's departure. Soon Anna was walking toward the market place.

The open market seemed different to Anna. The shopkeepers were doing business as usual, the people were milling around looking at the produce as usual, yet something wasn't normal. Anna went around picking up vegetables and other cooking necessities.

"Today I shall buy a small pheasant for supper and surprise mother with it," she thought. She began to cross the large avenue to go to the butcher's on the other side, making a wide swing around the large ancient oak tree that marked the center of the plaza. She did this in order to avoid the begging children that always hovered around. She avoided even looking in that direction as to avoid any possibility of meeting the gaze of some poor beggar child. She eventually chanced a quick glance over as if her human nature wouldn't allow her to ignore the dismal scene completely. When finally she had glanced over at the "beggar's tree" instead of continuing on she stopped and stared. She wasn't staring at the usual poor wretched street urchins with sullied faces and rags clinging to their dirty little bodies that were faithfully present, but instead, found herself staring at nothing. For indeed there were no beggars, not one.

Anna took a minute and scanned the whole marketplace. There wasn't one single child begging anywhere. She couldn't ever remembering a time when there weren't any children begging. As she looked more closely, it even seemed as if there were less children in general. A little puzzled, she continued across the plaza until she got to the butcher shop.

Anna knew the butcher well and therefore spoke to him directly. "Gillard, has begging been outlawed or something?"

The question caught the kindly man a little unprepared. "Excuse me, mademoiselle? " he said back as if he hadn't heard what he thought he heard.

"Has the king asked the beggars to leave?" asked Anna again.

"I don't understand. Why would they ask the beggars to leave?" remarked the butcher as he caressed his thin mustache inquisitively.

"Well," continued Anna feeling a little embarrassed, "the beggar tree; it's empty. I don't see any beggars at all." Beggars weren't a topic that people usually talked about. It was bad luck to talk about those less fortunate than yourself, but this obvious change of the usual environment seemed to make it O.K.

Gillard looked out at the tree and paused just long enough to raise an eyebrow before scanning the other side of the marketplace. "That's odd," he said as if thinking out loud. "Berni, look at the tree," he yelled at a man in the street and pointing over to the beggar's tree.

The man glanced over at the tree and then back over to the butcher's shop. "Yes, a little while ago they all went off toward the cathedral."

"Today's not hand-out day," said Gillard as the other man walked closer to the shop. "Today's not some sort of holiday, is it?"

"No," said Berni "and what's a bit strange is that some adults went that way too. Not beggars either. But all of the beggar children went." They all looked down the street that led to the cathedral and noticed that there still was a thin but steady stream of people going that way.

Almost without realizing, it Anna also began to walk down the street toward the cathedral. There was something hypnotizing about the silent stream of people all walking in one direction. As Anna walked on she could hear the voices of Gillard and his friend discussing the possible reasons for the mysterious disappearance.

Phillip was between classes at school. This day his class was held at St. Genevieve's school of theology. He heard the noises in the outside courtyard. He saw what was happening and remembered the news of a boy from Cloyes who was said to have a message from God about a special crusade for children.

"That's right. The boy was to be in town this week to try to talk to the king about it." Phillip moved to a better vantage point but stayed clear of the growing crowd. Still fresh in his memory was the Easter of a few months ago. He knew that a mob of people could easily be manipulated into an emotional response and he wanted no part of it. For the past few months Phillip had uncomplainingly fulfilled his duties but with very little enthusiasm or desire.

After a few minutes of viewing the strange goings on, Phillip watched as the boy stopped speaking and stepped to one side to allow a small-framed priest his turn to speak. Phillip's eyes continued to follow the boy from Cloyes as he got down from the cart and practically collapsed into the arms of another priest standing close by. The crowd did not notice because the priest speaking had already captured the attention of the eager listeners.

Phillip sat at a distance far enough away that he only caught selected words of sermon being given. At that moment, he also noticed for the first time that a great majority of the listeners were children of varying ages. He had seen crowds gather before but never one quite like this.

Phillip stopped trying to listen to the priest on the cart and began eyeing individuals among the crowd. How interesting people were. "I wonder what everybody out there is thinking right now?" he asked himself.

"The Lord has allowed the first crusades to fail so that He can prove to the world that it is not by the strength of men that He will regain His promised land for His promised people," shouted the boy that was in the cart. "God will use the slight strength but great faith of children in order to fulfill his plan. This crusade of children can not fail because it is not of man nor of men's ideas." The large crowd began to murmur amongst themselves. Anna knew that her mother would not approve of her being here. She remembered last Easter when the crowds had gathered and her mother made them leave. Still, for some reason she stayed. Maybe it was just to hear this boy speak. How strange it was for a young boy to speak with such conviction and strength. Soon she found that she was not just watching the show but also listening to the words being spoken.

"We must listen to the voice of God. He has spoken, what else can we do?" Holding up the letter in his hand he continued, "We have God's very words here in this letter to guide us. He will continue to guide us and He will protect us if we do His will." With those words the boy staggered a bit as if he were going to faint. A nearby priest caught him and whispered something in his ear. The boy was let down off of the cart and allowed to sit down.

Immediately a young priest got up on the cart and began to speak. "The things that young Stephen has said are true and you would be well to listen. I can testify that he came to me in my church and told me all that he has told you. I felt that a spirit was guiding me to listen, and as Stephen spoke I felt his words to be true. Later, I saw with my own eyes as the spirit fell upon him and he was led to write the words on the letter. I am convinced that the child speaks the truth and that the Lord would have us fulfill his will in this matter." The priest barely took a breath before he continued on with his message. He spoke of the gift of childhood and how God had made children with such unwavering faith. With this faith, God would conquer his enemies.

While the priest was still speaking, some guards along with an official pushed their way up to the cart and spoke to the boy and the priests there. Without waiting for a response, the official and the guards pushed their way back out again.

After the official left, the priest did not say another word but simply got down from the cart and began to make their things ready to leave. In a few minutes word got back to Anna that the official had asked the boy to leave and go home. The crowd stayed and watched for a little to see what the boy and priests would do, but soon it was obvious that they were just readying themselves to go. Without any announcement or dismissal the crowd began to slowly dissipate.

From the back of the crowd Anna turned and walked back towards the marketplace not really knowing what to think. Soon she heard two little beggar boys racing from behind her, "If we get back first," one said breathlessly to another, "we can sit on the root."

"Yeah," said another, "let's hurry."

Phillip's concentration was broken as an official of some sort, along with two guards, pushed their way towards the cart through the crowd. The crowd of youth was easily divided by the large guards and soon the official was saying something to the priests and the boy who was sitting down slumped over. Phillip strained to hear but could not. It seemed that after the official left everything froze where it was for about five minutes before the crowd began to disband.

As the people began to slip away, Phillip saw something that he hadn't seen before. He sprang to his feet and started out toward the crowd leaving his things where they lay. "Anna," he shouted. "Anna, wait."

Anna stopped and turned to look if the call was meant for her. In just a moment she saw the figure of a young man trotting in her direction waving. "Anna wait, I want to talk to you."

"Phillip," Anna whispered to herself as she recognized who it was. It had been so long since she had seen him and yet her heart still sprung to life. Phillip slowed a bit as he got closer to her and walked up to her with a smile on his face.

"Anna, I'm so glad I caught up with you," Phillip started. "I hope I didn't startle you, coming up to you so suddenly, but it's been so long since I've been able to talk to you or your mother and when I saw you . . . well I just wanted to see how you both are doing."

Looking downward Anna said, "I'm glad you did."

"You probably have to get home with that food so I don't want to hold you up, but may I walk with you for a while?" Phillip asked Anna, who still seemed a bit startled by his sudden appearance.

"I heard that you were busy with your classes," Anna replied, beginning to take a step toward home. "Don't you have classes today?"

Phillip fell in beside Anna and reached down to help her with the basket of food she was carrying. "Yes, I have classes, but sometimes things come up and you just can't make it. Nobody will mind," Phillip said with a sparkle of mischievousness in his eye.

Anna smiled. She had never known Phillip to ever think of skipping a class or shirking any responsibility given him to do. For him, this attitude seemed a little odd, but she was glad that he was walking with her. "I have heard that Madam Christina won a very nice contract with Sir William and that work has been steady for you," Peter began.

"Yes," Anna said, "that is true, but we have even had more blessings." Anna told Phillip a little of how her mother had gained much work because of the Madam Madeline and how she was now working on her daughter's wedding dress.

At this news, Phillip looked away from Anna because he couldn't let her see that it bothered him.

"Is everything all right?" Anna asked noticing Phillip's change in countenance.

"Yes, of course, I was just thinking of something for a moment. I'm sorry, Go on," Phillip said regaining a bit of a smile. They walked on as the passing carts kicked up a thin layer of dust into the air.

Suddenly, as if he remembered something, Phillip stopped and said to Anna, "What was going on in the cathedral square earlier, and what did you hear?"

The thought caught Anna equally off guard. She stopped, but for a moment could find no response. "I truly don't know," she finally answered.

"But you were there."

"That's true, but for only a little while at the end." "Why were you there?" Phillip went on inquisitively.

"I'm not sure," Anna responded, but could see that Phillip still had a questioning look on his face. She went on, "Many people were walking toward the square and I just followed to see what was going on." With this, Anna felt a little of her shyness return and she didn't look back up at Phillip.

"Did you hear anything that was being said?" Peter persisted.

"A little."

"Well, what did they say?"

Still looking down she replied, "They said something about a crusade of children going to the holy land."

"It is true then," was Phillip's only comment.

"What's true?" Anna asked finally looking up.

"I heard from Louis that there was a boy named Stephen from a city near Orleans that claimed he had received a vision and had a letter of proof that Christ wanted him to lead a crusade of children to recapture the holy land." Phillip looked directly at Anna, "What did he sound like?"

"I don't know exactly. He sounded very confident, but it frightened me a little."

"What did he say to frighten you?"

"Nothing that he said or even how he said it. I think I was frightened after he stopped speaking."

"I don't understand," Phillip said.

"While he was speaking I felt like everything he said was, without question, the truth. After I began to walk away I wasn't sure anymore. Doesn't that seem strange to you," She said, "that for one moment you are sure something is true and then a few seconds later you're not sure?"

"Maybe next time he speaks, I will listen a little more closely to what is being said. It sounds interesting." Phillip paused for a moment and without speaking the two young people turned and continued walking down the street. "Did you notice that most of the crowd were children?" Phillip asked while looking ahead down the street.

"I did notice that all of the beggar children were there listening to every word that was being spoken. How interesting it all was. I think I will discuss it with mother. But not tonight."

They walked the next two blocks without talking. With the days strange events talked out, Phillip began to think about Anna. She spoke with intelligence, she was gentle, she was strong of character for a girl her age, she even walked nicely, and she was very attractive. For the first time Phillip noticed how fair and clean her skin was. Her dress was also very nice as if she had worn it for the first time this morning.

Why had he talked so freely with her? He didn't know. She was a lot like her mother in that regard. Christina had always talked freely about things and did not judge people or situations very quickly.

Anna was thinking of how nice it was to talk with Phillip again. She remembered some of the conversations that he had with her mother while he was coming by to bring food. Anna had never said much but enjoyed listening and thought Phillip to be handsome and smart. Right now he seemed more than that. He seemed real. He had never really seemed to notice her very much in the past and now he was talking with her as if they were good friends. In Anna's life only she, her father, and her mother seemed to be real people. Everyone else was just there. They didn't have a lot of character or emotions. They just existed. Anna liked that Phillip also now seemed real.

Suddenly she remembered that Phillip was studying to be a priest. She looked up at him from the corner of her eye as they were walking. Phillip noticed and smiled gently back at her. "How could Phillip be a priest and be real," she thought. "Priests never seemed to be real to her."

"Phillip," Anna whispered almost afraid to be the first to break the silence, "what will it be like to be a priest?"

Phillip had to quickly change his train of thought in order to answer the surprise question. He began to open his mouth and give a standard response, but before he said a word, he caught himself. He closed his mouth and had a quick flash in his mind of himself wearing priest's robes, but there was no pleasure in the thought. "For me, I don't know. I guess everyone is different."

Neither one said anything more until they reached the front door of Anna's house. "Thank you for allowing me to accompany you to your home, Anna," Phillip said, "I enjoyed talking to someone other than a seminary student or priest for awhile."

"No, thank you Phillip, Mother and I have talked of you often and wondered how you have been. She will be glad to see you."

"I really must return to classes or I will be missed."

"Oh, you simply must say hello to mother. She will be hurt if she knew you were here and did not at least say hello," Anna added convincingly.

"Yes, but you must help me get away at once. Every time I come here it seems that I end up staying longer than I had originally intended," Phillip commented with a smile.

Although Christina was very busy, she stopped working and took time to visit with Phillip. Christina was as beautiful and kind as ever. "Maybe even more so now than before," thought Phillip. It was good talking with Christina about the many things that had happened to him during the past many months, and he opened up and talked much more than he had planned. Unlike the priests and others, she seemed to understand and care. Anna spoke very little, but sat listening intently to the conversation between Phillip and her mother. Phillip did indeed stay longer than he had originally intended.

A few miles outside of Paris the crisp night air settled over a camp of about sixty people huddled in a circle sleeping on the ground or in carts. With the silence of the night mixed with the rhythmic sounds of nature one would never guess that only a short distance away was the huge metropolis of Paris.

"Aaaaaaaah, Noooo!," pierced the calm as if an assassin's arrow had pierced an unexpecting victim. The once peaceable camp suddenly was alive with confusion. In a few short seconds most of the adults were crowding around one of the carts trying to look over one another to see what had caused "God's messenger" Stephen to scream.

In wrinkled priest robes, already on the cart, and with his arm around the boy, was Father Gilbert. "What is it?" he was asking gently to Stephen. As he held his arm around the youth, he felt him trembling uncontrollably.

Stephen just sat there trembling with his head in his hands. Father David who stood at one side of the wagon saw what was happening and turned to the onlookers with a smile. "It is all right. Stephen has just had a nightmare. I'm sure he will be fine. Please, everyone try to go back to sleep."

As the people began to relocate their sleeping places, Father David got up on the cart with Stephen and Father Gilbert. The floorboards creaked and the cart shifted a bit from side to side as the slightly built priest lifted himself up. "It is all right Father Gilbert, I will stay with

Stephen for a while."

"No, please stay," Stephen finally spoke clinging on to father Gilbert. Father Gilbert looked over at Father David.

"All right," began Father David, "but I will want to talk to Stephen first thing in the morning." Father Gilbert stayed close to Stephen without saying a word, but just holding him as if trying to keep him warm. It took Stephen another two hours before he finally fell back asleep.

"He said what?!!" screamed King Phillip II.

Not daring to look into the face of the monarch, the royal secretary repeated the message that he had received from the Pope Innocent III. He opened up the letter as to read it word for word and he began again. "The Holy Father says, 'We have not received any special word from above that the Father in Heaven has chosen to use children to recapture his holy land. However, in all honesty I feel deeply in my heart that the zealousness of these children to do the will of God, puts us to shame. Surely, we can take a lesson in faith from such as these.'"

"Why, why, why would he not simply have discredited this fanatical boy and his followers and have left it at that." Looking around at the few trusted men in the room, he continued, "that statement of 'putting us to shame with their faith' is a spark I tell you. With that spark of hope, I fear a fire will start. A fire that will burn many."

"Geoffrey, I want you to send word to the priests in Orleans to tell the boy that the Pope has not ordained this vision and I, as King, order him to cease his preaching," ordered the King to a man to his left.

Before Geoffrey could respond to the affirmative a young man who sat against the far wall spoke up. "Excuse me, your Majesty," he interrupted. The King shot a glare in his direction. "Please, your Majesty, I must inform you that you will not find the boy nor his followers in their home towns." The King raised an eyebrow. "I'm afraid you will find them right here in Paris." King Phillip stood up straight and remained silent waiting for the young man to explain. "You see, your highness, the boy left, but only for one day. He is in the city preaching his vision to whoever will listen. The Pope's words have already reached the streets and I'm afraid, your majesty, that our spark has already ignited the common people into a fire."

Phillip had skipped classes for the past two days but so had many of his fellow seminary students. Almost all of the priests and bishops disagreed with what was going on but were afraid to stop it. The comment of the "Holy Father" had indeed turned a gentle breeze into a whirlwind that looked like it was going to head south toward the holy land. The boy Stephen was preaching continually but now from the grounds of Notre Dame. People, and especially children, flocked to hear him speak. The priests, David and Gilbert, were at other locations of the city spreading the news and pointing people towards Notre Dame. Every day outsiders poured into the city hearing of the news of the crusade being organized.

Only a few days after the Pope had said that the faith of the children put the adults to shame there were thousands of children buzzing around Notre Dame. For a few nights many slept there as if they were camped out in the country. The weather was beautiful and was taken as a blessing of God. Tomorrow the children's crusade would march.

Phillip had listened closely to the speeches of Stephen over the few days and found what was said to be very moving. The talk of how God had waited until just the right time and chosen just the right ones was exciting. The fact that the other crusades had not turned out like were planned because of the corruptness of man. During those crusades kings and nobles wanted to not only gain the Holy Land, but also wealth, power, and land for themselves. The motives of children were pure. They wanted to take the holy land because it was what God wanted. Their faith in God would conquer all.

It was astounding how this twelve-year-old farm boy from Cloyes had mastered the art of preaching better than any of Phillip's well-seasoned mentors. Surely he was led supernaturally. Everyone said that he was. You could almost see the fire in his eyes when he spoke, and the weight of his words would hold captive the attention and vision of even the most independent thinker.

Before night fell, Phillip knew for sure that he too would be a part of the Crusade. It was his destiny. It was exciting to think of reigning in the Holy Land with Christ instead of being stuck in some preprogrammed position in the Church. It was all clear now. He dreaded the thought of being a priest. He loathed the work that he was being called to do there under the strong unyielding arm of St. Denis. The path to the Holy Land was the path to freedom.

Many of Phillip's friends had already made commitments to go on the crusade. Some of the priests had also been called along with a number of monks who had recently heard of the adventure and had come to the city. Phillip wasn't sure how many would finally end up going, but it was already obvious that many thousands would make up this noblest of God's armies. Of all the people that were committed to go, there was still one that had not come. Phillip had not seen Anna or Christina at any of the gatherings, and in his heart he knew that he would not.

Christina and Anna ate their supper without speaking. The streets had been bustling like harvest time, but now there was an unnerving calmness as if something great or something disastrous was about to take place. "They will be leaving tomorrow from what I hear," Anna started. She didn't have to say who "they" were, because nothing but the crusade had been on anybody's mind for a number of days.

Christina was obviously a bit agitated. "I wish we could talk about something else," she said looking up at Anna from her bowl of vegetable soup. Again the two ate without saying anything.

"Mother," Anna said putting her spoon down. "I went and heard Stephen of Cloyes speak."

Christina stopped eating and put her spoon and bread down on the table. "Anna, you know I asked you to stay away from all of this. Why did you disobey me?"

"I didn't disobey you mother. I heard him speak a few weeks ago before much was known. I didn't even know what was going on until I was there listening."

"Why didn't you tell me about it?" Christina responded.

"Remember the day that Phillip came over to visit for a little with us?" Christina nodded. "It was on that day that I heard Stephen speak. Phillip saw me there and walked with me home. I guess I didn't tell you because I remembered how much you were frightened on Easter with the mob of people there. I didn't want you to worry."

"Why are you telling me this right now?" Christina probed. "I had wanted to talk to you many times about it but I know how much this whole children's crusade business upsets you and I was afraid to bring it up. I bring it up now only because I can't act like nothing is happening anymore. We should have at least gone to listen to some of the speeches like everybody else. How do we know that this is not of God and that He doesn't want us to help in some way?"

"I have never said that this wasn't from God, Anna, and you are right, it does frighten me," began Christina, with tears welling up in her eyes. "I do not pretend to know the mind of God. I am not a spiritual person, nor do I know much about the workings of the Church, but I am a mother. The thought of children marching off down some unknown path to some unknown land abandoning families, friends, and safety tares my heart out." It was apparent to Anna that even though her mother had not said anything about the goings on of the past weeks, she had thought much about them.

With her mother so animated, Anna would normally accept her mother's words and leave it at that, but Anna found that she had a response. It was a response that she remembered Stephen giving while he was preaching. "Mother, have you ever considered that it is those very things that God is relying on to win this crusade?"

Christina was a bit stunned at the answer of her daughter. "Have you ever considered that God wants to use the weak things of his kingdom in order to conquer the stronghold of the enemy? Have you ever considered that God, in asking His people to give up their most precious possessions, their very lineage, is testing us to see if we really will trust in Him? Does it not seem that it is not only possible but logical that God would choose children to bring the reign of His own Son back to Earth?"

Christina was speechless and, to Anna, seemed weak. Obviously her words made an impact. She expected her mother to respond with her usual wisdom but was surprised to hear, "That is enough! Go to your room and prepare yourself for bed." Anna quietly obeyed her mother.

6

MADOC

Little Madoc had found himself a comfortable place to lay his blanket down among all of the other children. For a boy of 11 he was unusually small and frail. Even though he had a mother, she had never shown much interest in him except for the fact that as a beggar he brought food home to share with her. He spent his whole day out at the market begging for food with the rest.

Up until last year Madoc had been one of the principle targets of diversion for many of the other street kids. He seemed an easy target because of his small size and the fact that he really had no gang to run with. Last year after being roughed up by a larger boy, who said that Madoc had stolen one of his "regulars," he was forced to beg in other places. One day he had wandered to the West bank of the river in order to eat a little bit of bread that he had been given. Near the water's edge he heard the unmistakable whimpering of a puppy.

Madoc made his way through the tall grass and carefully down the bank to the water. There in the muddy grass lay a little puppy. The puppy was all wet and lying on its side with its two back paws still touching the gently flowing water. The puppy had thin black hair covering its little sick body. One could count each rib.

Madoc made his way down to get a closer look at the suffering animal. When it heard him coming, the pup turned its head slightly and looked up directly into Madoc's eyes. The meeting of these two poor pathetic creatures in that instant changed both of them. Somehow they knew that they had finally found someone who would love them, and having someone to love them made them somebody. Whereas before they had only existed in God's realm of things, much as a blade of grass or a stream of water, now they were alive.

For the months to follow, Madoc had to find various hiding places for "Hungry" so that his mother would not know that he had adopted a dog. Hungry grew to be a fine looking animal. He had surely been lost by mistake. Madoc didn't know much about dogs, but someone mentioned in passing that Hungry was some kind of hunting hound that was usually owned by a rich landowner for sport.

With Hungry by his side the other kids around decided that Madoc was not as good a target for their children's pranks and harassment as he once had been. Hungry was extremely loyal but did not interfere with Madoc while he was begging or talking with others. In fact, Hungry turned out to be very helpful in scavenging for food around houses and stores. The only problem was that Hungry ate a lot.

Madoc's mother noticed that he had not been bringing home as much food or other things as he used to and told him to stop being lazy. Nick, his mother's boyfriend didn't have a regular job and he was especially adamant that they "Needed every little bit extra." When the food supply did not increase, Madoc's mother decided to follow him to see why his begging was not going well.

Down a few blocks of the slums, jumping over open sewers and dirty alleys she followed him. She knew that he was not going directly to the market like he usually did. Instead he took a detour down a street that was behind one of the larger textile factories in the city. When they reached a part of the back wall where two of the wooden slats where broken, Madoc stopped.

"Hungry," Madoc shouted to the wall. "Come on, boy." At once a black hound bounded over the broken slats and almost on top of little Madoc. After a fond greeting was exchanged between the two, they continued on toward the market place. Madoc's mother had seen enough.

Later that day, at dusk, Madoc folded the flap back that acted as a front door for his home and stepped inside as usual. While Madoc's eyes were still trying to adjust to the darkness of the little room he felt a sudden crack across the side of his face! "You little thief!!!" shouted an angry man's voice. It was his mother's boyfriend.

He was a short, stout man with shoulder length black hair. Madoc never liked him. He treated he and his mother like slaves ordering them around whenever he was sober. He never made any money for the family but always seemed to have enough for cheap wine.

"Pick yourself up off of the floor you little thief," he continued. With the side of his face burning, Madoc picked himself up off of the dirt floor only to be knocked down again.

The man reached down and pulled Madoc up by his shoulders. He stuck his face in Madoc's and with the stench of wine on his breath said, "If I ever hear that you have a dog again, I'll kill the mutt and cook it for supper."

"No!" shouted Madoc in the man's face.

Madoc's mother tried to butt in, "Please Nick, I think he's got the idea." She saw the rage in her boyfriend's eyes.

Red faced, Nick held the whimpering boy out at arms length and once again knocked him to the floor.

"Stop it!" cried Madoc's mother, but Nick wasn't finished teaching him a lesson. He reached down to pick Madoc's limp little body off of the floor in order to hit him again.

Nick pulled his arm back ready to strike when suddenly the flap of the door snapped opened. Nick turned in time to see the silhouette of a black beast leaping in bearing sharp teeth and growling viciously. In a split second Hungry had knocked Nick off of his feet and against the far wall. It was all Nick could do to raise his arms up to defend himself. Hungry was ripping at the man with reckless abandon. His powerful jaws were tearing flesh from bone.

"Hungry! Stop!" cried Madoc as soon as he could muster the energy. Hungry obeyed immediately and trotted over to the beaten boy lying on the ground.

Looking wide-eyed at Madoc, his mother kneeled down by the heap of human flesh that was her boyfriend. "He's still breathing," was all she said horrified by what she saw. Still looking at Nick she went on, "Madoc, you must leave here. Leave and never come back. I'm afraid that when he recovers he will kill you." Finally she looked over at her son who was propping himself up on the floor. "You must go, now!"

Madoc had left his house deeply wounded, but not because of the beating that he had received from Nick. He would never go back.

Since the fight, Madoc and Hungry had found a place of their own to live. It was inside the Jewish quarter by the river. From that time on, Madoc constantly looked over his shoulder in fear expecting that any-time Nick might sneak up on him from behind. Hungry never left his side. Madoc had nightmares about Nick killing Hungry and then try-ing to kill him.

Now as Madoc sat there on his blanket with the other children, ready to march on the crusade, there was, for the first time, hope and purpose in life. Madoc had been reluctant at first to go and listen to the preaching of Stephen. He had always thought that God hated him. Now he felt that maybe God cared about him after all. Stephen said that God had prepared these special children in order to carry out His special purpose. Madoc had never had anyone call him anything but a worthless beggar. If God thought that he was special, then he would do what God wanted of him.

7

LAST PREPARATIONS

Phillip was up before sunrise laying on his cot and thinking of the seriousness of the venture that he was about to set upon. He was stiff from sleeping on the ground and sat there stretching for a few minutes before attempting to get up.

He would be leaving everything that he'd ever known behind him. He probably would never see many people that he grew up with again. He wouldn't see the priests, most friends, not even his own family. He would not see Christina or Anna.

He thought about Christina and Anna for a while. He hadn't seen either of them in a couple of weeks. He would miss them.

The thought struck him that he might still be able to run over and at least say good-bye. It would be pushing his departure a bit but he had to chance going and making it back in time.

Soon Phillip was walking quickly down the road that would lead to Madam Christina's house. The great city of Paris was still dark and still asleep. It would be dawn soon and the sleeping giant would come to life as usual. The crusaders also would be waking up and awaiting orders to march.

A short while after the sun had peeked up over the horizon, Phillip was standing at the door of his friends. Lights were on inside. Phillip had no time to hesitate, so he rapped firmly on the door with his knuckles.

Behind a closed door he heard the voice of Anna, "Who is it?"

"It's Phillip."

Phillip heard the inside bolt slide to one side and the door opened. "Phillip, I can't believe its you," said Anna. "I was sure that you would have joined the crusade and we would never see you again. I'm glad you're here."

"That is the very reason that I am here Anna," said Phillip. "I have joined the crusade. But I couldn't leave without saying good-bye to you and your mother. You have been so good to me. I just had to come by."

Anna's head slowly dropped and tears filled her eyes. "Phillip, must you go also?"

"Yes, I must go," Phillip said unwaveringly. "I know that I was meant to go. I feel a calling within me that I cannot refuse, and now, do not wish to refuse."

Phillip was moved by the obvious grief that the news had brought Anna. With tears in his eyes, he reached out his hand and put it gently under Anna's chin. Tenderly he lifted her head until they were looking at each other. "I am sad to say good-bye, but I am glad that you care. May I say good-bye to your mother also?" Phillip added.

"I'm sorry Phillip, but she just left with Mr. Geno to take the wedding dress up to the castle Velva. It will take a day or two for her to put on the finishing touches." Anna paused. "She will be very upset that she missed you. She thinks that you are a fine person."

"I must go now," said Phillip taking a step back. He turned and rushed off toward Notre Dame and his destiny.

Anna went inside, sat down, and cried. She didn't just cry because Phillip was leaving but she cried because he was free to go and she was not. She too wanted to be a part of this spiritual crusade. Thousands would go on to victory in the Lord, but she would be left behind trapped by her mother's "close minded" viewpoint.

Anna stopped crying and feeling sorry for herself. This "madness" as her mother had called it was nothing less than the most spiritual event of her time and possibly of all time. She was here at this in time in history and would only be able to watch as the crusade marched off to the Holy Land. Surely God would hold her accountable for refusing to go.

By now Anna was sitting straight up in her chair entranced in thought. "I must go," she concluded. "I can't go and leave mother here by herself," she rebutted. "Why does mother need me? She has her contracts, her house, her work, and there are plenty of fine gentlemen who would be glad to marry her."

Anna slumped back over. "If I leave, it will break mother's heart," she thought. "Maybe I am actually holding her back. She could definitely marry up in class and live a better life." Anna's thought shifted to a spiritual vein. "Surely the Lord will bless mother if I go on the crusade. Maybe the Lord will curse us if I do not go."

After a grueling half-hour, Anna had convinced herself that she would be dooming her mother if she did not go on the children's crusade. Soon she was in her room packing clothes, a few personal items, and a little money that she had saved. Before she could change her mind, she wrote out a quick note and left it on her bed. Then she walked out her front door and down the road toward Notre Dame.

Madoc and Hungry were looking over the camp that was about to march. The multitude of people was incredible. Madoc was sure that the crusade had doubled in numbers between the time that they had fallen asleep last night and the time that they woke up.

Madoc was hungry, but as he looked at the rag tag group of crusaders all around him, he was sure that he would have no luck begging from them for food. He and Hungry set off one last time to the market place in the square.

Madoc was very glad that he had come to the square to beg this morning. There were no other beggars and all of the people seemed to be especially generous. He even received a few coins. As Madoc was enjoying his success he caught, from the corner of his eye, the movement of someone coming directly at him at a run. It was Nick!—and he was looking right at Madoc with vengeance in his eyes. Madoc ran. As he ran by a nearby alley, Hungry joined him.

Madoc ventured a glance back over his shoulder as he ran and saw Nick gaining on him. Nick was carrying a club in one hand while the other arm bounced limply at his side. "I'll catch you, you little assassin.

I'll catch and beat you and that animal of yours into dust!" he yelled breathlessly.

Madoc ran for his life. As he jumped over ditches and jotted between people, he dared not look back. This was just like one of his nightmares, but with one big difference. He knew that there would be no waking up from this one if he were caught.

Though Madoc knew the alleys well, the speed and strength of Nick would soon overtake the small boy. When all seemed lost, Madoc and Hungry burst out into the open courtyard of Notre Dame. Without stopping, the two weaved their way in and out until they were in the middle of the crusaders. If they would have turned around they would have noticed that Nick never entered into the crowd. Nick may have been an evil man, but even he feared God and his wrath.

At mid-morning, word spread among the group of crusaders that they would soon begin their journey. In only a short period of time everyone was gathered around listening to Stephen as he stood atop the balcony of the almost finished Cathedral of Notre Dame.

"Today we start on a journey that will lead us to the center of God's will for each of us." Began the boy leader. "It will not be easy and many will sacrifice much...or all. All of us have prepared ourselves for this crusade in many ways. We will start this journey by marching to Vendome where we will make our vows in that most sacred place."

Father David, who only a month ago was an ordinary perish priest, stepped forward and addressed the thirty thousand young crusaders. "Let us pray...Almighty God, hear us and accept our complete and absolute dedication to you and your will. We go forth to conquer the Holy Land for your sake. We now march so that the Christian banner will fly over Your great city. Amen."

The people in the crowd shouted with joy and raised their hands up in the air. Father David yelled out, "For God and the Church . . . For God and the Church . . ." over and over until the whole crowd was crying out, "For God and the Church."

Phillip was shouting with tears in his eyes, "For God and the Church!"

At another place in the great body, Anna was shouting, "For God and the Church!"

Madoc was holding his frightened dog with one hand and shouting, "For God and the Church!"

The thirty thousand crusaders along with the many thousands more of spectators kept shouting as Stephen made his way down to the courtyard. When he was finally on the ground and then in his wagon, he motioned with his arm and shouted once more, "For God and the Church!" The sea of crusaders began their march out of the Cathedral grounds and out of Paris like a giant wave.

After the cheering, enthusiastic sounds of the crusade passed down the streets and out of the city, a different kind of sound filled the air. A deep mourning arose from every corner. Mothers, fathers, brothers, and sisters were in the streets, sitting on steps, and behind closed doors, mourning.

From a window high up in the royal palace King Phillip Augustus watched the day's events in disgust. In all of his many years as a prince, diplomat, crusader, and king, he had never felt so weak and powerless.

8

ON THE MARCH

The crusaders made pretty good time on the first day and were more than 10 miles out of Paris before nightfall. The children who were not waiting at the wagons in order to receive a little of the food that was donated by supporters, were scrounging around trying to find some food on their own. Nothing was very orderly at first, but a few of the priests began to put some of the adults and older youth in charge of food wagons and other supplies. Soon things had some semblance of order and the first night's rations were doled out.

Phillip had been put in charge of a bread wagon because of his age and reputation with the priests. He took to his task very well and only gave the rations that the priests suggested. When Phillip looked up at the long lines of children behind his wagon he stood up and shouted, "Some of you will have to go to other wagons to get food." If he fed all of these children from his wagon, he wouldn't have enough to last two more days.

Phillip kept working handing out the meager rations but when he stood up to take a break, he noticed that none of the children from his lines had moved to other wagons. "Why don't some of you do as I ask and go to another wagon?"

A boy from the middle of the line stood out and shouted back, "The other lines are just as long as this one. Why should we lose our place here?"

Phillip took a minute and squinting a bit in order to see better, took a look around at the other wagons. There were only a scarce few wagons, and indeed the lines behind them were at least as long as the line behind his wagon. For the first time Phillip realized that they did not have enough food. There was nothing to do but go back to work handing out bread to the grubby little hands reaching up for their share.

As if in response to Phillip's disappointment at the lack of food, Stephen and Father David walked up to the line of children that was behind his wagon and with smiles and calm words began reassuring everyone that God would provide for all of their needs and not to worry. After a few words of blessing, the young leader walked on to the next wagon with his small group of followers that were always around him.

Feeling a little better, Phillip began to reach for another of the large burlap sacks that kept the bread. As he grabbed the next bag in the stack he found that he couldn't move it. A bit puzzled, Phillip grabbed the heavy sack with both hands and pulled it toward him. The sack rolled out of Phillip's hands and tumbled down the other sacks until it burst open on the bed of the wagon.

Phillip stood back in shock. There lying on the bed of the wagon was Michelle, the daughter of Lord William. Michelle turned her head and looked up to see who it was that had discovered her. She too was taken back as she recognized Phillip.

For a moment, the whole scene caused a bit of a stir around the wagon as some of the children crowded in to see what was going on. But as they glanced in and saw the stow away girl dressed in common clothes getting up and dusting bread crumbs off of her, they all lost interest and got back in line to wait their turn. Phillip, on the other hand, quickly guessed what was going on with Michelle and not wanting to draw more attention, said nothing to her.

"Andre, would you take over for me while I see to our new found crusader?" Phillip asked a friend who was helping him.

Andre, looking at the pretty girl now standing up in the wagon gave Phillip a little smile and responded, "Sure Phillip, anything for a friend." Andre then stepped into Phillip's place on the wagon and Phillip jumped down and extended a hand up to Michelle.

Anna was standing in line behind a boy who was obviously a beggar. His clothes were rags, his hair long and scraggly, and he smelled. Anna thought how strange it was that only a short time ago she went to the market place and tried to avoid children like this. Now she realized that this crusade made all persons equal. In this line there were no rich or poor. Everyone was hungry and tired.

The richer children would not be sleeping in warm comfortable beds, nor would they be eating hot home-cooked meals. The beggar children actually seemed a little better off out here in the open. In the countryside, they at least had fresh air and a little food given to them. Anna felt that this was much better than the gutters and slums of Paris where the begging children were malnourished and starving.

This particular beggar boy seemed a little odd though. While the rest of the children had their attention completely fixed on the food wagon ahead, this boy was continually looking out into the darkness of the countryside as if he were expecting someone.

Madoc had been a bit worried about Hungry. His dog had run off about a half-hour before and hadn't returned. Madoc wanted to go out and look for him but he thought it would be wiser to get in line and make sure that he got some bread.

A slight noise in the brush next to Madoc caused him to look over. Out trotted Hungry. Madoc's eyes grew large as he noticed that Hungry had something in his mouth. It was a large rabbit and it looked as if Hungry hadn't mauled it too badly. Hungry arrived at Madoc's side and dropped the rabbit right at his feet.

The hungry Madoc reached down, picked up his gift, and slipped it into a cloth bag that hung on his waist. He looked around to see how many others were staring at him. Fortunately, not very many had even taken notice of what had just transpired. The teenage girl just behind him obviously saw everything but tried to act as if she hadn't. Then Madoc got an idea.

He looked up at the girl behind him and greeted her. "Hello, I'm Madoc and this is my dog Hungry."

Anna looked down kindly at them and responded, "My name is

Anna. It is good to know you."

The beggar boy obviously had a reason for starting up the conversation so Anna kept her attention on him. He looked around and lowered his voice, "You see this rabbit I got here. I'll share some with you if you help me cook it."

Anna smiled. "All right," she whispered back. "I'll tell you what. You give me the rabbit and I'll get a fire going, clean the rabbit, and cook it for us. You stay here in line and get some bread."

Madoc's smile dropped to a frown. He wasn't sure about handing his supper over to this stranger and then allowing her to get out of his sight. He was about to suggest that they forget about the bread and both prepare the meal when Hungry took a few steps over and nuzzled the girl on the leg. She cautiously reached a hand out and stroked Hungry's head and neck.

"Hungry trusts you," responded Madoc. "I'll get the bread." Madoc untied the bag from his waist and handed it to Anna.

Phillip hunted for a good place in which he and Michelle could talk without being heard. He found a tree stump for Michelle and signaled for her to sit down, while he sat on a large stone. "I'm not going back," Michelle said stubbornly.

Phillip looked down at the ground and started scribbling in the dirt with a small stick, "Mademoiselle, what are you doing here? You can't just run away. You're the daughter of a lord."

"Maybe I can't, but that's exactly what I did. I thought it through a hundred times," said Michelle. "I knew that I would be leaving home. I just wasn't sure how until this crusade thing came along. When I found out that Father Jacque was sending some charity wagons for the crusaders, I knew that my chance had come." Michelle went into detail about how she had gotten peasant clothes and about how she had found a hiding place among the bread sacks. She changed the truth a little in order to leave out the parts where she had received help from a few of the servants in the castle. She didn't think that Phillip would tell anybody, but she wanted to make it seem like she had done it all herself.

Phillip was a bit surprised at Michelle's determination to leave the castle. Many people didn't like arranged marriages, but it was a fact of life that all seemed to get accustomed to eventually. "So you're really not going back?" Phillip shook his head. "What is a lady like yourself going to do on a crusade?"

"Oh, I don't plan on going on any crazy crusade. I'm just along for part of the trip." Michelle went on, "I have a cousin in Lyon. We grew up together and were very good friends as children. She married the brother of Sir Stephen there almost two years ago and I'm sure that she will keep me with her for as long as I like."

"I take it then that she doesn't know you're coming," interjected Phillip.

"No, but I know there won't be any problem," Michelle said confidently. "I couldn't have risked sending her a correspondence and besides there wasn't time."

Phillip looked right at Michelle and raised his voice. "Mademoiselle Michelle, this is a crusade. You can't just catch a ride with us as if this were some sort of caravan that just happened to be going your way. You have no idea of the difficulties involved. We'll be walking all day in the sun. There won't be any comfortable beds or clean sheets to sleep on at night." Lowering his voice again he added, "And we only have enough food to last another couple of days...if we are lucky."

Michelle's haughty expression didn't change. "Mademoiselle Michelle, I don't know how religious you are, but I don't think that God would approve either. I...I mean...that this is a very sacred event." Phillip didn't know how to express what he felt. He felt that the presence of Michelle somehow cheapened the whole crusade. She wasn't there to be a part of the holy undertaking. She was just there because it was a convenient way to escape.

"Nobody here knows who I am except you, Phillip," Michelle said matter-of-factly, as if what he had just said had no importance. "Help me stay anonymous and I will be out of your affairs in a couple of weeks."

Phillip sighed deeply. "All right, your secret is safe with me Mademoiselle Michelle," he said trying to show his reluctance, "but maybe you'll change your mind before we get to Vendome."

Michelle smiled. "Now, I suppose that if we're going to keep my identity hidden, I should use another name...maybe a common name like Anna."

"No," Phillip said immediately. Michelle looked at him and raised a questioning eyebrow. "You don't look like an Anna," said Phillip.

"All right then, how about...Mary? That's common enough, or don't I look like a Mary either?" Michelle said mockingly.

"Mary's fine," said Phillip. "Now let's get you settled."

The camp rose with the dawn. The morning air was a bit cool but most of the crusaders were anxious to get up and get a good start.

Phillip had arranged for Michelle to sleep in one of the wagons, and he spread out his bedding underneath. Phillip got up early to make sure that the horse was ready to be harnessed up to the wagon. As the camp got closer to leaving time Phillip went back and awakened the sleeping Michelle.

"Go away and leave me alone," Michelle said still half asleep. She gave a disgusted look to Phillip and pulled the covers over her head.

"Mary," Phillip said shaking Michelle again, "Mary, its time to go."

Michelle pulled the covers down again exposing a puzzled expression. She then looked around at the scene of the camp all around her. "Oh yes," she said as she remembered where she was. "Why are we leaving so early? The sun just barely got up itself."

A few of Phillip's friends who were watching the whole thing began to chuckle amongst themselves. "Mary," Phillip whispered at Michelle, "we need to talk a little before we get moving." He wanted to make sure that they had the same story about who she was before his friends started asking questions.

"All right, all right, I'm getting up," Michelle said throwing the covers off. "Where can I go to have, you know, a little privacy?"

Phillip turned and pointed to a little make shift tent that was set up between two trees. "Over there, but I'd hurry if I were you before it gets taken down." Michelle looked at the privy with disgust, but finally got out of bed and made her way slowly over.

"That girl has been spoiled," said one of Phillip's friends as they watched her stumble her way over to the privy. "A few more days as a crusader should cure her of that though."

"Yes," said Phillip, "a crusader." Turning back to his work, Phillip shouted to another young man about his age, and that he'd seen before at St. Denis', "Antoine, let's get that horse hooked up or we'll be the last in line."

Madoc had been ready to go for quite a while now. He and Hungry were sitting down under a tree, watching the rest of the people get everything done. It was amazing how many children there were and how lightly they had packed. Of course he didn't bring anything either, but he did have his dog, and "that was enough," he thought as he reached over and petted his friend.

Anna was still straightening things up and shaking her bedding out as thoroughly as possible. She couldn't believe how dirty things were after just one day and night on the journey.

Anna had found a place to sleep near the boy and his dog. They had eaten well together but the boy wasn't much for talking. Anna had tried to talk to the boy, but he didn't respond with many words, mostly grunts of yes or no. However, he had been very kind to include her in his special meal. She also felt that the dog liked her and having him close by made her feel much safer.

"Oh look at this dirt!" Anna said trying to brush off her clothes. "Mother would go crazy." Suddenly Anna stopped and her expression went blank. "Mother," she whispered to herself. Tears came to her eyes.

Christina had gone to the castle of lord William in order to put the finishing touches on his daughter's wedding dress. However, without the bride present, her trip proved to be almost completely useless.

Christina thought back at the chaos in the castle when she arrived. The princess had simply disappeared. Everyone had stopped what they were doing and a massive search was being carried out. Christina had spent the entire day setting in a waiting room staring at the walls.

Lord William's coach now pulled up to her house in Paris. The coachman opened the door and helped her down. It would be good to be home. She missed her comfortable house. Here she could get back to work on some other projects that had been piling up. Most of all though, it would be good to see Anna. She hadn't liked leaving her, but Anna was old enough to stay by herself and there was plenty of food in the house so that she wouldn't have to go out.

"Anna, I'm home," Christina called out. There was no answer. "Anna," she called out louder. "Where could she be?"

Christina glanced in Anna's room before going to put her things away in her own room. All of the windows in the house were shut up tight and there was a bit of a musty smell. She walked into the kitchen and saw a piece of bread and some breadcrumbs on the table. She picked up the hard stale bread as her heart pounded inside of her.

Christina ran into Anna's room and froze as she saw the note lying on her bed. She reluctantly picked up the piece of paper with writing on it, "Mother, I love you. I will miss you, but I had to go."

"Anna!" she screamed as her eyes burned with tears. Frantically she made one more futile search through the house, and then she threw the front door opened and ran into the street, "Anna!" she screamed. People stopped in the streets and some opened the doors and window of their houses to look out.

"Anna, nooooooo !" Christina shouted and then she fell to her knees and began crying convulsively. Many of the ladies in the street came over to her. Neighbors came out of their homes. Nobody had to ask what had happened. Many who had cried in private over the past days now joined her there in the street and they grieved together openly.

With Stephen in the lead wagon, the crusade set off again down the dusty trail that led south to Vendome. Renewed chants of, "For God and the Church!" rang out.

Phillip was in the middle of the group and walked beside his wagon. He had secured a spot for Michelle beside the driver.

Anna and Madoc were toward the back of the group and they began moving fifteen minutes after the leaders. Waiting behind all of the other groups was a large number who were waiting for the first sections of the crusade to get a good head start. This last group simply did not move. When the bulk of the crusade was out of sight they started back towards Paris. They had already had enough. The great children's crusade would have to go without them.

After three more days of marching, the crusade reached the city of Vendome where they set up camp on the outskirts of town. The priests and Stephen had already decided that they would stop here for a couple of days and have Mass before they made their vows and started off again. Not very far from Vendome were the cities of Orleans and Cloyes. The priests were hoping to pick up more supplies. They also planned to extend an invitation to the children of the area. This was Stephen's home territory and the people here had been hearing his preaching for a couple of months.

The people indeed supported them well. Even though not many new children joined the crusade, the kindly neighbors brought wagonloads of provisions.

After a very emotional Mass held on the second day, the crusaders took their holy vows. Father David led them to kneel and pray, "Dear God, we have heard the cry of the Holy Land for liberation. We now solemnly vow to take up the cross and follow Thee. We vow to be used as Your holy instruments in the retaking of the Holy City. We, now put our lives and immortal souls in you hands."

Stephen and the priests then exited the middle of the circle and the rest of the crusaders fell in behind them as they marched straight east along the Loire river. The leaders had not thought about bringing maps so they had to follow the giant landmarks that would eventually lead them east to Lyon and then south to the sea.

The beginning of the summer had been dry so the river routes were obviously the best way to go. They calculated reaching Lyon in less than a month and then going along the Rhone-Saone valley to the port city of Marseilles.[1]

---

[1] The approximate distances between the major cities of the crusade were: Paris to Vendome 90 miles: Vendome to Tours 30 miles: Tours to Lyon 270 miles: Lyon to Marseilles 140 miles. Though these distances seem short to us, travel in the 12th century was slow and hard. It could easily take a large caravan a couple of months to travel these distances.

9

TROUBLES/NO TROUBLES

Father David looked over at his companion. "Well Brother Gilbert, it looks like God has shown you the folly of worrying about how the crusade would survive." The two priests walked side-by-side just a few paces behind Stephen's wagon.

"Yes, it seems that God has supplied our needs for now, but even these new provisions will only last another three or four days. Then we will be far from any major cities," answered Father Gilbert looking straight ahead.

"You surprise me Brother," answered Father David. "You of all people should have faith that God will continue to supply."

"I suppose you are right. It is just that I cannot forget about the last day before we reached Vendome. We had no food and little water. I can not forget how all of those little hungry eyes looked at us."

"No doubt that God was using it to test our faith. And look what happened. Our faith was rewarded with new provisions. Brother Gilbert, we cannot let our followers think for one moment that we doubt God's ability and desire to meet our needs," said father David staring more intently at Father Gilbert. Father Gilbert did not say anything but just stared ahead as if he were in deep thought. "Brother, I have faith that when these provisions run low, God will again meet our needs; and then again; and then again."

With a smile of realization, Father Gilbert looked over at Father David, "Of course you are right. Do me a favor Brother."

91

"Yes, whatever you wish."

"Preach that same message to the children tonight before we pass out the provisions. I'm sure that if I needed it, they must need it even more."

"You are a wise servant Brother, a bit cautious, but wise," said Father David as he resumed his pace. "I think it would even be better if they hear it from Stephen. I will talk with him about it this afternoon."

Phillip's hands had been full over the past few days watching over his wagon and even more so watching over Michelle. Phillip's friends were sure that there was something going on between the two. They spent a lot of time talking alone, and they were always bickering with each other. Phillip gave her a little more rations than the others, he made extra stops for her when she needed it, and he even gave her his own blanket when she complained about the nights being too cold.

"How's the princess this morning?" asked Antoine to Phillip a few days out of Vendome.

Phillip stopped dead in his tracks and turned pale. "Wha...what did you say?" he asked stuttering.

"I asked how princess Mary was doing this morning that's all." He paused and looked at the expression on Phillip's surprised face. "Are you all right?"

"Yeah, yeah, I'm all right, but why did you call her princess?" asked Phillip.

"Oh, us fellows were talking last night and we decided that you treated that girl more like a princess than just an ordinary girlfriend, so we decided to call her the princess."

"Do me a very large favor Antoine and don't call her that again," said Phillip smiling, "things are bad enough as it is. If she hears you calling her that she'll probably expect you to treat her as a princess."

"All right," laughed Antoine, "we couldn't possibly put up with her if she got worse, but you're the one who pampers her."

Phillip turned his head and breathed a sigh of relief. Then when Antoine left Phillip said to himself, "Phillip, you fool. Your own actions are announcing to everyone the very thing that you wanted to hide."

He decided right then that he would have to treat Michelle just like everybody else.

Anna stood at a good distance as she watched Phillip. It looked as if he were in deep thought. She wondered what he was thinking, and wanted very badly to go to him, but she didn't.

It was on the second day out of Paris that she spotted him for the first time. He was walking in front of a food wagon. That night when the crusaders had stopped to rest she was going to go to him. When she got close, she noticed that he was sitting very close to a pretty young lady. She watched for a little while. He seemed very focused on everything that the girl was saying. Anna decided that she would not bother him that night. There would be the next day. As the days came and went Anna wanted to, at least, tell Phillip that she was there, but the girl was with him most of the time, and somehow she just couldn't get up enough courage to break in.

Even though she had to admit to herself that she was disappointed, Anna reassured herself that even if Phillip had a girl that he cared for, her friendship with him was too important to her to let go. She would go to him...but when?

"Anna, there you are," said Madoc, "have you seen Hungry?"

Anna took her gaze off of Phillip and turned to see Madoc walking up to her. "No, no Madoc I haven't. Has he been gone long?" she asked as they walked off together to find him.

Before heading off to his wagon, Phillip briefly scanned the area around him. His eyes stopped when they came to rest on the figure of a girl walking off in the other direction with a younger boy at her side. His heart leaped a bit, "Anna?" he asked to himself. "Impossible, she's at home with Madam Christina." Still, he began to take a step in that direction in order to follow.

"Phillip," came a call from behind him. He turned back toward the wagon. "Phillip, come here please."

Phillip turned and walked over to where his wagon was being hooked up to the oxen, took one more glance at the girl walking away with the boy, and then looked back toward the wagon. "Yes, Mary, what is it?" he asked.

"Phillip, I'm hungry. May I have a little bit of bread before we get started?" Michelle asked expectantly.

Phillip began to reach into a sack for some hard bread, but as he did, he caught the smiling faces of Antoine and Andre looking at him from the buckboard. Phillip pulled his hand out of the sack empty. "Mary, you know that we can't give out anymore food until lunchtime."

Michelle looked at him with an astonished look on her face, "But I'll get weak."

"I'm sorry Mary, but we all get the same amount. Besides you get to ride on the wagon. You'll just have to wait like the rest of us."

Antoine and Andre almost couldn't contain themselves from laughing. Antoine looked back at Phillip and mouthed the word 'princess' at him. Phillip scowled at him, but that made them laugh out loud.

"I don't see what's so funny," said Michelle pouting. "I may faint from hunger and fall right off this stupid wagon." Antoine and Andre laughed even louder.

On the fourth day after a disappointing stay at the city of Tours the crusade decided to stop a little earlier than usual in order to set up camp. The situation began to look difficult again. Some of the trails they had used were not very good for the large group and the wagons had difficulties crossing. Once the crusade came to a narrow pass. The only place to go through was a thin passageway that only allowed two or three to go at a time. When they camped that night, it took the rear of the group an hour to catch up with the front.

Walking beside the nearly empty wagon, Phillip could hear the wooden slats on the bottom rattle every time it hit a bump or ran over a rock. The only thing emptier than the wagon, Phillip thought, was his stomach. The unusually hot day added to the misery of hunger. Many fainted or simply got sick, so the crusade made very little progress.

That evening as Phillip and the others solemnly went about the task of getting the wagon ready so that they could pass out the remaining food. There would only be enough to feed 1,000 or so from his wagon if they gave half rations. Since the amount that was normally given was not really enough, half of that only assured the crusaders that they would go to sleep hungry.

It was their usual custom to stop and take an hour or so to get camp set up before the food was distributed but this evening the children bypassed setting up their camps and went directly to the wagon to get in line. Pushing and shoving ensued. Phillip told Antoine, Andre, and Michelle to help him immediately before things got out of hand.

The children didn't talk or joke as they waited in line. No one was happy with the little portion they received, but the situation was serious and everybody accepted it as much as possible. The rations were being passed out quickly because, as was their habit, Phillip and the other helpers ate last, and they were hungry.

"Phillip, I think that you had better look up a minute," said Andre tapping Phillip on the shoulder. "Look at the end of the line."

Phillip looked up at the line and followed it with his eyes tracing it from the front to the end, but there was no end. "What's this?" he asked standing straight up.

"It looks as if some of the other wagons didn't ration out their food very well," whispered Antoine so that the children in line couldn't hear.

"I didn't plan for more," Phillip whispered bending down pretending to do something in the wagon. "We will run out way before we feed all of these extras."

When there were only a few pieces left, Phillip told his helpers to take their share and go. "I'll tell the rest that there isn't any left. Now go on." Phillip stood up tall in the back of the wagon and announced out loud. "I'm sorry but there isn't any more. You'll have to try to find food somewhere else."

Many began to break ranks and walk away, but some of the older ones gathered closer to the wagon. Finally one older boy of about 16 spoke up. "If you hadn't given them so much there would have been enough for all, he said pointing at a large group of children who had received their rations and were off to one side eating.

"Yeah, that's right," said a few others.

"That's ridiculous," said Phillip. "I myself haven't eaten all day. Now I suggest that you all go on and try to find another wagon that still has food before that is all gone also." Most of the rest of the band broke up and went on.

However, a small group of six boys came right up to the wagon. "I don't believe you," spouted off a short stocky dark haired teenager. "I've seen how it works. The wagon flunkies always eat a good helping before they start doling out the rest. I imagine they have a little extra stashed away too. What do you think guys?" The other boys looked around at each other and nodded in agreement. "I think we should just look for this fellow's stash."

One of the boys began to climb into the wagon, but as he was just about up, he was suddenly jerked back from behind. "Heh, what the..." yelped the boy as he fell to the ground.

Michelle stood there scowling at the boy on the ground. "I think all of you boys should have better manners. Here," she said flinging a piece of hard bread at the dark haired boy, "you can have my food if you want it so badly."

The six boys didn't go away. "That's a start," said the leader, "now let's get the rest."

Phillip reached down and in one quick motion pulled Michelle up into the wagon beside him. "You blaspheme our Lord by your foolishness," Phillip yelled to the boys.

"Stop!" came a deep manly voice from behind. The boys whirled around to see Father Gilbert standing there with his arms folded and with a stern look on his face. Antoine was standing to one side of the priest and a large group of other children started to form a circle around them.

Father Gilbert pointed a finger at the boys in the middle, "You troublemakers get out of here and don't bother this young man and young lady again." The six boys all stood there looking at their feet. "Do I make myself clear?"

"Yeesss Father," they all said in unison. They quickly faded out into the crowd.

"Thank you Father," said Phillip breathing a little easier. "I am sorry Father, that you had to come away from your other responsibilities to help us here."

"This is my responsibility," said the priest. "I am only sorry that you were treated in this way. We are very thankful for the job that all of you have been doing with the food supply. Especially in light of such hardship," he said looking down into the empty wagon.

"Father, may I ask you a question in private?" asked Phillip.

"Of course, but I must tell you that I already know what you are going to ask me," replied the priest. "You are going to ask me how we are going to feed everyone tomorrow. Am I correct?"

"Well . . . yes, but, how did you know?"

"Is there any other question on our minds today?" asked Father Gilbert.

"I suppose not," said Phillip.

Raising his voice, the priest said clearly, "Gather around my children. I want you all to hear the answer to your question." After about a minute he began, "I know that you are all hungry and tired, but please listen. I have faith that God will supply our needs. This is a faith journey and by faith our Lord will feed us. We must pray and we must believe." After a few more words, the priest walked away putting a hand of blessing on the heads of the children that he passed.

Phillip watched the robed servant of the Church walk away and then looked down to notice that Michelle was still glued to his right side, clinging on to his sleeve. "And thank you," he said looking at her. Then Phillip's expression changed to one of anger and he pulled his arm free. "Why did you do such a crazy thing? Don't you realize that you could have been hurt?"

"You're welcome," Michelle said sarcastically. "And excuse me. I think I'll go get ready to go to sleep." Phillip tried to help her down out of the wagon but she pushed his hand away.

Antoine walked over to Phillip and they both watched as Michelle left. Phillip spoke to Antoine, "She really could have been hurt by those fellows you know."

"Yes, I know," said Antoine, "and she knew it too."

"Do you think that she was right in what she did then?" asked Phillip. "I mean, I might have still been able to talk my way out of it."

"Maybe," started Antoine, "but Mary was willing to bet her supper that you wouldn't. I must admit that she's got a strong heart." Antoine paused a minute. "You know what Phillip?"

"What?"

"You're right about one thing. Princess isn't a good name for Mary. I think 'the lioness' is more fitting. And to think that for all of these days I doubted if she would be tough enough to go on this crusade. Huh, imagine that." Antoine started to get his things out of the wagon. "Good night friend," he said leaving Phillip alone.

Later that evening as Phillip put his blanket down below the wagon where Michelle was sleeping, he couldn't help but think about what had happened. Maybe he was wrong about her too. With an empty stomach and a full mind Phillip found it hard to sleep, so he got up and stared at Michelle lying there in the back of the wagon. "Goodnight . . . . . .lioness," he said.

10

CEDRIC

Whispering, Madoc shook Anna. "Get up. Get up. I think I hear him."

"Madoc, it must be the middle of the night," responded Anna in a groggy voice. "Look, the moon has moved half way across the sky."

"Yes, I know but I couldn't sleep. Hungry hasn't come back, and I'm worried."

"Don't worry Madoc. He'll come back. He always does," Anna said trying to get comfortable again. Hungry often went off looking for food and exploring. The last couple of days he had stayed away for long periods of time, but as much as Madoc worried, the dog always arrived with a reward for his waiting master.

"I knows it but he hasn't come back yet, and I swear I hear him yelping from up that direction," whispered Madoc as he pointed towards a canyon that emptied into the river basin. "Listen."

After a few moments of silence, an unmistakably pathetic sound of a dog howling and whimpering made its way down the canyon and to the ears of Anna. She sat up and looked at Madoc.

"I gotta go to him," said Madoc.

"No!" whispered Anna loudly. "Madoc you can't leave the safety of the camp. You have no idea of the possible danger out there. Besides, I need you here with me to protect me," she tried.

"You'll be fine here with the others." Madoc sat up and began putting his sandals on. "He needs me."

"Wait, I'll go with you." They quickly readied themselves and left the camp, stepping over a few annoyed friends who were previously sound asleep.

With Madoc in the lead, the two strays made their way up the first rise within fifteen minutes. "Please Madoc, I must stop just for a few seconds in order to catch my breath," wheezed out Anna. Putting her hands on her hips she inhaled deeply. As she stood there she took just a moment to look back at the sleeping camp. The almost full moon shone down on what was now almost 25,000 people, mostly children, laying down under the open sky. There were only a dozen or so tents scattered in among them, horses and oxen grazed on small patches of grass close to where they were tied, and a handful of children could be seen stirring around. The once proudly carried banners stood lifeless in their places where they had been put to rest for the night.

Sleeping quietly under the stars, this rag-tag army of God didn't seem so impressive and spiritual as it did on the great day they left Paris. It looked very much instead, like a great number of beggar children and orphans lost in the wilderness, miles from any hope of providing for its needs.

"Coming or what?" called Madoc, who had already advanced another fifty feet before realizing that Anna wasn't behind him.

"Coming," responded Anna turning and starting back up the gradual slope. After another five minutes, Anna said to Madoc, "Madoc, I haven't heard anything for a while. Are you sure the yelping came from this way?"

"Sure, I'm sure. Now hurry up. Maybe Hungry is hurt and can't call out to me," said Madoc picking up the pace a little.

Another ten minutes walking and Madoc stopped suddenly. "Look, Anna, there he is." Madoc began to run cautiously to where Hungry was tied up.

"Madoc, come back," Anna called out as she saw Hungry tied up to a bush and muzzled with a piece of soft leather. There to one side of the bush was a crudely built lean-to shelter. The shelter was half built into the side of the canyon and the half that was showing was made of sticks what looked like pieces of cloth and leather draped around the top and sides.

"Who done this to you boy?" Madoc said kneeling down in order to untie Hungry.

"Stop thief!" growled the voice of a man from inside the little hut. Then from the entrance came the shadowy figure of a person. A tall figure walked briskly over to where Madoc stood with Hungry. Hungry was wagging his tail and begging to be freed. The man spoke again, "Wouldst thou steal a soul's beast little man?"

Madoc stood frozen by fright. Anna, who was still some twenty feet back, also froze where she was. The face and clothing of the man now stood completely revealed by the moonlight.

The man was dressed as a knight ready for battle, but his protective clothing was tarnished, rusty, and torn. His rust spotted metal helmet covered the top of his head but bursting from all sides was a matted glob of long brown hair. A very long ungroomed beard covered most of his face and draped itself down over a chain-mail shirt[1] which was so rusty that one could hardly tell that it was made of steel. Between the soldier's chain mail shirt and body was some sort of brown cloth that had been a crude bed covering, or maybe a large sack at one time, and now provided an undershirt of sorts.

Around the man's waist was a large leather belt that held up his protective chain-mail pants, distinguishing the man as a knight. His chain-mail pants and the cloth underneath were full of holes and ragged on the ends. His feet were bare and dirty. Also hanging on the side of the man's belt was the scabbard for a sword, but the sword, or what was left of it was in the soldier's hand. The sword that he was waving in the direction of Madoc had been broken in half and the half of the blade

---

[1] Chain-mail armor was used in many cultures throughout history. It can also be thought of as chain-link armor and it allows for the work of battle better than rigid armor. It was made of mild steel and was prone to rust if not carefully maintained, There were various pieces of clothing made in this fashion of interwoven steel chain, everything from head covering to leg coverings. Once rigid armor was created that allowed for more jointed areas and freer movement, chain-mail armor became less desirable because it did not deflect sharp blows nearly as well, but quality rigid armor didn't appear on the scene for some time. Thus, at this time, only Knights were afforded the luxury of a full chain-mail suit of armor.

that remained was chipped and useless. The sight was enough to make anybody freeze in their tracks.

As the man was just about to reach for Madoc, the frightened boy began to take a step back but tripped and fell to the ground in front of Hungry. Hungry, with his make shift muzzle still over his mouth, leaped at the man, but he was restrained by the rope.

The man stepped back, dropped his sword to his side and looked at Madoc. "Look what thou hast done little man. Thou hast turned the beast against his master. Dost thou not know that a thief is in danger of Hell's fire?"

"Have not stole em. And he's not a beast, he's a dog," sassed back Madoc still sitting on the ground. Then looking at Hungry he said, "Here boy." Immediately Hungry obeyed and Madoc wrenched off the muzzle. Hungry gave Madoc a big swipe with his tongue.

The man now standing down to the boy and dog didn't seem so fierce to Anna. She moved forward. The sudden movement from behind startled the warrior. He whirled around and brandished his sword in the direction of Anna. In seeing the startled girl, he sheaved the sword, stood up straight, and laughed out, "For twenty years this lone soul hath lived here hidden from the world. Now in one fateful night he has been discovered and conquered by two children and a hunting beast."

"It will never be said about Cedric of Toulouse that he was a poor loser. Even if a night attack is not very chivalrous, it has proven to be effective at times." Madoc and Anna kept silent.

"Please, young warriors, you must honor this poor wretched soul with a bit of conversation," said Cedric looking alternately at the two. Finally he pointed to a clearing. "Please sit there while another sitting stone is looked for." Then he disappeared into the thicket.

Madoc and Anna looked at each other with uncertainty. "Let's get Hungry and leave before he comes back," said Madoc finally. He reached down and untied the rope.

Cedric then reappeared with a large stone in his strong hands and plopped it down in the clearing. Still the two didn't move. Cedric pulled something from a leather pouch and motioned to Hungry.

"Come here beast," he called. Hungry trotted over to the man and was eating from his hand before Madoc could call him back. Both Anna and Madoc then slowly made their way over and sat down beside one another on a fallen tree trunk.

"Get over here Hungry," scolded Madoc. The dog came. "Your stomach will be the death of you boy...gotta learn who is and who isn't your friend."

"A ha," said Cedric perking up his eyebrows. "Thou dost injure a person with your doubts." He then slowly sat down on his stone looking more intently at his visitors. "It is probable that these two young friends have come from the camp below. It is puzzling, to think of a possible purpose for such a group." With this Cedric again paused as if to receive a response. None came. "There are banners, priests, and poor provisions. If the band wasn't full of children and void of weapons and horses, it would seem to be a crusade."

Anna finally spoke, "We are a crusade, and we are marching to the Holy Land to take it in the name of the Lord and the Church."

"Ha," responded Cedric with a smile. He looked at the faces of the children which did not change. Finally his smile dropped and his eyes glared. "Thou canst be serious...but you are." He buried his face in his hands and began to weep loudly. Madoc and Anna exchanged questioning glances. "Purgatory grows hotter still," he cried still not looking up.

Anna, not able to bear watching the grown man cry so, spoke up. "Purgatory? I do not understand."

"Yes, purgatory. Twenty years ago this soul came here seeking penance. Daily, he whips himself with sticks and thorns. He sleeps in the cold. He survives on raw meat and tasteless bushes. He stays here alone. He does not bother God with prayers. He refuses to return to his home and to those who once loved him. He has refused himself any type of pleasure. All this he does so that purgatory's fire will be less painful and his time there a little shorter. Now," began Cedric standing and waving his hand in the direction of the camp, "now children march off to do the job that he was to much of a coward to do. He didn't even have the good fortune of dying while trying. No, instead he returns with broken vows and shame hanging over his head: And now this. It is too much for one to bear. Surely God in his justice will use this children's crusade as an example to cowards like him in order to make his sentence more severe."

"God 'd do that?" questioned Madoc after listening to the emotional outpouring. "Of course He would," said the man. "That is what God does."

"He would not," contradicted Anna. Cedric looked over at Anna. "Yes, God is just, but God is also love," she said. Cedric seemed shocked at the words. Anna continued, "My father said that God's Word teaches that God's love is patient, long-suffering, and forgiving to those who will accept it."

Cedric took a step toward Anna. His mouth dropped open a bit as he stared respectfully at her. "Thou ardst a prophetess then."

"Of course I am not," she said a little startled by her own words.

"Yes, yes thou ardst. Thou knowest the Words of God, and thou hast shared them with me," answered Cedric. "Dost thou know more?"

"Well, yes. Yes, I know some more. My father constantly taught my mother and I. He was not a servant of the Church but he learned the languages of the Bible as a boy from one of the priests at St. Denis. He would spend hours going to the Cathedral in order to copy and memorize scriptures. As the bishops changed they later forbade him to study, but he had already copied and memorized great portions. What I know are only the bits and pieces that I can remember from his talks. I don't believe that it will be much."

Madoc interrupted, "We have to go back to camp Sir. We'll march in the morning."

"No matter," said Cedric ignoring Madoc and inviting Anna to sit down again. "The birds have tried to sing God's Words to these ears, but no matter how the ear strains, it can not understand. The wind has whispered its message also but to no avail. This poor wretched soul has spent many hours with his head underneath the cool flowing waters of the river trying to divine its secrets about the Almighty, but the river refuses to reveal them. Twenty years have come and gone and God has not revealed himself. If thou, will refuse to tell me God's words, then I feel that I will never know." He paused and looked earnestly at Anna. "Please, if thou knowest but one word. Tell it. If thou knowest but ten. Tell them also. In thy heart and mind thou hast more power than all of nature. Reveal to me what the sun and moon cannot. I beg you?"

Anna looked at Madoc, "I am compelled to tell him, Madoc. You do not have to stay."

"We will not leave," responded Madoc, and almost as if to give his answer also, Hungry laid down at the feet of Madoc who sat on the tree trunk.

Anna turned to Cedric. "Where do I start?" she asked.

"Tell me again that God is Love," was all the worn out knight said, and then he waited for Anna to begin.

"Yes, God is love," began Anna. "God loves so much that he sent his Son Jesus from heaven to live among us, die as payment of our sins, and then rise again to show us that he has the power and desire to resurrect us and take us to heaven to live with him there." Anna continued to speak the words that she had heard. As Cedric listened, tears ran down his cheeks, but he never allowed his eyes to look away from Anna for a moment as if she would disappear if he dared.

Hour after hour Anna spoke. She was shocked at how much she remembered. She would picture her father speaking to them at the dinner table or in the living room, and all of the words he said came back to her. She spoke of man's sins and God's desire to still know his fallen creation. She spoke of the impossibility of man to renew that broken relationship with a holy God, and then of God's plan to send his perfect Son in order to pay sin's price for all men. She spoke of God's grace and of God's love.

Hour after hour Cedric sat there with a continual river of tears coursing down his cheeks dampening his long beard. He said very little. Only a few times did he have a question, but every time, Anna had an answer from what God's words said.

Finally as the sky in the East began to lighten, Anna said, "That is what I know of God from what He has revealed to us from His Word." Anna glanced over at Madoc and noticed that Hungry was gone, but that Madoc was wide awake and with tears in his eyes also.

Cedric finally allowed his head to drop and look at the ground between his feet. With a deep sigh, he said to himself, "If only this soul could deserve such a wonderful salvation as that, but surely it cannot be."

"Why not?" asked Anna.

"Hast thou this gift? This gift of salvation?" He asked honestly to Anna. Madoc looked at Anna also. Both waited an answer.

"Yes. When I was ten years old I accepted the gift. I accepted Christ," she said.

"Then at ten, you deserved the salvation of God," asked Cedric.

"No," responded Anna quickly. "We never deserve it." At that another scripture came to her. "The scriptures say that while were yet sinners, Christ died for us."

With that, Cedric's face brightened so suddenly that the expression startled Anna. Then jumping to his feet he ran up the side of the canyon and out of site.

Anna said out loud, "How very odd!" Then she looked over at Madoc who was still sitting on the log. He had a fearfully serious look on his face. "What's the matter, Madoc?" asked Anna worriedly.

He looked up at Anna, "I always thought God hated me. I never knew why, and I thought Him to be mean. God doesn't hate me. He hates my sin, but He loves me. Doesn't he Anna?"

"That's what the Scriptures say Madoc."

"I want to have salvation like you. I want God to be my Father. Can I?" asked Madoc to Anna.

"The Holy Scriptures say that any person who will ask God to forgive them of their sins and ask Him to save them, can have salvation," answered Anna moving over to sit by him.

"How would I ask?"

"When I asked, I just prayed and asked God like I would ask my own father something," answered Anna.

Madoc stood up and looked up into the still star lit sky and began, "God," then he hung his head until his chin was touching his chest. "God," he began again. "My sins are bad but you said you could forgive them. Forgive me and save me." With that he looked up at Anna. Anna smiled. Madoc smiled.

Anna remembered the day that she asked God to save her. When she told her dad and mother they both cried with joy. Now she wondered what her father was doing in heaven. She wondered if he had been watching while she was telling the soldier about God's words. Then she thought about her mother. She had to turn suddenly so that Madoc would not see the sudden look of anguish on her face.

At that moment the familiar sound of Hungry coming through the bushes was heard. As he came into the clearing both Madoc and Anna went toward him in order to retrieve the rabbit that he brought with him.

The two of them decided to go ahead and stay there and cook the rabbit while they waited for the soldier to return. Day broke, the two had a very much-needed breakfast, but Cedric had not returned. They then decided to hurry on back to the camp and get ready to move on with the rest. Since they usually were all the way at the end of the crusade, they figured that they would have time before the rear began to move.

Anna led the way down the canyon with Madoc and Hungry tailing behind closely. As they got closer to the camp, the low cloud of dust that was visible told them that the camp was definitely up and moving. Finally they topped the last little hill and could see the entire camp, but they didn't stop to look long, for the front section had already begun to march on.

Just outside the camp a little service was being held for a child that had died the night before. This was not uncommon. Many children and adults who were sick and dying had come along on the crusade in order to receive a miraculous healing if possible, but if not, to die on the crusade. To die on a crusade almost assured someone that they would be swept directly into heaven.

Anna and Madoc passed the little burial ceremony in process and found their usual place in the group. The few other people that Anna had gotten to know had watched over their things. It was not long before they also were on the march.

"Freeeeeeeeeeeeeeeeeeee!"

Everybody suddenly stopped what they were doing in order to look off to one side and up on a rise about 200 yards away. There was a crazy man dressed in rusted knights armor and rags jumping up and down, waving a broken sword in the air, and yelling.

Madoc and Anna gasped at the same time, "Cedric." There was the knight jumping around with his eyes sparkling brightly and an unmistakable smile shining from beneath his bearded face.

Finally he stopped, yelled out clearly, "I...am...free!" and hurled his sword as far as he could into the air. He then whirled around and disappeared.

11

FINDING A WAY

Phillip had gotten up just before dawn in order to try to find food. He was not the only one. Others were also out early combing the countryside for anything that looked eatable. Most were trying to catch fish in the cool waters of the nearby river. You could easily tell what children had grown up in the cities and which had grown up in the country. The city children splashed a lot but had very little success. The country children made nets out of vines and plants or waited patiently in shallow pools for the fish to swim close enough for them to gig them with crude wooden spears.

Phillip watched the country children for a while and then decided to imitate what they did. He pulled out a knife from his pouch that he had bought at Sir John's mercantile before setting out on the journey. He found an acceptable branch and whittled out a point.

After many failed tries, a boy younger than himself, came over and said, "Any luck Cap'n."

Phillip looked up and with drops of water dripping from his face responded a little curtly, "Not at all. I've seen a few and had a few stabs but no luck."

"Let me see your spear a moment Cap'n," the boy said advancing. "Ah. Tis no wonder. Your stick's to green and soft and you forgot to put a gig on the end." Phillip didn't know what to say. The boy began again, "Come on. We'll find you a suitable stick and I'll carve you off a good point."

A half-hour later Phillip and the boy were walking back to camp together carrying six fish between them. "I forgot to ask you your name," Phillip said as they walked.

"My name is Achaire, but my friends call me Acky," responded the boy. "I come from the city of Metz."

"How did you learn to fish?" Phillip asked.

"Well Cap'n, my family works a large piece of land for the duke on the outermost edge of the limits. I always went into the outlying area with my father in order to hunt and fish for extra food for the family. I lived off the land while I was traveling from Metz to Paris. I'd say that I was getting' pretty good at it."

"One more thing, Acky," Phillip asked.

"Sure, what is it?"

"Why do you call me Cap'n?"

"Oh, its that I noticed you were the fellow in charge of our food wagon," began Acky. "Did a good job too. I just figured that kind of makes you the captain."

The two were getting close to the camp now. "I see," said Phillip smiling. "Thanks a lot for the fishing lesson."

"Phillip, you're all wet," was the first thing Michelle said as the two came walking up. Then she saw the six fish hanging between. "Oh Phillip, you caught us some breakfast. I am so hungry that my head hurts."

"Actually Mary," said Phillip, "this is Archaire and he caught the fish."

"Acky, missy," corrected Acky while nodding to Michelle.

Phillip continued, "Acky will take his fish and help feed some friends of his."

"How many are yours Phillip?" Michelle asked.

Phillip hesitated, "One," he said pointing with his spear to a small fish on the end. Michelle's expression of joy vanished.

"No worries missy," said Acky with a smile. "I can spare one of mine this time." He removed Phillip's fish and then a good-sized one from the stringer and handed them to Michelle.

Michelle pulled her hands back, made a funny face, and said, "Uuh," in disgust.

"Thank you very much Acky," said Phillip taking the fish by putting a finger in each one's mouth. "We had better get cooking these things."

Acky left with his catch and Phillip and Michelle built a quick little fire. The fish was very good. Phillip wondered why he hadn't tried to catch fish sooner.

That day and the next the crusaders made their way through the countryside with food wagons getting more and more full, but not with food. As Phillip had thought, his wagon alone now carried about a dozen sick or hurt children. Everyone was scrounging for food as they went but many were not able to find it.

Small villages on hearing of the coming of the crusade would simply put out the little extra food that they could afford on the outskirts of the village and close up all of the windows and doors of their houses. The children would converge on the piles of food like vultures converging on a dead animal. Then at the orders of the leaders they would move on. The summer had seen almost no rain, crops had failed and farm animals had died.

In general, the villagers feared the crusade. In their hearts they wanted to help, but from past experience did not want to be victimized. Many still remembered the crusade of Phillip II and Richard the Lionhearted some twenty years ago. The soldiers had come to believe it their God-given-right to take whatever they needed in order to carry out their crusade. It was bad enough that King Phillip had levied a high crusade tax in order to pay for the venture, but those who had the misfortune of living close to the route that the soldiers were taking also found themselves stripped of everything valuable that they had. Crops, animals, tools, wagons, and various others things were confiscated for the sake of the crusade.

For the first time since the organizing of the crusade there was widespread complaining. Fights were breaking out every time the group stopped to set up camp. Many children left the crusade in order to stay in a village or try to find their way back home. Many others had succumbed to illnesses and little mounds of dirt and rock with makeshift crosses marked the path in which the crusade had passed. Complete chaos seemed the next logical step.

There was, however, one group of about one thousand children who seemed to be holding together pretty well. That group was surviving with only a few casualties. That same group had had no fights and still carried their crusade banners high.

When Acky had called Phillip "Cap'n", an idea came to Phillip—the idea of structure. Phillip found eight young men, a priest, and an older man whom he had noticed to be natural leaders and who seemed to have good characters. He called the ten of them together and proposed a plan to them. Each one of them would lead a group of one hundred.

He proposed that the leaders of each group would call their group together and find out who had abilities in certain areas of need. Who could hunt, who could fish, who knew what plants were edible, who knew what plants would be helpful medicinally, who could care for the sick, etc. Each area of need would have a leader. When it was time to look for food, the group would divide up with their leaders and hunt, fish, or find vegetation. When it was time to cook, those who knew how would prepare the food and cook for their smaller group.

When the group captains first surveyed their group of one hundred, they found that they had to swap some people around in order to have a good balance of skills. In just two days the plan was working better than even Phillip could have imagined.

Not only were the groups helping each other to fulfill their duties, but also the children were doing something that they hadn't done before. They were helping each other with every little task. They would find firewood together; set up tents together; make nets, spears, and traps together; they were doing things for each other instead of just themselves.

Within a week of setting the plan into effect, hundreds of others came to Phillip asking if they could join in one of the groups. Phillip formed ten new groups with ten more leaders in order to meet the need.

The leaders would come to Phillip throughout the day asking what they should do in this case or in that case. Even the older boys and men

asked Phillip for advice on what they should do to solve certain problems. Many of the problems were similar and Phillip would have to
repeat himself often. Finally Phillip told the leaders that they would all
meet once a day in order to talk about problems that were common to
all. As it turned out, Phillip would start the meeting and then the leaders would talk amongst themselves and find the solutions to their
problems without Phillip ever saying anything. Only every once in a
while would Phillip have to interrupt and put things in order when
everybody tried to talk at the same time. At the end of the meeting all
of the leaders would go shake Phillip's hand and thank him as they left
to join their groups.

Phillip walked back to the smaller campfire that Michelle and a few
others were sitting at. "Ahhhh, peace," he said as he sat down with a
sigh.

"How did things go at the meeting tonight Phillip?" asked Andres.

"You know, I think they're getting better every night. In a few more
days they won't even need me," he said. "Then I'll be able to join in one
of the groups and just be normal."

"Impossible," said Michelle looking at the fire.

"What?" asked Phillip.

"I said, impossible. I've seen the way everybody has begun to treat
you and talk to you these past days," said Michelle looking up at
Phillip. "Why do you think we're at this fire over here by ourselves. You
can't be just like everybody else now." Phillip watched the flames of the
fire with a straight face as Michelle spoke. "You have saved the lives of
these people and they know it."

"That's ridiculous," started Phillip taking his gaze away from the
fire and looking at Michelle. "I've done nothing. They're the ones who
are doing it. You've seen the way they have pulled together. It's them."

"She's right, Phillip, and you know it," said Andres. "Without you
we would be like the rest of the crusaders; no food, no friends, and no
hope. I wonder if the leaders of this crusade have noticed what's going
on here?"

"It must be stopped immediately," said Stephen to the two priests standing there. "I will not have it! I will not allow one section of the crusade to form their own little groups and have leaders. I am the only leader of this crusade. Do you hear?"

"As I tried to explain before," began Father Gilbert, "they are surviving together while the rest are divided and falling apart. This young man, Phillip, has set into order no small group. It is working."

"No, no, no," raved Stephen, his high voice now loud and shrill. "I am the called one. I am the chosen leader. There can be no others."

"Of course you are. And you will still be," said Father Gilbert trying to calm down the boy. "I am just suggesting that we talk to Phillip and find out what he has done."

Suddenly Father David's eyebrow perked up and he held up a hand as to stop the other two from talking. "I think I have an idea that will make both of you happy," he said with a smile on his face. "We will find out exactly how this young man Phillip has organized his section of children and tomorrow Stephen will call the whole mass together and announce that he has had a revelation from God."

"What! Don't you see that the children will see right through that?" said Gilbert unbelievingly at Father David.

"They will see what we want them to see," said David, "and the children will love and follow Stephen more vehemently than ever."

"I don't understand," said Stephen with a puzzled look on his face.

"You will," said Father David. "You will."

That night the crusaders stopped a little earlier than usual in order to camp on a wide open plain. The news began to spread that Stephen and the priests wanted to have a very important meeting with the whole crusade. Stephen found himself a place half way up a hill so that everyone could hear him. It took all fifteen thousand about a half an hour to find places to sit.

At first some of Phillip's leaders complained that they would not be able to do their jobs before dark set in if they had to go to the meeting. Phillip had to remind them that they were only part of a much larger much more important group. The larger group and its leaders took president. They all attended. Phillip noticed that the smaller groups all found places to sit together.

Phillip took a place in front. From where he was sitting he could look back and see the entire crusade. This group of ragged looking children didn't even look like the same group that had left Paris almost three weeks ago. It was smaller by almost half and everyone looked very tired, very hungry, and very dirty.

"Please, everyone we need silence," yelled out Father David, who had just climbed the little incline in order to take his place by Stephen's side. He was waving his hands high in the air in order to get their attention. "Please, everyone we must have quiet." Slowly the noise of talking and rustling around came to an acceptably low volume. "Thank you. Now listen." He looked over at Stephen and nodded.

The young boy stood to his feet and looked out over the crowd. He had not been exempt from hardship. He looked thinner and his clothes were dusty and worn. His voice, however, had not suffered. Within two minutes after he began speaking, he had everybody's complete attention.

"Last night I had a dream. I dreamt that we were not crusaders marching into the Promised Land, but that we were Moses and the children of Israel walking in the desert toward the Promised Land. I saw the children of Israel hungry and complaining. They fought with each other over old tribal disputes. I saw myself the old and wise Moses looking over his people with a broken heart. I was trying to lead the people and settle disputes. I was trying to judge between people who were angry at one another. I saw myself tired and worn out sitting on a rock on the side of a mountain overlooking the chaotic numbers below. Then I saw a man older still than myself coming up slowly to meet with me there. He saw how tired I was. He began to speak, 'Moses you cannot lead these people in this manner for much longer. It will be the death of you.' I asked the older man what I was to do. He answered me thusly, 'You must elect leaders to rule over the ten thousands, leaders over the thousands, leaders over the hundreds, and leaders over the fifties in order to help you lead this people.' With his words I felt a tremendous weight rise off of my shoulders. His words were right and true."

"This morning, as I awoke, I remembered the entire dream," continued Stephen shouting out to the masses. "Throughout the day I thought about it in relation to our situation here. Father David helped me realize that it was not just a dream, but direction from God. God was telling me that I, like Moses, must put leaders in charge of groups so that we can carry on this crusade. With a good structure, we can help each other find food and water, cook, and care for the needs of the sick. It will work."

With that Stephen took a long pause in order to scan the reactions of the crusaders below. Most were smiling, nodding their heads in approval, and murmuring excitedly. The noticeable exception was a large group sitting to the far left side. They were talking amongst themselves also but with puzzled looks on their faces.

A few of the group leaders tapped Phillip on the shoulder at the same time, "What do you think of this Phillip?"

Phillip was caught off guard for a moment but didn't let those behind him see the expression on his face. When he caught his composure he turned around and smiled. "Sounds like a good idea. Let's listen to what else he says." He then turned around and looked back up at the boy and the priest. "That's odd," Phillip thought, "Stephen is almost always with both of the priests. I wonder where Father Gilbert is?" He took a moment to look around. Phillip saw Father Gilbert at the front right with some other crusaders but quite a distance away from himself. Suddenly Father Gilbert turned his head a little and looked directly at Phillip. For a split second their eyes locked but then the priest looked away abruptly.

"This very night," began Stephen again, "we will come through and appoint leaders and groups. Now go and find a place to camp. We will be coming through each area appointing the leaders who God directs us to appoint." With that the boy sat down as if exhausted, and Father David began talking to him in hushed tones.

Everyone slowly got up and began the process of finding a place to set up camp. All at once there were twenty young men surrounding Phillip. "They will elect different leaders and split up our groups," said one. "All that we have worked so hard to build will be destroyed," said another. Everyone began to talk at once.

Phillip raised up his hands. "Please, please. Nobody is going to destroy anything." They quieted down and listened. "When they realize that we have already set up a good structure, they will be pleased that they don't have to change anything."

"Realize," said one young man. "Realize. I think they already "realize" what we've been doing. They saw it working and used this dream thing in order to have an excuse to take it into their own hands."

"No!" said Phillip angrily. "That cannot be true. We can never think that they would do such a thing. The truth is that I have been praying for several days now that God would show the rest of the crusade our plan so that they all could benefit. To me this is an answer to prayer."

The leaders nodded their approval at this thought. "You are right young man," added a leader who was an older man. "But still, what if they try to break up our groups?" The others joined in again with their disapproval.

"Don't worry," said Phillip. "When they come to our camping area, I will explain to them what has been going on. Surely they will see that advantage of keeping things as they are." Phillip paused for a second and said, "Now go back to your groups and tell them what we've talked about here so that they will not be upset." The leaders went off in the direction of their camp still talking amongst themselves.

Phillip turned to go also but from the corner of his eye he caught the side view of a familiar face standing in the midst of the crowd no more than a hundred feet away. "Anna!" he shouted out waving in that direction. He started pushing his way through the crowd. "Anna!" he shouted again. This time she heard him and looked directly at Phillip.

Phillip froze for a second. It was really her.

Suddenly a hand grabbed Phillip. "Phillip you have to come at once. There's trouble," said Antoine.

"Not now," Phillip said pushing away Antoine's hand. "Anna, it's me Phillip," he shouted in her direction.

"Phillip, you must come now!" Antoine said grabbing his arm. "Some of the groups are talking about abandoning the crusade when we get to Lyon. Now Phillip!"

12

FINDING FRIENDS

He saw her. Phillip called her name. Anna froze. She could not respond back to him, even though she wanted to. No words came to her lips. Now another young man about Phillip's age was dragging him off in another direction. Phillip kept looking back at her. One more time he mouthed her name, "Anna," and then she didn't see him anymore.

About four days earlier, Anna and Madoc had joined one of the newly formed groups under Phillip's leadership. Madoc and Hungry were naturally a great help in hunting for and finding food. With Hungry's help tracking they even brought back two small deer one day.

Anna had taken a place doing various things, mending clothes and sandals, and at dinnertime she helped prepare food for the others. They had both fit in very nicely and had made a few more friends.

Anna had seen Phillip many times in the past four days and found herself hiding whenever he came by. She didn't know why she hid, but for some reason she felt it would be best if he didn't know she was there. People talked about him often, but Anna refrained from making any comment about Phillip or telling anybody that she knew him personally.

That girl was always with him wherever he went. Anna found out that her name was Mary. As Anna would watch them in the distance, she noticed how different the girl was. She carried herself differently than the other girls. She always walked with her head up and shoulders squared back. She looked proud as she walked and even as she talked. As Phillip and Mary would walk around talking to the leaders of the groups, she could not help but think how noble they looked together.

That night no one went to bed early. Everybody wanted to be there when the leaders were chosen. The sun had long set over the scorched land before Stephen and some of the other leaders with him visited the area that Anna and Madoc stayed. Anna noticed that even though Phillip stood to one side of Stephen and the others when they began choosing the leaders, Phillip looked very calm.

When everybody was in position to hear, Anna could hear Stephen begin to speak. "We have been notified that some of you have already formed loose groups and chosen leaders. We have looked into your choices and found that they are good ones, and I can not see where the Lord would lead us to change things." Stephen looked around to see pleased faces and then finished with, "We will have a meeting of all the leaders tomorrow afternoon." Stephen and his little group then walked off towards the next area of campers.

Phillip stayed for a minute after Stephen and the others left and looked into the crowd as if looking for someone. Finally he looked down, sighed, and then left in the direction that Stephen and the others had gone.

Everybody seemed very happy with what had happened. They were laughing and talking a lot more than normal. Madoc didn't talk much, but Anna could see that he was satisfied also. Madoc reached down and patted Hungry on the head and said, "D'ya hear that, boy. Tis good. Tis good. Tomorrow we'll get up early and see if there's any food around here."

That night Anna laid in her bedroll thinking about all that happened that day, and came to a decision. "Tomorrow I will find Phillip and talk to him." She opened her eyes and stared at the stars sparkling in the night sky. How beautiful and infinite they were.

The crusade was up and going on time the next morning, but practically nobody had had anything for breakfast. The events of the day before helped to give the children some new hope, but the reality of their hunger soon brought back to them the seriousness of their situation.

As the crusade proceeded on, children constantly left the ranks in order to try to find some sort of food. Later in the morning there was a girl of about ten years who found what she thought to be something good to eat. About fifteen minutes after she ate it her stomach started cramping horribly. The poor girl cried in pain for about two hours and then her screams suddenly stopped and her clear blue eyes stayed fixed opened, as if entranced by the clouds above. She died while being attended to in one of the wagons.

The death of this little girl really effected Anna. She'd seen others die on the journey but somehow watching that girl squirm and cry in the wagon and then suddenly stop was very hard on her. The people in the front part of the crusade didn't even know what had occurred, and therefore marched on as if nothing had happened.

Anna didn't know the girl personally but stayed with a small group of others to bury her on the side of the trail. The girl's bed coverings were used to wrap her in, and the limp little body was put into a shallow grave. The priest said a few words, a wooden cross, (made out of two sticks tied together), was hammered into the ground with a rock, a mound of dirt was piled over her, and the small group of mourners quickly broke up in order to catch up with the rest.

Anna lagged behind all of the rest and thought more deeply about the girl's death. She thought of the girl's family at home crying because she had left. She thought of the girl's dreams about reaching the Holy Land with the crusade. Would anybody ever know what had happened here with that little life on this summer day?

She found herself picturing her own body lying beneath the cool earth in that shallow grave. She pictured her mother weeping for her and never knowing what had happened to her. Tears stung Anna's eyes as she walked.

Suddenly Anna felt the earth under her give way. Everything happened so quickly that she was not sure exactly what had happened. Somehow she had taken a bad step and fallen into a deep ditch. She lay there a little dazed and with a great pain in her right leg.

When the dizziness faded she tried to shift her weight so that she could get a better look at her leg. The pain was so intense that she could barely move it around in order to look at it. It was hurt badly. Her knee and shin were already starting to swell.

"Oh no," she thought, "the whole crusade is a long way off by now." Maybe some of the people who had stayed back for the funeral were still close enough to hear her yell. "Help! Heeelllllp," she yelled with all of her strength. She was weak from a lack of food and from her injuries and somehow her voice just did not have the force needed.

After about fifteen minutes of screaming and crying for help, Anna gave up screaming. Now the thoughts of death came rushing back to her like a flood. "There's no hope," she thought. Then she remembered something that her father had said to her. He had told her that only those who do not know God have no hope.

Anna sat there and began to remember the things that she had learned from her father and mother. "God help me," she prayed calmly. From that time on, even though her head told her that the situation was hopeless, her heart was calm. She even thought of how nice it would be to be able to see her father again, but somehow she felt that she would not die. She remembered songs that she had learned at church and began to sing them out loud.

"Phillip, we will probably reach Lyon tomorrow afternoon," said Michelle calling down to him from the wagon.

"Yes," he responded without breaking stride. "I guess things are going to change for you soon," he said smiling up at her. She was not smiling. "What's the matter, Mary? I thought you'd be ecstatic about seeing friends there?"

"You have friends in Lyon?" asked Antoine overhearing the conversation.

"Yes," said Michelle looking over at Antoine who was driving the cart. "I am hoping to be able to speak to them while we are camped outside of the city."

"I sure hope your contacts are good ones," Antoine went on. "We could sure use some fresh supplies."

"I don't know, Antoine. I hope that my friends are still friendly," finished Michelle. "Phillip, can you help me down? I would like to walk for a little while."

Without saying anything, Phillip reached up, and with both hands around Michelle's waist gently lifted her off of the moving wagon. "Are you sure you can walk? You haven't had much to eat in the last few days."

"It's all right. We only have another hour or two to go tonight," she said. Then she motioned with her head at Phillip to move away from the wagon. "I want to talk to you about something," she whispered.

When the two were a little ways from the wagon Michelle grabbed Phillip's sleeve. "Phillip, I want you to stay with me in Lyons," she finally said.

Phillip immediately looked down at her. In her eyes was something that he had never noticed in her before. That proud sassy look was gone. In her eyes was deep concern and caring. "What?" he asked as if he had not heard.

"Phillip, you must not continue on with this crusade," she said. "How can you say that?" responded Phillip.

"How can I not continue on with it? I have made a vow, and I must fulfill it."

"No Phillip. This whole crusade thing is nothing but hunger and death," she said. Phillip was going to respond but Michelle continued on. "Phillip, I fear that if you continue on, you also will die."

"That is a possibility, but sacrifice and even death has always paved the road to final victory."

"Phillip, you must not die," Michelle said as a tear began to form in her eye. "You are young and full of life. Your life is worth something. How can you just be willing to throw it away like this?"

"Michelle, I was hoping that after all of this time with the crusade, you might begin to understand the importance of it," said Phillip. "I was hoping that you would feel a calling within yourself from the Lord. I was hoping that you would feel the importance of this event for all of human kind and especially for the sake of Christ. I must admit that I was hoping that you would chose to go on with us."

"No, Phillip, I can feel no calling or burden," said Michelle. "The truth is that I am more convinced than ever of its folly. A bunch of dying children marching off to the sea is all that I see. All this trip has done for me is make me feel deeply sorry for all. Especially you, Phillip."

"You just don't understand the crusade, Michelle" was all Phillip could say.

Michelle's face began to turn a little red with anger and more tears filled her eyes. "Phillip, I understand all to clearly about this crusade," she began in an excited voice. "I understand how the nobles and bishops all laughed and scoffed at 'those poor fools marching off to their doom' without lifting as much as a little finger to help. Oh yes, they gave a few wagons and a little food. Just enough to get you out of the city and ease their consciences a little." Now Michelle and Phillip were standing in one place while curious onlookers passed by. "The truth is, Phillip, that I also laughed and scoffed at the whole thing for a while, but then it dawned on me that this crusade would be a perfect cover for my escape. No one would ever look for me here."

Phillip kept listening to Michelle as she continued. "Yes, I laughed. I laughed at this boy prophet, Stephen and everyone who believed him. I am not laughing any more though. Not because I have come to accept it or believe it. I stopped laughing because I found out that a lot of good people are being led into starvation, disease, and death." Phillip was amazed at the passion in Michelle's voice. He knew that trying to defend his position while she was like this would only cause the already staring passers-by to hear more than they should, and so he kept silent.

Finally Michelle stopped and just looked at Phillip and then sighed. She then took his sleeve again and began walking with him. After only a few steps she began to whisper up to him, "Phillip, I know that I can find you a very good position in Lyon." Phillip looked down at her with a frown. "No, now don't interrupt," she went on. "Listen to me. You have proven yourself to be intelligent and honorable. I'm sure..."

"No, Michelle," Phillip whispered back to her. "You know I can't do that. I must see this through."

"Then you'll see it through to your death," said Michelle angrily.

"Then so-be-it," said Phillip back. They walked on for a while longer before either of the two spoke up again.

"Phillip, don't you understand that I really want you to go with me to Lyon?" Michelle asked finally in a shaky voice.

"I understand Michelle. I understand that you think I am a fool who is marching off to his destruction. I understand that..."

Suddenly a voice broke in from behind, "Phillip! Phillip, please hold for a moment." Phillip stopped and turned around to see one of his former group leaders running up to meet him with a small boy and dog running with him.

"What is it?" asked Phillip.

"This boy says he must talk to you immediately," responded the tall skinny young man with respect.

Phillip looked down at the panting boy. "What's so urgent, little fellow? I'm sorry, what is your name?"

"Madoc. Name's Madoc. I got to talk to ya 'cause they won't go back to get her." Madoc breathed out heavily.

"I'm afraid I don't know what you're talking about," said Phillip probing for more information.

"Its my friend. She's lost and these people say that she probably just left like the others." Said the boy. He could see that he still hadn't been understood. "Please Mister, I know she wouldn't just leave."

"Well how long has she been gone?" asked Phillip.

"Bout an hour and a half I suppose," said Madoc.

"That's not much time. She might just be off the trail a bit looking for food," responded Phillip trying to comfort the boy.

"No, she's not like that. Besides, I feel like there's something wrong and Hungry here feels it too," said Madoc looking down at the dog and patting him on the head.

"Why did you come to me?" asked Phillip.

"It's just that I thought you knew Anna," said Madoc. "She told me that you were friends."

Phillip's face got serious. He bent down to the level of Madoc and looked him square in the face, "Anna is the name of the girl who got lost?"

"Yes, and I'm afraid she might be in trouble or something."

"What does she look like?" Phillip asked.

"Well, she's kind of tall with long dark hair," Madoc said. "Please, we need to look for her right now!"

"O.K. let's go look for her," said Phillip with a smile.

"Phillip, we aren't finished yet," said Michelle trying to catch Phillip before he left.

"What more can I say, Mary?" he said, straightening up and looking at Michelle. "You asked me if I understood what you were trying to tell me. I do understand, and again I say that I must see this thing through. I'll be back tonight." Then Phillip quickly turned and trotted after Madoc and Hungry.

Michelle watched him hurrying off and as a tear rolled down her cheek she whispered out loud, "No, Phillip, you don't understand. You don't understand that I want you to come with me because I love you."

Phillip, Madoc, and Hungry walked back along the trail that the crusaders had just come through calling out Anna's name the whole time. For almost an hour they zigzagged back and forth looking down ravines and behind trees. They began to lose hope of finding her. In the one hour they covered the same amount of ground that the slow moving caravan of children covered in two hours. They stopped calling out, but kept looking.

Hungry stopped and perked up his ears. Then he began to whimper. "Did ya find something, boy?" asked Madoc. Phillip stopped and came over to where Madoc and Hungry were.

"What is it?" asked Phillip. "Did he find something?"

"I don't know?" said Madoc. "He seems like he hears something but he's not moving. "Go on boy. Go find Anna." Hungry finally started to move slowly. Phillip and Madoc followed at a jog.

Soon Phillip heard something. It sounded like singing. He began to run. As he got closer he heard the distinct sound of a girls voice singing a scripture song. "Anna!" he shouted. "We're coming!"

"Help!" came the girl's voice. "Help me. I'm hurt." Hungry reached the ditch first but couldn't find a way to get down into it. Phillip came running up to the edge and only stopped long enough to gauge the depth of the ditch before he jumped in. In a split second he was kneeling down beside Anna.

"Phillip! Oh Phillip, you came!" Anna said weakly but with a smile on her face. "My leg is hurt Phillip. Please help me." Then she reached up and put both arms around Phillip's neck and laid her head on his chest.

Phillip held her gently for a moment, not able to believe that it was really her. Hungry's barking from above made Phillip remember that the situation was serious. "Anna," Phillip whispered gently in her ear, "let me look at that leg." Anna did not move. "Anna, we need to look at that leg." Anna still didn't respond.

"Anna," Phillip said pulling her away from him. She lay limp in his arms. He quickly checked her breathing. He sighed a sigh of relief as he heard her steadily inhaling and exhaling.

"Madoc," Phillip yelled up. "We need to get her out of this ditch. Walk down the ditch a little and see if there is a way out."

"All right," said Madoc as he ran along the side of the ditch.

Phillip laid Anna down on the ground and pulled a blanket out of her bedding that lay near by in order to put it under her head. Phillip then looked at Anna's leg. It was twisted at an odd angle, but there was no bleeding anywhere. For just a moment Phillip felt afraid. He didn't know what to do for Anna, and all the people who had any kind of knowledge of ailments were hours away by now. "Calm down Phillip," he said to himself. "Use your head, and think through this. What is Anna's most serious need?" He looked down at her tearstained muddy face. Her eyes were closed but her breathing was calm. For an instant he looked at her. She was beautiful to him, even though he didn't know why at a moment like this he thought so. It wasn't something that his eyes told him.

"Now," he continued, "what is her next urgent need?" Again he looked at her. Her leg was hurt badly and that would have to be stabilized, but first she would need water and food."

Soon Hungry came running up the ditch to Phillip and Anna. The dog looked down at Anna and licked her on the face. "Stop that, dog!" said Phillip to Hungry. As soon as Hungry licked her face she moved.

Madoc came running up just in time to see Anna open her eyes. "Madoc, you came back for me," She said looking up at him.

"Of course I did," he said back to her. "I'd looked all day and night if I had to." Anna smiled.

"It's all right now Anna," said Phillip reaching for her hand.

Startled, Anna looked over at Phillip sitting at her side. "Phillip, it is you, and you're actually here! I thought that I had dreamed it."

"I'm no dream, Anna," said Phillip with a smile, "but neither is this ditch that you stumbled into. Now here, take a drink of water from my pouch."

When Phillip finally had tied two sticks to either side of Anna's leg, which caused them both a bit of embarrassment, he lifted her up and carried her out of the ditch. Phillip carried Anna for a little while, but it soon became obvious that he could not carry her much longer.

"Anna, I have to put you down for a while," he said. "How are you doing?"

"I'm doing all right but my leg hurts a lot. I don't think I can go on Phillip," said Anna.

"It will be dark in about a half hour and the crusade must be at least two hours ahead of us," said Phillip looking at the sun as it sat low in the sky. "Madoc, you stay here with Anna while I go and look for something to eat."

"O.K. but maybe Hungry can find us something," responded the boy.

"Maybe so. You send Hungry out if you want, but I'm going to look for something also." With that Phillip turned to Anna. "Will you be all right until I get back?"

"Does this mean that we're going to stay here for the night?" asked Anna.

"Yeah, I think it would be best," said Phillip. "If we can get a good night sleep and a little food, maybe we can leave tomorrow morning early." As Phillip was leaving he said, "I'll be back soon."

Phillip looked all over. There were no plants that were edible that he could find. The river was too far away and the lack of rain meant no ponds or brooks would have water for finding fish. It was dark before

Phillip gave up and went back to where he had left Anna and Madoc.

As he walked into camp he noticed that there was a fire going and meat cooking over it. Madoc was sitting on a large rock and Anna was lying by the fire propped up on one arm trying to cook. The fresh meat was a very welcome gift to all of the campers.

They talked until the fire died out. Anna told Phillip about all that had happened to her and Madoc since they left Paris. She had to move constantly because her leg felt uncomfortable as she recounted the stories. Madoc didn't say much but added a few things that Anna had left out. Finally they situated themselves the best that they could and fell asleep.

Phillip woke up early the next morning before the sun had even begun to lighten the morning sky. The moon was nowhere in sight and the sky was partly cloudy. He woke the other two up and said, "If we want to catch up with the others today we had better get started now. Anna, how does your leg feel?"

"I think it is a little better," she said sleepily. They got their things together in just a few minutes and were on their way. After about forty-five minutes Phillip could not carry Anna anymore. He was about to suggest that they rest when they heard a familiar sound coming toward them. It was the sound of a wagon.

Phillip quickly found a soft spot to put Anna and then straightened himself out and yelled out, "Hello there. Hello there in the wagon."

An immediate response came back. "Phillip, it's Antoine and Mary. Are you all right?"

"Yes," yelled out Phillip. "I'm here with Madoc and a hurt girl." In just a few minutes the wagon was there and Phillip and Antoine were lifting Anna into the wagon. Then they all jumped in, turned the wagon around, and began back toward the main body of the camp.

"Thank you for coming and getting us," said Phillip to Antoine and Michelle. "I don't think we could have caught up with you by ourselves."

"I would like to take the credit, but I have to admit that it was Mary's idea," said Antoine. "She insisted that there must be something wrong and that we come and get you. Have you ever tried to tell her no?" Antoine said with an exhausted look on his face.

Phillip looked over at Michelle who had a self-satisfied grin on her face. "I know what you mean, Antoine," said Phillip still looking at Michelle, "she can be very convincing."

As the sky began to brighten, the wagon rattled along. Phillip gazed back at Anna lying down with Madoc beside her, and then looked to his right where Michelle sat.

13

MADEMOISELLE MICHELLE

By nightfall the crusade was camped outside of the grand city of Lyon. They crawled into a large clearing just before the sun had set up, and now, little campfires dotted the area like an army readying itself to lay siege to the city and castle. To the night watchmen from atop the castle walls it seemed a strangely ominous group.

"What do you think, Thomas?" asked one of the guards to another watching the twinkling campfires.

"Seems a sad picture to me," Thomas responded still looking out at the camp. "They call it a crusade but I only see a few banners waving and a few scattered tents not arranged in any particular order littering the ground."

"How many do you think there are?" questioned the first, guard again. "We'd heard report of about 25 to 30 thousand leaving from Vendome."

"No, can't be that many. I'd say half that at best," replied Thomas. "Lord Robert was heard saying that they'd never make it this far. Said, 'First time they get a little hungry or hear the howl of a wolf the little pretenders will run back home to mommy.'"

"I heard that he and the Baron had a little bet goin' about the whole thing."

"I guess the Baron won then eh?" said Thomas looking over at his partner.

"No, they both lost. Neither of them thought they'd make it here, they were just bettin' on how many days it would take 'em before they gave it up."

Thomas chuckled. "Well, to my way of thinking, the lord and baron don't want this crusade of common children and priests to succeed." Thomas lowered his voice. "The nobles are scared to think that a group of common folk, and children at that, could show any courage and bravery without a lord or handful of knights gallantly leading them on."

"There's more to it than that Thomas," started the second guard. "The bishop and his learned group of religious second men aren't too happy either."

"Really? I hadn't heard that," responded Thomas. "Why not? I mean, the Pope himself seemed to be in favor of this crusade."

"The bishop is upset that an unlearned farm boy and a handful of parish priests are trying to usurp his "position" of holiness. The bottom line is that he, like all the rest, are scared that this crusade might actually be of the Almighty and that would mean that they and their precious positions don't mean a thing."

Thomas thoughtfully turned and stared back out at the humble encampment below. "I hope they make it to the Holy Land."

"My lord, the baron to see you," said the well-dressed chamberlain[1] entering Lord Robert's readying chamber.

"Yes, of course," grumbled the lord as a servant finished putting a decorative red overshirt on his master. "I was wondering when he'd get here. Paul, show the baron into the receiving room next to the main hall. I'll be right there." The chamberlain nodded respectfully and exited the room.

A little later, as the lord entered the room, the baron rose to his feet and began speaking, "My lord. I suppose you know that our guests have arrived and are camped outside of the city at this moment."

"Our guests, my dear baron?" questioned lord Robert. "Did you invite them here?" he asked sarcastically. He waited a second before he

---

[1] A chamberlain is the male counterpart of a chambermaid, an attendant for a sovereign or lord in his bedchamber, or a chief officer in the household of a king or nobleman

continued, "I didn't either," he said answering his own question.

"Still, they are here," stated the baron.

"Maybe if we ignore them, they will go on their way."

"Maybe," said the baron putting his finger up to his chin, "but it might be a good gesture to send out some essentials for them in the morning." The lord turned and looked down at a decorative wooden chair and ran his hand over while he thought. "It's been a lean year."

"That's true, but it hasn't been so bad for us as it has been for our neighbors to the west and to the south. If you wished it, we could let go of some supplies without it hurting us too much."

Lord Robert turned to the baron and began to speak angrily, "What I wish is that every one of the little beggars would drown themselves in the river. That's what I wish," he finished pointing a finger at the baron.

The baron walked over to lord Robert and dropped his formality of speech. "Robert, I too wish nothing more than that they would disappear before the morning sun broke over the horizon, but the fact is that outside of our perimeter are camped thousands of hungry little crusaders. I fear that if we turn them away without even the pretense of kindness, that the people and the episcopate will frown at us."

"Let them frown," said the lord in response. The baron walked back over to the other side of the room and took a seat. Lord Robert looked over at him sitting there as if in deep thought, "Well, maybe we can do a little."

All of the crusaders watched intently as about twenty wagons full of supplies made their ways through the city gates at late morning. They were first met by Stephen, Father David, and Father Gilbert, along with the leaders in charge of the larger groups. After a little discussion, the wagons split up with the group leaders. The wagons were quickly unloaded and then immediately afterwards lines were set up in order to give out the fresh rations to the crusaders.

As Phillip helped hand out rations to the last of the crusaders in their line, he took a ration for himself and found his old wagon in order to eat with Michelle, Anna, and Madoc. Anna and Michelle were in the wagon talking when he arrived. Madoc was on the ground close by.

As Phillip arrived at the scene, he decided that Anna and Michelle looked like they were busy so he took a seat next to Madoc. "How's Hungry today?" asked Phillip to the little dust covered boy.

"Guess he's all right," responded Madoc still holding a piece of hard bread in his right hand.

"Where is he?" continued Phillip trying to spark a little conversation with the boy.

"Don't know. He comes and goes a lot. Since I'm not allowed to feed him any of our rations he has ta find his own."

"Yeah, I guess that makes sense," said Phillip. Phillip finished his food without talking for a while. When he was finished he wiped his hands together and leaned back with his two arms extended a little behind. The sun was already well above the horizon and was shining its warmth down without the hint of a cloud anywhere. It felt good to have his stomach full.

Phillip was awakened out of his day dreaminess by the laughter of Michelle. He looked over and noticed that she and Anna seemed to be hitting it off very well. He got up and walked over to where they were. They were in the back of the wagon because Anna's leg was still very swollen and had to be kept straight.

Michelle saw him coming and with a smile said, "Hello Phillip. Anna was just telling me a few things about her life in Paris."

"Did you learn anything interesting?" Phillip responded congenially.

"Oh yes, quite a few things. It sounds very interesting living in the big city," said Michelle back.

Looking at Anna, Phillip asked, "How's the leg doing this morning?"

"It's doing all right," said Anna, "but it still hurts. Old Tom says that the swelling will go down in a day or two and then he will be able to tell me better how hurt it really is. Thank you again Phillip for finding me."

"Well if I've counted correctly," began Michelle almost chuckling, "that is something like the twentieth time in a day-and-a-half that I have heard you thank him."

Anna turned a little red, "It's just that I'm...I'm thankful."

"Oh," said Michelle waving her hand at Phillip, "I'm sure he was glad to do it. Saving damsels in distress is part of the job description of these hero type guys. However, I must admit he would look the part a lot better if he had armor, a sword, a shield, and was mounted on a splendid white steed instead of wearing these worn out peasants clothes and riding atop a buckboard in one of the oldest and most worn out wagons in all of France."

Tossing a half disgusted look in the direction of Michelle first, Phillip then looked at Anna and with a little nod he said, "You're welcome, mademoiselle."

Phillip then looked back at Michelle and said, "Mary, may I speak with you for a moment."

"Of course you may, Monsieur Phillip," responded Michelle in a snobbish upper class tone.

"You imitate a noble quite well Mary," said Phillip. "Now may I speak with you?"

"All right," said Michelle getting up.

When the two of them were a little ways away from the wagon Phillip turned and stopped. "Mademoiselle, don't you think it's time you become a damsel yourself again? I mean, I thought you'd have been trying to scale the castle walls or something by now."

"Believe me, if I'd have found a way to get in by now, I would be in," began Michelle. "I can't just go up to the castle gate and announce who I am."

"Why not?" asked Phillip honestly.

"First of all, they would never believe me, and secondly, if by some strange chance they might believe me, I'd be worse off than you can imagine."

"I don't understand," said Phillip with a bit of a puzzled look on his face.

"Let me explain it to you this way," began Michelle. "How do you think the arch bishop in Paris would receive a man dressed in a parish priest's dirty brown robe, but claimed to be the bishop of Orleans?"

"Hmm, I think I see what you mean," responded Phillip. "He'd be laughed at."

"And what if it turned out to really be the bishop of Orleans?" continued Michelle.

"It would be embarrassing," said Phillip finally.

"Of course it would. Now help me think of a way to get in."

Early that afternoon Phillip made a few visits. First of all he visited Madoc and talked the reluctant boy out of a good-sized piece of his soft cured deerskin. Then he went to a fellow that he knew to be a dyer. "Would you happen to have any dark colored dye?" Phillip asked the young man plainly.

"The truth is that I do," he responded. "I'm always on the lookout for plants and flowers that I know to produce dyes. It gives me something to do."

"May I have a little please," asked Phillip kindly.

"Sure," the young man said reaching into a thick pouch and pulling out a few small jars. "Here's a nice dark blue. Will that do?"

"Perfect," responded Phillip.

Phillip found a nice sunny spot out of the main stream of people and with a freshly discovered quill began to write on the leather piece. He wrote slowly and carefully so as not to smudge the letters he had already penned. After he was done he laid his work out on a patch of grass and watched it carefully as it dried. As he watched the blue stain darken on the light brown deer hide, he felt a tinge of pride as an artist might after finishing a painting.

Later, as Phillip appeared, he had the leather piece rolled up nicely and a piece of wound string around it to keep it in its rolled up shape. As he strolled into the little camp area with his scroll held to his side he tried to look nonchalant. Instead, everyone stopped talking and looked straight at him.

"What'd ya do with my deer hide?" questioned Madoc, not knowing that it wasn't polite to be nosy. The truth is that everyone else wanted to ask the same question. "Why'd ya roll it up like that?" continued Madoc probing.

"I wrote something on it," said Phillip, knowing that he wouldn't be able to ignore everyone's questioning stares.

"What did you write?" asked Anna.

Before Phillip could answer, the usually silent Madoc said a bit perturbed, "You mean you put words on it? Why did ya do something like that? I could'a used it for something useful."

Phillip looked at Madoc and the rest. He could tell that now they were really curious. He decided that he would tell them the truth. At least part of the truth. "It's a message for Mary's cousin in Lyons. Since crusaders are forbidden to go into the city, I figured that the only way to get a message to her cousin from out here would be by sending a letter with one of the city's people as they went in."

Michelle looked at Phillip with a mixed expression of puzzlement and surprise. The answer seemed to satisfy everyone else.

"Can I see what it looks like?" asked Madoc. "I haven't gotten to look at much writing before, and never by someone that I know."

"O.K.," said Phillip with a smile. He gently untied the string and unrolled the leather strip. Because everyone else was straining to look by now, he held it out so that everyone could take a look at it. "Well, what do you think?"

Even though nobody could read the perfectly formed Latin words, they nodded their heads in approval. Madoc was the most impressed. "Wow, I never thought just plain words could look so pretty," he said. Then he added with a little pride, "It looks especially pretty on my deer skin."

A little later in the day as the others were busy doing other things, Phillip took Michelle aside and told her his plan. "I will send this message to one of the priests in the city. I know that it will be received, or at least read, because it is written on leather." Michelle nodded and waited for the rest of the plan.

Phillip continued talking for ten minutes more when he realized that Michelle had made no comment. "Well, don't you think that the idea has a chance?" asked Phillip.

"It's a good plan Phillip," Michelle said. "I'm sure it will work."

"You say it will work and yet I don't see you jumping for joy over it. What's wrong?"

"I really don't know. I just got a glimpse of myself back at the court, and for some reason instead of my heart rising inside of me, it sank."

Phillip, looking a little disgusted, replied, "I must admit that that surprises me a bit. You have done very little but complain since I rolled you out of that bread sack. I have listened to you talk about how miserable this crusade has been for three weeks, and now you say that your heart sinks when you think of going back to the good-ole-days."

"Oh, believe me, I won't miss the crusade, Phillip. I have never been a big fan of dirt, sickness, hunger, and death, and that hasn't changed." Michelle paused and looked at Phillip, hoping that he would begin to understand without her having to say it. "No, I will not miss the crusade, but I don't know that I am ready to go back either."

"Well, by tomorrow you will be able to decide what to do from inside the castle walls," said Phillip. "Michelle, I know that this crusade is not for you. You don't believe in it. Your life is with ladies, lords, and nobility. Once you get back to that life, you'll forget about this short time of suffering and probably forget about the whole crusade until you hear news that we've entered the Holy City."

Michelle didn't answer, but she knew that Phillip was wrong. Though she had acted tough, the things that she had seen over the past three weeks would never leave her. She also knew that the crusade would never reach the Holy City, and she wondered if Phillip really believed that it would.

"Tomorrow morning then," Michelle said to Phillip.

"Yes, tomorrow morning," Phillip said to Michelle as she turned to leave.

A couple of hours after dawn Phillip came walking back into camp. He walked to where Michelle and Anna were talking and when they saw him they stopped. "They're going to let you in to visit," Phillip said to Michelle.

Anna's mouth dropped open a bit, "I can't believe that your letter really worked. With strict orders from lord Robert, I thought that you were just dreaming when you said that you'd try to get Mary in to see her aunt and uncle." She looked over at Michelle with excitement and said, "Congratulations. We will miss you while you are gone."

Michelle tried to smile and act excited with Anna. Phillip said,

"Shhh...nobody else should know because it might cause a problem. Now gather your things and let's get going before someone changes their mind." Michelle didn't move. Phillip looked down at the blanket that Michelle had been using and the few other pitiful things that she had and said, "Just leave your things there. We'll watch out for them while you're gone."

Phillip started to walk off, but Michelle stopped and turned suddenly as if she had forgotten something. She took a few steps towards Anna and gave her a long sincere hug. "Tell Madoc and that dog of his good bye for me, will you?" Michelle said.

"Of course Mary," replied Anna. As Anna watched Michelle and Phillip walk off, she almost asked Mary to bring her some material and thread but stopped herself. She also suppressed the fact that she was a little jealous of Mary for getting to leave the crusade for a few days. Surely she would be able to bathe properly, change clothes, and sleep in a real bed. Anna, still watching her friends walking away said to herself, "I guess it's better that its her than me. I'm not sure that if I had the opportunity to leave that I would return."

"Father Louis, we are not even sure if this girl is the daughter of Lord William at all," said the bishop to the priest who always worked at his side. "You meet her at the gate with this," he said, handing him a letter with his seal on it. "The guards will let her in, but bring her straight to me. If the girl is a Lord William's daughter, this must be handled delicately as not to be embarrassing to her. If she is not who she says is, then I don't want anybody to think me a fool."

"Of course Bishop," replied the priest. "I will do as you ask."

"You may go now," said the high church official, but before the priest had a chance to turn around completely, the bishop added, "Oh, Father Louis, one more thing."

"Yes, Bishop?"

"Make sure the priest who wrote this letter comes with the girl. The way that he writes Latin, I would guess that he is much more than a parish priest. His testimony will be important in validating the girl's claim."

"Yes, of course. That is a good idea Bishop," replied the priest.

Father Louis left and the bishop went back to his desk and looked over the letter again. After looking at the well written lettering, he said to himself, "Yes, I would like to talk to you, Father whoever-you-are. And I will give you a piece of my mind about this crusade of children."

When Phillip and Michelle arrived at the gate, Father Louis had already been there and spoken to the guards. He nodded to Phillip and Phillip nodded back with a smile. The well-dressed priest came over to receive Michelle. "Is this the girl?" he asked the guards.

"Yes," Michelle replied. "I am Mademoiselle Michelle. The daughter of Lord William of Velva."

The priest inspected Michelle's ragged appearance and grunted, "We shall see." Then Father Louis deliberately looked past Michelle and Phillip as if he were looking for someone else.

"Are you looking for someone Father?" asked Phillip.

"Yes, young man, the bishop wanted to talk to the priest who had written the letter that he received," said Father Louis. "Young man," he said, looking at Phillip, "if you see the priest please let him know that his testimony might be needed to verify the girl's claim.

Michelle, seeing an opportunity, responded before Phillip had a chance to say anything, "Father, this young man wrote the letter for me." The priest looked over at Phillip. Michelle then continued, "His name is Phillip and he is the third son of the Marquis Gerald of Orleans." Phillip turned quickly to Michelle and was going to say something when Michelle continued, "My father and his are good friends."

"Mmm," said Father Louis. "This is interesting. Come then. Both of you."

Michelle walked next to the priest while Phillip followed in silence a few steps back. A few times Phillip was going to stop the priest and tell him the truth, but he knew that if he did, it would put Michelle's story in jeopardy. He would have to fix it later.

"Why didn't you consult me before you gave them permission?" scolded Father David to Father Gilbert. "If this is a lie, it could get the whole crusade in trouble with the bishop of Lyon, and that would just add to the obvious disdain that Lord Robert already has shown."

"It's not a lie," began Father Gilbert. "The young man doesn't seem the sort to try something like that. After he told me the story of lord William's daughter I knew that it was true. From the first time I saw her I knew that she was nobility."

"Still, I wish you would have told me about it," said Father David again. "If she is Lord William's daughter, we could have used that information to get more supplies."

Father Gilbert stared at Father David for a moment. "You mean walk up to the gates and tell them that we have graciously returned Lord William's daughter. Now, will you be so kind as to give us some food?"

"Friend," said Father David, "will you never stop looking at the individuals of this crusade as more important than the crusade itself? Allowing the young lady to return to her class without embarrassment is chivalrous but not practical. God knew that she was here and that we would need more supplies. Her embarrassment could have filled the bellies of every crusader here for two or three days."

Father Gilbert just stood there with a confused look on his face. He wanted to say something, but as usual, Father David's argument confused him with its logic. Without responding, the kindhearted priest walked away.

Lately, Father Gilbert spent hardly any time with Stephen and Father David. He had become tired of listening to them play on people's emotions and manipulating every situation. They were constantly maneuvering people and supplies, "For God and the Church." Gilbert, however, enjoyed talking to and being with the children and other crusaders, so he spent almost all of his time encouraging and helping. In the case of Phillip and Michelle, what Father David said made perfect sense, but for some reason he was still glad that he had let them go unnoticed.

A young Friar monk came into the waiting room and informed Father Louis and Michelle that they were to enter the bishop's hall.

Phillip would need to wait outside. This made Phillip nervous because with the lies that Michelle had already invented, who knew what more she would say. He had tried to get her attention a few times on route to the bishop's hall but Michelle stayed close to Father Louis and refused Phillip even a glance.

The fifteen minutes that Phillip had to wait outside in the hall seemed to last forever. He paced continually. Five steps forward, turn, five steps back. Five steps forward, turn, five steps back. His worn out sandals made a hollow clicking sound on the cobblestones as he paced. "Michelle, what are you telling them about me?" he asked to himself. "This is the bishop. You better not be lying to the bishop," he continued. "What were you thinking? I had it all planned out. It was a good plan. Now what am I going to do?" Five steps forward, turn, five steps back.

The young friar entered in the corridor again. The rustic dress of the friar seemed out of place in the castle. "You many enter now," he said with a kind smile.

Phillip took a breath and walked through the door from the corridor into the elegant bishop's hall. The hall was not too large but it was very ornate. The furniture was exquisite and the carpets and drapes were beautiful. It reminded Phillip of how some of the higher church officials in Paris decorated their rooms.

It shouldn't have been so impressive to Phillip, but after almost a month away from the pomp and wealth of St. Denis's in Paris, Phillip had almost forgotten that this world really existed.

When Phillip entered the hall, the bishop was still turned toward Father Louis and Michelle, so Phillip stood silently. The bishop finished and turned to address Phillip. "Awe, here is the young man," began the bishop with a smile. "The son of a Marquis hmm. Over here we have mademoiselle Michelle, Lord William's own daughter, and over here the son of a Marquis studying for the priesthood. I don't wonder that if we went down and looked through the rest of the crusaders we might find a prince or two."

"If I might be permitted to explain Your Honor?" began Phillip.

"Don't worry young man," said the bishop. "As crazy as it sounds,

I believe you. You see, I knew the Mademoiselle Michelle when she was a little girl." Looking in Michelle's direction the bishop went on, "I recognize her face even through the dirt and tanned skin, and with her personality, the story she has just described to me of her escape is not surprising."

The bishop addressing Michelle then said, "I'm sure your father will be happy to know that you are all right." Michelle smiled and nodded in agreement. Then to the friar the bishop said, "Friar please dispatch a letter to Lord William immediately of his daughter's whereabouts." The friar nodded and left.

Phillip stared at the friar as he left. The bishop, noticing how Phillip was staring at the friar, commented, "So you're wondering why a friar would be under my service here."

"If you don't mind me saying, he does seem a little out of place Your Honor," said Phillip.

"I don't mind you saying," began the bishop, "and the reason is simple. He is an excellent secretary and is extremely religious. I found him, recognized his worth, and asked him to stay. Obviously he accepted."

"Mademoiselle Michelle has informed me that she will be staying here. As soon as we can get her properly attired she will be presented to the court," said the bishop, controlling the conversation completely. "She also tells me that you might consider staying in Lyon."

Phillip was obviously struck by this statement. He looked at Michelle. She had a pleading look in her eyes. "With all respect to mademoiselle Michelle, Your Honor, I believe that she has confused my intentions."

"You mean that you want to continue on with the crusade?" asked the bishop looking intensely at Phillip. "I have gotten the idea that there has been nothing but misery along every path and behind every rock. Why would you possibly continue on?"

"Simply, Your Honor," responded Phillip firmly, "I have made a vow to God and the Church." He paused a moment and added, "A vow is a vow."

The bishop relaxed his stare and smiled, "Yes, a vow is indeed a vow. Young Phillip, I would like to talk to you some more before you have to leave. Quite honestly, this crusade of children interests me, Looking over across the room to Father Louis, the bishop said, "Father, please arrange a place to stay for brother Phillip when we are done here."

"Yes Bishop," responded the priest.

Phillip again responded, "Respectfully, Your Honor, I would like to get back to the camp with the others."

"I don't see why," the bishop said a bit curtly. "I will not keep you from your crusade when they decide to leave. Has this crusade created in young men a disregard for the requests of their spiritual leaders?"

"Of course not Your Honor," said Phillip, backing down to his superior. "I hope you forgive me."

"Forgiven," said the bishop. "Go with Father Louis. He will make sure that you have clothing and a place to stay. I will send a message to you later this afternoon, but until I do, you are free to do as you wish."

As Father Louis and Phillip walked through the door, Phillip heard the bishop's voice fading, "Now young lady, we will get you presentable and have you back in court..."

14

OF KNIGHTS AND LADIES

Lord Robert's castle was much busier and more impressive than the castle of Lord William. "I would like to see more of it later," Phillip said to himself.

Phillip felt a deep twinge in his belly and suddenly remembered how hungry he was. Just before Father Louis left Phillip in his sleeping quarters he had mentioned to Phillip that he could eat with the lower clergy in their food court.

Phillip spent more than a half hour trying to wash up. The water in the water basin, when he was done, was dark brown when he finally finished. He quickly changed into the simple cloak he was given to wear and was on his way to find food.

Phillip followed Father Louis' instructions on how to get to the hall. When he walked into the door that Father Louis had indicated would lead him to the food court, his nose led him down the few remaining corridors.

When Phillip opened the door to the food hall a dozen pair of eyes looked over at him. There were eight or nine priests standing around one table while at the smaller table to the side stood three ladies. They all nodded politely as Phillip entered the room. Phillip nodded back respectfully.

There were a few empty places around the larger table, and as Phillip entered the room the Friar that he had seen earlier nodded for him to take the seat to his immediate right. "You look quite different," said the friar in almost a whisper.

"Yes, I guess I look a lot more presentable now," responded Phillip.

"I don't know," said the friar seriously. "I didn't see anything wrong with the way you were dressed earlier."

Phillip looked a little puzzled. At that moment Father Louis entered in and said. "Please be seated." He then said the blessing for the food, and sat at the head of the table. Phillip picked up his spoon and began to eat the soup that was placed before him. It was excellent. There were at least three different types of vegetables and small chunks of meat. The bread was fresh. It was a pleasant change from the hard stale bread that he had been eating over the past weeks.

Phillip had finished almost all of his soup and his bread before he even remembered that there were other people in the room. He slowly looked up. Everyone was staring at him. They were not looking at him with contempt or disgust. Some of the priests smiled kindly as he looked at them. One older priest on the opposite side of the table had tears in his eyes.

Phillip couldn't help but be embarrassed. "I'm sorry. I didn't realize...the food was so good that I...uh...I," he stuttered.

"No, no, no that's all right," everyone said.

Then the young friar spoke, "Do not be embarrassed Phillip. We are the ones who are embarrassed." Phillip looked puzzled.

The older priest who sat on the opposite side of the table from Phillip said humbly, "Son, I marched with the crusade of Phillip Augustus and Richard of England. There were days of hardship and hunger for us like there have been for you. The difference is that as the soldiers came upon farms and cities they took what they needed for supplies. You have no one to champion your cause. I can only imagine how hungry all of you are."

Phillip thought for a moment and then responded back to those in the room, "Yes, it has been difficult and we are constantly hungry. We cannot take what we need by force nor can we take the holy city by force when we arrive at its gates. But we do have a champion for our cause. It is God Himself. We believe that He will sustain us on our journey and that He will throw open the gates when we arrive at Jerusalem."

There was another moment of silence as the priests thought about what the young man had said. Again it was the friar who spoke, "We can see that you are a person of faith, young Phillip, but where is your faith placed?"

"I do not understand your question?" said Phillip. "I place my faith in God and in the Church."

"Is it God and the Church that have called you, personally, to go on this crusade?" asked the friar pointedly.

Phillip was about to give a quick response when he realized that he did not have one. He wasn't sure what God wanted with him and he knew that most in the "Church" were against the crusade. He was stunned to realize that he really didn't know where his "faith" in the crusade came from.

After a nervous minute passed without a response from Phillip, Father Louis spoke to his companions, "We are being unfair to this young man. He could not have known, as he walked into our dining hall, that his crusade has been the major topic of conversation amongst us for a week before it left Vendome and for every day since then." Turning to Philip, and speaking directly at him, he continued, "You probably aren't even aware of the great theological tremor that this crusade has sent through all of Christendom."

"Well, I know that the bishops, Archbishop, and all of the priests at St. Denis had talked about it, but I never thought about what others might be saying."

One of the other priests, who had not spoken yet, then said, "There are but a few of God's servants here in this place. We have talked about this crusade for weeks. We have looked at every angle and every possibility."

The older priest spoke again, "Until now the crusade has just been a point of debate. But now with it here; you here; it has become more."

"You see," started the friar again, "by walking in here, you have just dispelled many of our guesses about the crusade. It is not a crusade of rebels against the Church. It is not a crusade of demons, nor of angels posing as children.

Phillip was speechless. He had never considered too much what

others were saying of thinking about the crusade. After they left
Vendome, he mostly thought about survival. "I don't know what to
say," finally came out of Phillip's mouth.

From behind, one of the ladies spoke up, "Don't say a thing more
son." Phillip turned to see a heavy set, stern-faced, middle-aged woman
staring the priests down. "Obviously the boy is flesh and blood," said
the lady. "I don't know about all of that religious talk but after being a
cook all of my life I do know when someone's hungry."

The lady turned to one of the other ladies and said, "Martha, why
don't you get the boy another bowl of soup." Shortly there was another steaming bowl of soup setting in front of Phillip.

Michelle was ready. Her cousin had secretly sent her an outfit
along with her own personal chambermaid, and now the time had
come to be presented.

Outside of the dinner hall was a larger hall for relaxing and talking. As Michelle entered the hall, ready to be announced, she thought
of how the scene was much like what it would look like back at her
father's castle.

Michelle walked proudly into the large dinner hall and made brief
eye contact with Lord Robert who was seated at the head of the table.
Around the lord were seated a half dozen well dressed nobles who were
probably guests for the day. There was a small group of ladies on the
side who were standing and talking and at the far end of the table were
the younger members of the families.

Finally, the Chamberlain began to announce, "Mademoiselle
Michelle of Velva." Everyone in the room stopped talking and nodded
respectfully in Michelle's direction. All of the gentlemen that had been
sitting stood.

"You are welcome here Mademoiselle Michelle," said Robert officially. "Please join us as our guest."

As was correct, Michelle curtsied and replied, "Thank you your
Lordship. You are most kind,"

With the brief formalities out of the way, Michelle's cousin trotted
up to take her by the hand and give her a kiss on the cheek. Smiling,

she said, "Michelle, you look awful. Now come over with me and I'll introduce you to a few friends of mine."

After what seemed like forever, Michelle smiled her last smile and curtsied her last curtsy. It was almost time to dine, but as the group began to ready themselves, one of the young children asked Michelle out loud, "Did you really have to eat other children to survive?" Immediately, the mother scurried over and shushed the child.

Michelle's cousin said to Michelle with a controlled chuckle, "I guess that news travels fast doesn't it?"

Michelle forced a smile and responded, "It sure does Amelia." As they began to find their seats Michelle thought to herself, "I'll bet you didn't wait two minutes after you heard of my predicament before you started spouting off." Gossip was one part of the life at court that Michelle couldn't stand. She remembered back at her own castle when the gossipers feasted on the news about her and one of the castle guards. Everyone with their smug little smiles and their laughter when they thought that Michelle wasn't listening. A tear came to her eye.

Amelia took Michelle's arm and whispered loudly, "Don't feel badly cousin. Nobody will think badly of you. It must have been pure h-e-l-l for you." Then giggling a little added, "I can't wait to hear about it."

"I'll bet you can't," Michelle said smiling.

Madoc's heart was beating fast as he hid behind a couple of bigger kids sitting around a small fire. A stocky black-headed boy walked quickly into the area. He was looking for something. He stopped and took a good long look around. After he seemed satisfied that what he was looking for was not there he moved on.

Madoc stayed put for a few more minutes before he dared to move. It was already dark and he hoped that he would be able to slip by without being noticed. "Hungry, when I get a hold of you," he said to himself, "I'm going to have to give you a serious talking to."

Madoc moved from campfire to campfire careful to stay far enough away as to not be seen clearly. "Surely they know where I'm staying," he thought. When he got close to his own campsite he slowed down and found a good position a few yards out that would allow him to see without being seen.

From his vantage point Madoc saw two of the boys that he was trying to avoid talking to Anna. Andre and Louis were there beside Anna. Madoc knew that he should go over to them and explain what had happened, but he couldn't work up the courage to move. He waited and watched. Finally they left.

When Madoc entered the camp, Anna saw him coming and motioned him over to the wagon. "Madoc, you've got to do something about Hungry," Anna said. "He stole again."

With his head bowed, the little dirty beggar boy responded, "I know Anna. He's bad that way lately. We got food but he's havin' a hard time findin' it for himself."

"Maybe you should find some twine to tie him up with," said Andre from the side.

"He'll go crazy," said Madoc. "I never tied him up afore. Besides he'll starve for sure that way."

"We won't let him starve Madoc," said Anna, "but we have to tie him up. We'll help you . . . . ."

"There you are you little twerp," yelled the stocky black headed boy as he walked into camp. He walked straight at Madoc.

Madoc was about to run when Louis stepped in front of him and held the intruder up. "Wait a minute."

The boy stopped but didn't take his eyes off of Madoc. "I won't wait a minute. This twerp's dog stole two pieces of bread from me and I want my food."

At that moment Andre recognized the black-headed boy as the one who tried to cause trouble for Phillip. He knew this could be real trouble. Andre said, "Listen, we'll pay you back but there's no need to get rough."

The boy turned to Andre, "You listen to me. All of you. Nobody steals from me and gets away with it. Nobody touches my stuff. If that mutt even comes close to my stuff again I'll kill him." After having made his point, the boy straightened up and said, "Now where's my food?"

Anna produced one piece of bread, put it in the boy's hand, and looked around at the others. Madoc felt bad because he had already eaten all of his. Finally Louis got some bread that he had been saving for later and stuck it in the boy's hand.

"I should ask for more," the boy said, "for all of the effort it took me and my friends to find him." The boy then looked around hoping that some of his friends might be around to back him up. Finally he turned to leave, "If that dog so much as sets foot in my camp again, he's dead."

The group of friends stood silent until the boy was well out of their camp and then everyone stared at Madoc. Madoc bowed his head and said, "I'll get some twine or something."

As things were settling down about Hungry, Anna's mind turned to the fact that Phillip hadn't returned yet. Nobody else said anything about it, so she decided to keep silent also.

When Hungry lumbered into camp that night he was met by a rope. It was a miserable night for everyone because Hungry wined and whimpered all night. The other crusaders who were camped close by and who were thankful for Hungry's hunting before were now upset by the noises he was making. Various shouts rose up: "Shut that dog up." "Put something it its mouth." "Get that dog out of here."

The morning's sun peeped through the window in the room where Phillip was staying and a beam of its light slowly worked its way up Phillip's face until it reached his eyes. Phillip woke up disoriented. His mind tricked him into thinking that he was out with the rest of the crusaders. When his eyes cleared enough to see that there were four walls around him, he sat there startled. "Oh, yeah," he grunted to himself as the previous day's events came flooding back.

After he'd eaten with the priests he went out and looked at the city. Lyon was a beautiful city. The markets were full of people and there seemed to be plenty of food and other goods for sale.

Phillip didn't talk to many people. He just watched. He watched as the people carried on their daily routines. He wondered if anybody even knew that there were thousands of hungry people outside of the city walls.

Every once in a while Phillip picked up bits and pieces of conversations about the crusade. "I don't even know why they're still here," said one lady to a man selling fresh vegetables from a cart.

The man replied, "I would say that there are two possibilities. They either want our food or our children; or both."

The lady had considered that they would want food but the idea of the crusade taking some of their children startled her. "They had better not try to take our children. Lord Robert and every knight here will surely see that they don't." The lady, who had a hand bag full of goods, then quickly turned to go home and check on her children.

The scattered bits and pieces of conversations like this one made Phillip think more and more about the crusade. He had not really considered what this crusade had done to families in and around Paris. "It must have been devastating for some of them," he thought.

He thought about Madam Christina losing Anna. He envisioned her in her house crying and broken hearted.

Yesterday had been a hard day. Phillip was forced to think through his decision to go on the crusade. How was he so positive about it when he decided to go in the first place?

Now, here it was morning and he was still inside the city walls. The bishop would probably call for him this morning and he would be able to get back with the others outside later in the day. He was feeling guilty about the fact that he had two good meals and a nice place to sleep.

When the bishop didn't call for Phillip in the morning he decided to go to the church library. He told Father Louis where he'd be when the bishop called to talk to him.

When someone finally did come to call on Phillip at the library it wasn't one of the clergy. Instead, it was a young man about Phillip's age. He had a strong build and had on the distinctive costume of a squire.[1]

"Hello Phillip," the young man began, "I am Squire John, son of Roland and nephew of Lord Robert."

---

1. A squire is a shield bearer or armor bearer of a knight, a ranking below a knight and above a gentleman.

Phillip stood up and put down a book that he was reading. "Hello squire John. It is a pleasure to meet you. May I be of service to you?"

"Yes you may," said John. "I would appreciate some of your time. I would like to speak with you."

"Of course."

"Come with me," the other young man began. "I know of a good place to talk." Phillip follow the squire out of the library and through what seemed like a maze of hallways until they came to a door somewhere in the back of the castle.

John hardly stopped to push the heavy door aside before he walked through. Phillip followed. The room was the castle armory. It was large with many weapons hanging on the walls and stacked in large orderly piles.

John walked right through the room without stopping. On the other side was another door that was already opened. Phillip again followed John. Inside the smaller room, which they had just entered, was the armory of some knights, probably those who stayed in and around the castle.

Phillip hardly noticed the half dozen pages and squires sitting around, because the armor was spectacular. The Javelins, swords, shields, bows and other weapons were impressive. Even the colors were amazing. The symbols of recognition on the shields were finely detailed and real works of craftsmanship.

When Phillip entered in with John, the others in the room stopped polishing their master's armor and stood respectfully to welcome him, and then sat down and continued their menial task.

John turned to Phillip and invited him to sit down on a small stone bench. "I hope that it was not rude of me to pull you away from your studies, but we have been talking today about the crusade of children and wished to have some firsthand information."

Phillip responded, "I will tell you what I can," said Phillip. "You may be disappointed when you find out that I don't really know that much. I am not even in the lead group. I am just a simple follower."

"I think you are trying to be quite humble," said John. "We've heard some of the things that you have done already."

Phillip looked puzzled. "I'm sorry master but I don't understand."

"Last night, my sister told me a number of things that you have done along the crusade in order to save lives. She told me that when the crusade was destined to fail, how you stepped in and saved it from its doom," John said enthusiastically. The other boys nodded.

"Aha," thought Phillip. "Michelle, you have set me up again." Then Phillip said, "I'm afraid that any stories that you have heard might be exaggerated. I have only done my part. Many others have done much more."

Phillip's reply was ignored. John, who was obviously the older squire and the leader among the group, put his finger to his chin and stated, "We've heard some of the lord's knights debate the issue of heredity and knighthood verses divine election and knighthood." Phillip was taken back by the change of topic.

"We've heard that you were the third son of the Marquis Gerald and therefore you were chosen to the priesthood instead of the knighthood. The question, therefore, is, 'Who chose you to the priesthood, God or your parents?'" Phillip still wasn't following the line of questioning.

John looked at Phillip briefly and went on, "What we're trying to ask is; have you ever considered the fact that God may have wanted you to be a knight but your father chose for you the wrong path?"

Phillip was beginning to understand what the squire was getting at now. For many years the debate had gone on about who should be allowed to be a knight, and who should not be allowed.

In the past the knighthood had been very restrictive. Only certain young men that were born of noble birth would even be considered to be able to attain it. Now, with all of the crusades and military campaigns it had become practical to open the ranks a little and allow more in.

The Church had more influence and so did money. Men wishing to become knights took up the cross immediately showing their devotion to God and Church, and those of known poor moral character were being challenged as to whether they could be knights or not. Sons of rich merchants sometimes were able to buy their way in.

Naturally, a number of questions were being debated among all of Christendom, but the main one was theological in nature. Could man interfere with God's plan for the knighthood or was one's fate predetermined and unchangeable?

Now that Phillip had clued himself in to what the group had been discussing he simply said, "I have never considered the knighthood for myself nor have I thought that it is what God would want for me."

The squires looked at each other and then John asked, "Are you convinced then that your father has chosen your correct destiny?"

Phillip did not answer. He thought to himself about how misguided the question was and yet how much it really hit the mark. These young fellows had no idea that Michelle dreamed up this whole Marquis thing, but the question that was just asked was a valid question, even for him. "Did my father, when he dropped me off at St. Denis act under the will of God for my life? Was I destined to be a priest?" Then Phillip answered the boys, "I'll have to think on that a bit." The group seemed pleased that they had asked such a wise question that demanded contemplation.

John smiled. "Who knows, you may be squire material yourself."

"I doubt it," replied Phillip.

"Here hold this," said John reaching behind him and pulling a sword off of the wall.

The other boys laughed when Phillip gripped the sword. "Whose armor is it," asked Phillip. "It's exquisite."

"It's mine," said John proudly. "I will be nineteen in two days, and on that day I am to be knighted."

"Congratulations, Sir John," said Phillip bowing his head.

"No, no, no," said John with a smile. "Let's not get ahead of ourselves. Bad luck, you know."

"Now," said John changing the subject, "tell us more about the crusade."

As the squires and pages closed in to listen, Phillip began to tell them bits and pieces of the things that had happened along the way. He purposefully left out negative events and personal opinions. As he recounted story after story of what happened, he began to realize himself that it had been quite an adventure already.

At lunchtime Phillip went back to eat with the priests. The food and conversation were both good. He was still the topic of conversation but he didn't mind so much this time. He had had time to think through things from a different perspective and was able to respond with more confidence. There were still some questions that he couldn't answer though.

Later that day Phillip went to the church to pray. There were other people praying also. Phillip spent some good time there asking the Lord some earnest questions.

When he got up to leave, he noticed that two rows behind him Michelle was bowed in prayer. He had the desire to whisper to her but refrained out of reverence. Phillip started down the aisle to leave when Michelle looked up and saw him. She immediately made the closing gestures on her prayer and stood to meet him.

Michelle followed behind Phillip until they reached the vestibule outside of the main church area. When outside, Phillip turned and faced Michelle. She smiled.

Being falsely polite Phillip said, "What a pleasure to see you again mademoiselle."

Someone walked by and Michelle whispered to Phillip so as not to be heard, "Phillip, I had to see you. I wanted to explain."

"Oh, you wanted to explain," Phillip said. "Explain what? How you lied to the bishop! Why you have been telling everyone ridiculous stories about me and the crusade!" Phillip's voice was getting louder. Michelle looked around to see if anyone was noticing.

"Phillip, we are not out in the wilderness," Michelle whispered loudly. "Please don't speak so loudly. I told the story about you being the son of a Marquis so that you could get a proper rest and some food. I at least owe you that."

Phillip began to calm down. Michelle went on. "And I didn't tell the whole world stories about you. I just told my cousin Amelia, in strictest confidence, you understand. How was I to know that she would tell others," Michelle said trying to look innocent.

Phillip sighed, "Michelle, at first the whole thing angered me. I started to have very unchristian thoughts about putting my hands around your delicate little neck. I do admit though that I am thankful that I have had this opportunity to think through the whole crusade from a different point of view."

Michelle, seeing a ray of hope, asked, "And what has this different point of view told you?"

"I don't know exactly," said Phillip. "I honestly don't know. Things that seemed so clear and sensible two days ago, almost seem ridiculous now."

Even though this made Michelle happy, she was careful not to show any pleasure. Instead she added, "Phillip, it will do you good to stay here a few more days and think completely through this." She paused. "Come on, you can walk me through the market and back to the castle." At first Phillip resisted the idea of walking around in public with a lady. Michelle then said, "It's all right, young master Phillip. You forget who you are."

As the two walked together, Phillip felt uncomfortable. People in the market place showed the young couple a degree of respect that he had not been used to. Michelle led Phillip to look at the stores of precious merchandise. They never got close to the food markets. Worrying about food was a servant's chore.

That night Phillip waited for the bishop's summons but it never came. He felt like he wanted to stay a little while longer, but the desire made him feel guilty. All of the other crusaders were outside sleeping on the ground and eating what little they could scratch together.

Phillip found out earlier that the crusade had made no attempt to break camp. Lord Robert had sent out another load of food for the crusaders that morning. At mid morning, Squire John came by the church and asked Philip to pray with him and then go out and talk again.

The young men enjoyed the morning together talking about different things. They talked mostly about the one subject that was dominating John's mind—the knighthood. John asked about the knights in the Paris area. Phillip told him that he didn't have many dealings with the knights, but told him what little he did know.

John asked Phillip again if he might consider changing from the priesthood to the knighthood. His reasoning was that in Lyon his father the Marquis would not even have to know the change until it was too late. Phillip smiled and said that he didn't think that he was suitable to being a knight.

"I don't know," said John. "The ability to use a weapon doesn't matter as much as you think. My father always told me that a knight was primarily," John held up his index finger, "brave and chivalrous. Secondly," he held up his middle finger, "a knight is pious and loyal to Church and lord." Then John held up his thumb and leaned over and whispered, "And thirdly, a knight appreciates the beauty and charm of a lady. Of course this last one," he said still whispering, "isn't one that is commonly spoken of."

John went on to inform Phillip that his father had said that learning weaponry was just a matter of practice. John said that Phillip could get his body in shape and learn the basics within a couple of years.

Phillip tried to say a few things that might change John's desire to convert him, but to no avail. "Nonsense," said John. "I heard my father talking about the crusade. He said that it was no wonder that the crusade had made it this far. He said that a crusade of priests and children alone would have fallen apart within the first week. My father said, when he heard about you, that there were probably a number of young knights amongst you who were commissioned by the archbishop to keep the crusade together.

"Excuse me for saying it, John," began Phillip, "but that is ridiculous. I don't mean any disrespect but I am only a young theology student and I don't believe that I've met any knights in disguise or anyone who might be confused for one in the whole crusade."

"Don't get excited," said John. "I figured that out. I just wonder if God might have chose out a few "knights" of his own choosing in order to protect the crusade." Phillip started to shake his head but John said, "I mean it. Look, you said yourself that you are loyal to the Church and you are obviously pious." He held up his index finger. "And if half of the stories that I've heard about you are true, then your actions have proven you to be brave, chivalrous, and cunning." John held up another finger. Then whispering again he added, "And number three is just a matter of time."

Phillip said, " Has it ever occurred to you that a priest can be brave, courteous, cunning, and loyal?"

"Not really," said John. "None of the priests around here are like that. They are all dull. They go about doing their church duties, but never really do anything creative or exciting."

Phillip had a frown on his face and was about to speak when John saw that he might have offended his friend and spoke before Phillip had a chance, "I don't mean anything bad by that, you understand. Service to the Church is highly commendable."

Phillip wondered to himself why this young man had never heard of all of the great and brave things that men of the Church had been doing for centuries before there were knights. Phillip then tried to give John a brief lecture on some of the "heroes" of the Church in times past.

John was only partially interested. He figured that priests used to have to be brave and do courageous things because there were no knights around. Now that there were knights, priests were basically ornaments of the Church. He couldn't figure out why anyone would actually choose the priesthood over the knighthood.

The discussion finally ended with John having the last word. "I still don't see why you won't even consider the knighthood. You're of good birth and you have the two most important qualities already."

Phillip chuckled in frustration. "Come on John," he said standing up, "its time to eat." When the two young men reached the place where they would separate and go their own ways, they found Michelle and Amelia standing there.

"It's about time the two of you showed up," said Amelia. Michelle thought you'd have come by here a long time ago." Michelle glared at Amelia. Then as if on cue Amelia said to her brother, "Come on John I'll walk you back home."

Amelia took her brother's arm and began walking him down the path toward the castle. As Michelle came toward Phillip, John turned around with a big smile on his face and held up three fingers high so that Phillip got the point. Phillip turned red.

"What was that all about?" asked Michelle.

"Never mind," said Phillip. The two of them walked back to the church together.

The bishop didn't call for Phillip that night either.

15

SIR JOHN

The next day the castle and church were very busy. Every one was preparing for the knighthood ceremony of squire John. Knights from surrounding cities were coming in for the ceremony and the mood of the people in the city was one of excitement. The general mood had been low ever since the crusade had camped at Lyon's doorstep. This event would be a breath of fresh air.

Phillip knew that the bishop would not be calling for him this day. The bishop would have a big part in the ceremony. He and his underlings would be preparing every detail so that it would be perfect.

Phillip stayed in his room and prayed during the morning because the church was full. John and the other knights would be there most of the morning saying their prayers.

At mid morning Philip enjoyed walking around by himself. At one point he found himself close to the front gate of the city. The thought entered his mind of just walking out the gate and back to his friends in the crusade. No one would mind.

As Phillip got closer to the gate, he began to feel panicky. He was struck by the overwhelming fear of leaving the city. He realized for the first time that he did not want to go back to the crusade. Phillip stood there for a long time.

At lunchtime there were only a few of the priests present. Phillip ate without speaking to anyone.

After lunch Phillip went to his room. He sat on his bed staring at the ceiling. He thought about Anna, Andre, Louis, Ackey, Madoc, Stephen, and all of the others. How could he just abandon them? He knew that he couldn't.

Phillip started daydreaming about how he could save his friends that were in the crusade and sneak them into the city. "Ridiculous," he laughed. "They all wanted to be in the crusade. Didn't they?"

Over and over Phillip thought about the possibility of staying in the city and how wonderful that would be. "No, it would be terrible. What about my vows and responsibilities?"

The afternoon sun told him that the time for the big event had arrived. Phillip knew that the church would already be full. He went out and found a place as close as he could to the church. He was stopped 100 yards short of the front doors by the multitude.

Phillip and people of his real class never got to actually see these sort of special events. They usually stayed back somewhere in the crowd and waited for the news of what was happening to get back to them. A few self appointed heralds would place themselves at strategic points in the crowd and as they received news of what was happening they would yell it back to those behind.

With about a half hour to go, Phillip had found for himself a descent spot to stand. He was wedged comfortably between an older man on his left and a portly middle-aged man on his right. After a bit of courteous conversation the fat man told Phillip that he was a baker in the city and that he had known John since he was born.

A narrow passageway was kept clear from the doors of the church and throughout the crowd. The passageway was for anyone "important" to pass through if they arrived late.

Two guards came out of the church doors with Michelle between them. They began to look around. Phillip guessed that they might be looking for him but he didn't really believe it. He didn't make any gestures. Finally, Michelle spotted him and said something to one of the guards. Within a few moments Phillip was behind Michelle, and the guards followed them back into the church.

The guards escorted Michelle and Phillip to a bench that was located towards the back of the auditorium. Phillip said a quick thank you to Michelle and then fixed his attention to the front.

Everything was ready. The cathedral was decorated with all of its special ornamentation. At the front on either side were two rows of knights decked out in all of their finery. Different colors, shapes, and symbols all made the knights look spectacular.

The first two rows were also filled with knights. Behind them were rows of nobles and some of the wealthier and more influential people of the area. The only commoners were a few servants who were needed, and a few sergeants who had won the privilege of position by long and honorable service in the army.

A small choir of boys signaled the beginning of the ceremony by singing a Gregorian chant of the Church. The sound of the boys' high-pitched voices echoed off of the high marble walls. In the middle of the song, John, accompanied by his father and another knight, entered the cathedral from a room on the left. At the close of the song the bishop, accompanied by his people, entered from a waiting room at the right and met John at the center front of the church.

Together, the two small groups climbed the few steps that led up to the platform. When every one was in their appointed places and the room was completely silent, the bishop closed his eyes and began the honorary opening prayer for the knighthood service. The bishop's Latin chanting had almost hypnotic effect as it sounded throughout the cathedral.

After the prayer, Father Louis presented John's sword to the bishop to bless. After the special prayer was given for the sword, John's banner, lance, and shield were brought for a blessing also. When all of the armor had been blessed, Sir Regenald took his son's sword and girded it around the young man's waist.

With John now standing erect and proud with his newly girded sword, the other knight that was with him and his father walked up and stood directly in front of him. The knight, who was probably in his mid thirties, began to remove the glove from his right hand in order to deliver the pommee.

John clenched his teeth and gave a stern look. The silver and white clad knight then raised his opened hand high into the air and brought it down with a crushing blow across John's left cheek. John stumbled backwards but was able to keep himself from falling completely to the floor. Then in a split second the red faced young John was back standing proud and erect in his place. For the first time the crowd inside and out applauded and cheered enthusiastically.

The white clad knight then bowed and stepped aside. John unsheathed his beautiful shining sword and faced the crowd. Then he kneeled. He began to deliver his oath of obligation, which listed the obligations that a knight was bound to fulfill with his life. "I, John," he began with a shaky voice, "vow to uphold all duties of the order of the knighthood. It is my solemn responsibility and duty by birth and by right to serve my country and my Church as God Himself has placed them over me in authority and under me for protection. As a knight, honor will guide me and righteousness will protect me. I will always..."

John's voice grew stronger and more resolute with every word. When he finished his speech he stood and raised his eyes and sword towards heaven in order to emphasize the sincerity of his vow. Again the crowd roared its approval.

The ceremony was impressive from the beginning to the end and Phillip could not help but be moved by the conviction in every word and every action. All participants in the ceremony performed well.

Phillip knew from experience though that a moving ceremony didn't make a good knight. Ceremonies and who performed them depended on position and wealth, but position and wealth often produced a poor product. Many spoiled and useless knights roamed around the country drinking too much and doing little to keep their vows. However, in the case of John, Phillip hoped that a real champion of the Church would emerge.

For a moment Phillip envisioned himself in full armor with a sword and banner, riding on a splendid steed. He would be a great champion for the Church.

Phillip's mind snapped back to the ceremony when Sir John put on his brilliant silver helmet, grabbed his lance, and walked briskly toward the back of the auditorium. Outside of the doors a guard was awaiting him with a young chestnut colored horse that was decorated with ceremonial saddle, bridal, and stirrups. On the saddle blanket that hung from under the saddle was the new signet of Sir John of Lyon.

Without breaking stride, John grabbed the reigns, put his left foot in the stirrup and swung himself and all of his armor effortlessly up onto the horse. He gave it a sharp kick in the ribs and the horse jumped into an immediate gallop.

Phillip, along with everyone else, began pushing to get out of the back doors of the cathedral so that he could get out into the courtyard where the quintaine would be performed. In the middle of the courtyard was an entire suit of armor hanging on a pole. John made several passes showing his steady hand with the lance and excellent horsemanship as the guests found places to stand and watch.

When most of the crowd was in place John made one final pass with the lance. Those who could not witness the official ceremony in the church were really enjoying the quintaine, which was performed out in the open air.

Pulling the chestnut up, John handed his lance to a squire and unsheathed his sword. The crowd cheered with anticipation.

For a moment the crowd noise died down and just before Sir John was to show his expertise with the sword a distant noise was heard that caught everyone's ear. It was the unmistakable sound of another crowd cheering about something, but it had come from beyond the south wall of the city.

John only flinched at the disturbance for an instant and then refocused on what he was doing. He began making passes at the suit of armor that was located in the middle of the court. With each pass John severed a different part of the armor from the rest. Every powerful stroke of the sword brought an invigorating cheer from the onlookers.

Phillip's own heart was racing as he watched. He felt proud that he knew Sir John. At that moment he was sure that he wanted to be a knight also. He reached out to the nearby Michelle and without looking at her, put his hand in hers.

Michelle's heart leaped. It was the first time that Phillip had shown real affection towards her since the beginning of the crusade. She didn't move. She lost interest in the quintaine and drank in the moment with Phillip.

When the knight had battered the poor suit of armor into nothing more than a heap of metal, he made one last mad dash atop the sweating Chestnut and waving the sword over his head at a full run he brought the weapon down with a crushing blow that decapitated the top part of the pole that held the helmet. The crowd was ecstatic. John threw back the visor to his helmet to reveal a giant smile. It was done, and he had done well.

Phillip took a moment to look around. Lord Robert and Sir Regenald were slapping each other on the back. The other knights also looked very satisfied as they nodded their approval one to another. Most of the young ladies had gathered in one place and were all smiles and giggles as they whispered back and forth to each other. Yes, it was a triumphal moment.

As the euphoria began to die down, that distant crowd noise returned. Phillip could see by the expressions on the faces of Lord Robert, the baron, the bishop, and the others, that they were clueless as to what it could be. Again the noise was heard. Lord Robert's smile disappeared and he caught the eye of one of the sergeants. The sergeant nodded in understanding and began off in the direction of the south wall with a small company of soldiers following.

The crowd in the courtyard began to talk among themselves and preparations were being made for other activities. The day had just begun. Many of the other knights would now participate in the program that included horsemanship, acts of strength, and exhibitions of skill with weapons.

The disturbance at the south wall got suddenly louder and clearer. It was the voices of children. The thoughts of the crusade came rushing back to Phillip as he listened. A strange sensation came over him.

Phillip began to drop Michelle's hand so that he could go with others in the crowd who were leaving to see what the noise was about, but Michelle hung on to him. "I'm coming too," she said. A quick glance into her eyes let Phillip know that she was thinking the same thing that he was. They set off immediately at a brisk pace passing others who were walking slowly.

While still a short distance from the wall, Phillip heard the distinctive voice of the boy prophet shouting out his message. "...is the perfect model of the biblical armies of God. Not by might of man, have God's people triumphed over evil. It has always been contrary to the force of man that God has triumphed. Did it not anger God when David numbered his army so that he could evaluate his own human power? Was it not God's own hand that guided Gideon to fight a hundred thousand of the enemy with only three hundred men of his own?"

Phillip stood beside Michelle listening. The boy preacher who was standing in his peasant's clothes atop a wagon was a stark contrast to the strong proud Sir John in all of his finery. Yet the proud look was much the same. The self-confidence and manner of speech was more compelling.

Stephen kept preaching, "The fact that the Lord God would call a crusade of children is not lunacy, as some might think. As we can see from God's history that quite the opposite is true. It is the only crusade that makes sense. Crusades of great armies and knights who are bound to countries and overlords could not possibly be the instruments of God for this task."

Phillip stood listening to the same words that he had listened to before, but now they were different. They were different because he was different. Before, the message of Stephen had not offended him. Now, it was as if Stephen was preaching at him directly, and maybe even against him.

He became indignant inside. "Who was this peasant boy to be preaching against him? He had no right." Why hadn't he felt this way before? Phillip's mind became very confused.

After watching the emotion well up in the face of Phillip, Michelle gently took his sleeve and said, "Please, let's go." Phillip obeyed her without acknowledging her. All the way back to the church area he said nothing.

When they finally reached the area in which they would part, Phillip stopped and looked as Michelle. Michelle did not like the look. It was not the look that she had been receiving over the past few days. It was not the look of growing fondness that she had been working so hard to cultivate.

"I need to be alone," began Phillip. "I think that I will spend the rest of the day in my room or at the library," he added with a polite smile.

Michelle felt panicky. Something inside of her told her that she must not let him go. "No, Phillip," she said. "The last thing you need is to be alone." Phillip snapped out of his self-induced trance and looked curiously at Michelle. "You need me," she said.

Michelle decided that she must put off playing the patient lady and make a bold move. The power that the words of Stephen had on Phillip was obvious and she had to act now in order to break it.

"Thank you Michelle but I'm afraid that if I don't think through some things right now, that I will not be good company to you."

"Stop it, Phillip!" Michelle said forcefully. "This is me you're talking to Phillip. Remember me, Michelle! I know what happens in that mind of yours. You can talk yourself into anything without regard to reality."

Michelle had not talked to him like this since they had arrived at Lyon. Phillip retaliated, "So what do you suppose I do then? Go talk to the bishop? You know that's impossible. Or maybe talk to one of the priests? Or maybe even Sir John? All impossible! No one can help me. No one understands what's going on! They close their ears to the message of the crusade. They turn their backs on the crusaders. They don't understand."

"Maybe they don't," said Michelle, "but I do." Michelle put her hand in Phillip's. "I will stay with you." The way Michelle said those last words sounded much more like the commitment of a lover rather than the concern of a friend. Phillip looked deeply into Michelle's eyes.

Phillip forgot about Stephen. The words of Michelle had aroused something in him that he had disciplined his mind to not dwell on. He caressed her hand gently and together they walked back toward the center of the city.

"We can't use force to make them leave," said the baron.

"I don't care how it is done," shouted the red faced Lord Robert at the baron. "I want that boy and that rabble out of here by tomorrow night. Do you understand me? In two days I am going to walk out that front gate," he said pointing in the direction of the main gate, "and I want to see trees and fields again. I don't want to see or smell that group of troublemakers ever again!"

The baron paused before he said anything. It wasn't very often that he saw Lord Robert this upset, but when he did he knew it was serious. "Do you have any suggestions, my lord," he finally asked.

"Truthfully, my dear Baron, I do not," said Lord Robert plopping down in a nearby chair.

A few moments passed without either man saying anything. There was a slight knock on the closed door. "Enter," barked the lord.

The chamberlain came in and announced that it was one of the lord's sergeants. Lord Robert told the chamberlain to let him in. The sergeant entered and stood at attention waiting to be recognized.

"Yes sergeant, what is it?" asked Robert impatiently.

"Your lordship, I believe that we have a problem," said the sergeant.

"What kind of problem?" asked Lord Robert, knowing that the sergeant would never bother him with something trivial.

"Sir, some of the children of the city have gone out to join the crusade. The people of the city are becoming afraid."

"So a few people are duped into believing this prophet boy and his ravings," began the baron, "let them..."

"No!" said Lord Robert standing up so suddenly that his chair fell over behind him. "That's it." Then he yelled, "Chamberlain!"

When the chamberlain trotted in, Lord Robert said, "Get me the bishop, Louis the tailor, Sir Regenald, and the rest of the city leaders immediately. I want a meeting in one hour. Now!" The chamberlain trotted back out of the room. Then looking over at the sergeant who was still at attention said, "You may also leave, sergeant."

When the sergeant had shut the door behind him the baron asked, "What's that all about?"

"Its all about, Baron," Robert said with a smile, "finally getting rid of our problem. By tomorrow morning the sympathy of our dear city toward those poor little suffering children will have turned into hostility. Our soldiers will have to ask the crusade to move for their own safety."

The general feeling of the crusaders after Stephen preached at the city wall was one of anticipation. Nobody was sure of what was going to happen but they were sure that something was going to happen. After almost a week of camping in front of the city, the group was getting into a routine. Father David felt that this feeling would only cause problems when it was time to leave. Therefore the sooner they left the better.

The fact that a couple dozen people from Lyon, mostly children, had joined the crusade after the preaching was a confirmation to many that it was still very much alive. A renewal of hope and duty was rising. Around the campfires that night people were talking about the Holy Land again.

Hungry had gotten used to his rope but still didn't like it. Madoc, Andre, or Louis would take turns taking him for a walk outside of the camp. When they were far enough away, they would untie him and let him roam around but they wouldn't let him get too far out of sight. A couple of times Hungry even brought a chicken back with him. Nobody asked where he might of gotten it from.

Anna's leg was doing well. Most of the swelling had gone down and she could get out of the wagon for longer periods of time. Tom made a better splint for her. Along with a set of crutches that a boy made for her, Anna could now get around pretty well. Even though she was more mobile, her friends noticed that as each day passed by, she talked less and less.

After the preaching service at the wall of the city, Anna, Andre, Madoc, Louis, and a few other friends were all sitting down together nibbling on some old bread and talking. They talked for a while about how glorious it would be to cross through the Great Sea and how the shops would have to stop just so that they could pass. They figured that after such a spectacular entrance, that the Moors would probably just run out of Jerusalem and all of Palestine.

A blonde headed boy said, "I'll bet that when we get there, the trees will be full of fruit. We'll get first pick at which house we want to live in also." Everybody nodded with a smile at the idea.

When the conversation had slowed down a little the same blonde headed boy asked, "Hey, I wonder where captain Phillip is?" When nobody said anything, the boy answered his own question. "I guess maybe he's not coming back, huh?"

The fact that Phillip had not reappeared in all of this time was something that all of his friends had thought a lot about but had not talked about.

"We'll, its been said," began Andre. "I admit that I didn't want to believe it, but it looks like Phillip and Mary aren't coming back." Nobody responded. Andre continued, "They should have never left in the first place."

Anna couldn't keep her emotions back any longer. She tried to get up to leave before the others saw her cry, but she just couldn't keep the tears from coming.

"Wait," said Louis to Anna as she grabbed for her crutches. "I'll help you." Louis jumped up and offered a hand to Anna. She pulled herself up, put her crutches under her arms and she and Louis left together.

Phillip slipped into the church grounds just before the curfew began. After what had just passed between he and Michelle, Phillip knew that he wouldn't be able to sleep. Contrary to what Michelle thought, his mind was in more turmoil than ever. He wanted to get to his room and think.

He knew his way around well enough now that he thought he could go through some of the less busy passage ways and get to his room unnoticed, but before he turned the last corner, one of the older priests stopped him.

"There you are young man," said the priest. "I was hoping to find you. I have come by your room three times in the last hour or so."

"Can I help you?" asked Phillip politely. He didn't really want to talk but how could he refuse to talk now. The older priest obviously had put some effort into finding him.

"I just thought that you should know that the crusade will be leaving tomorrow."

"How do you know Father?" asked Phillip shaken. "I mean, did they announce it or something."

"No, they didn't announce it," said the priest. "I don't even believe that they will be the ones making the choice about it."

"I don't understand," said Phillip.

"The people of the city have apparently asked lord Robert to force the prophet boy and the rest to leave. They have become afraid." The priest noticed that Phillip still was not following so he gave him the rest of the information. "After the preaching this afternoon by the boy, a number of our children left the city to join the crusade."

"Now I understand," said Phillip. He put his hand to his forehead and rubbed back his hair with a nervous action.

The older priest continued, "I wasn't sure if you had heard since it all happened so recently." He waited for Phillip to say something but he didn't. The priest added, "I thought that you might need to get ready to go. The crusade will probably be packed up and ready to leave by tomorrow afternoon."

Phillip rubbed back his hair again. He looked at the priest with a confused expression.

Reading the expression, the priest lowered his eyebrows and asked, "You are going on, aren't you?"

Phillip replied in a soft voice, "Of course...of course. Thank you for telling me." The priest didn't seem totally satisfied with the answer. Phillip regained a confident look and added, "I'm sorry. It's just that this has caught me off guard. I truly am grateful."

The older priest left and Phillip went into his room. For another two grueling hours Phillip's mind jumped from one choice to the other. Finally he dozed off.

Phillip was awakened by the sound of marching soldiers. He looked out of his small window down into the pre-dawn streets of Lyon to the vision of what looked like a full legion of soldiers marching toward the south gate.

Phillip threw his blanket off and swung his legs around. He quickly grabbed for his tunic. Then he stopped. Instead of putting on the nice tunic that he had been wearing lately, he reached down to the foot of his bed and unrolled his old robe and put it on.

He moved quickly through the cathedral halls as other people were beginning to stir. He didn't talk with or even look at any of them. Before he reached the doors to the outside, he noticed that the old priest who had talked to him the night before was standing to one side. Phillip stopped.

"I thought that you might be along soon," he said smiling. "You've made the right choice. I only wish that I were young enough to go. May I say a prayer for you?"

"Yes, of course," Phillip responded. The priest put his hand on Phillip's shoulder and prayed a long slow prayer. At first Phillip could not concentrate on the words of the prayer because he was still thinking about getting out quickly, but after a minute or so he began to really listen. The prayer was not any of the memorized prayers that Phillip knew. It was a personal prayer directed specifically for him.

"...and dear Lord," continued the priest, "help this young man find out what you are trying to show him through this crusade. Give him your strength and courage so that he will finish his part. I pray that as he lives that he will find You in all he does, and when he dies that he will find You waiting to receive him. And please..." the priest went on. When he said, "Amen," Phillip raised his head and thanked him. Then he asked the guard to let him out.

Phillip knew that he must follow after the soldiers towards the south gate. But when he got there, how would he get out? It would surely still be closed. He walked briskly but he noticed that his heart had slowed down and a calm had come over him.

He easily overtook the soldiers who were not in a hurry. It was a slow process for the small troop of soldiers to get through the thin streets and crowds. It was obvious that Lord Robert was making a show of force for the city so that the people would know that the problem was being taken care of.

Finally, the small troop of soldiers stopped and Phillip was trapped behind them. He quickly backed up and found a small side street that would allow him to go around the jammed street so that he could get closer to the gate.

When Phillip was finally only a hundred yards or so from the gate he had to rejoin the main street and hope to find a way out. The sun had come now and the crowd of onlookers was growing.

Phillip was beginning the slow process of squeezing between people so that he could get to the gate when only twenty feet away he caught sight of the unmistakable face of Michelle looking right at him. He froze. At that moment the crowd let up a little and Michelle got a good look at Phillip standing there in his old robe.

Michelle began to breath heavily as tears welled up in her eyes. "No! No! No!" she yelled as she moved towards Phillip. When she reached him, he didn't move or say anything. "You can't do this!" she screamed as she threw her arms around him.

The crowd began to stop looking at the soldiers and began to stare in silence at the strange scene that was going on. A young woman of obvious nobility was holding on to what looked like a young man dresses in an old ragged brown robe that was used by common church servants.

Phillip continued to say nothing. He stood there like a statue while Michelle cried convulsively into his shoulder.

Phillip finally moved when, from behind, a gleaming broad shaped sword tapped him on the shoulder. He turned and looked up to see his friend Sir John staring down at him from his horse. The two young men stared at each other for a few tense moments, and then John looked down at his weeping cousin.

"If you did not already know," John said looking directly at Phillip and speaking loudly, "there is a law against any crusaders entering the city. If you do no leave immediately, I will be forced to put you in stocks." The crowd murmured at hearing that the young man was from the crusade.

Phillip answered back humbly, "I ask your forgiveness sir. If I may be permitted to leave, I promise you that I will not return."

Michelle looked up at her cousin with tear filled eyes. He looked back down at her cooly. She had lost.

Michelle let go of Phillip and took two steps backwards. Phillip melted inside as he looked at the moistened cheeks and red eyes of Michelle. He began to take a step toward her but John again placed his sword on Phillip's shoulder. Phillip stopped and looked into the stern face of the knight.

John escorted Phillip through the crowd and the soldiers and then he had the gate opened up. When Phillip was finally out in the open he walked many yards before he dared look back. When he finally did looked back he saw Sir John staring at him atop his mount. Yes, John would make a good knight.

It was obvious that the crusade was preparing itself to move. Everyone that Phillip passed was either getting their things ready or had already done so. Nobody seemed frightened by the soldiers that were making themselves into a formation outside of the city walls. Children were talking to each other and carrying on as if it were simply another day.

Phillip was heading for the place that he had left his friends at many days earlier. He was nervous. He had no idea what he was going to tell them. He knew that if he tried to explain about Michelle, it would be like telling them that he had been lying to them from the very beginning. On the other hand, if he did not tell them, he would have to lie some more just to cover things up.

Soon Phillip stood just outside the little camping area of his friends. They were busy getting their things ready. Andre had already gotten the horse hooked up to the wagon. Hungry, who was tied up, saw Phillip first and began to bark. When Madoc and Anna looked to see what Hungry was barking at, there was Phillip walking slowly toward them.

Madoc yelled, "Look!" Every one around stopped what they were doing and watched Phillip come into camp. Andre and Louis both smiled and walked over to welcome him back. Others then noticed and came over to welcome him back. In the next hour, as the crusade was getting to the point to where they could depart, many visitors hearing about Phillip's return also came by to welcome him. Father Gilbert made a special effort to come by and talk to him. Phillip felt a stronger part of the crusade in that hour than he had ever felt before.

16

BITTER WATERS

Soon the crusade, which now numbered about twelve thousand, was on the move again. The dust that was being kicked up gave testimony to the fact that it had not rained in a long time. Phillip thought how incredible it was that such a large group could make so little noise. The only real noise being made was the rattling of some of the half-filled wagons being pulled along the bumpy road.

Phillip insisted on walking so he took up a position a few yards behind the wagon which Anna was riding in. It was during the first day that he realized that not only did Anna not greet him when he came back into camp but that she was avoiding looking at him. Phillip was actually kind of glad about it because he did not look forward to explaining to her the events that occurred to during that week in Lyon.

The next two days went on pretty much the same, but food was beginning to get scarce all ready and the hot summer sun was taking its toll. The group had walked as far as they could each day and at night everyone was so tired that they did little more than sleep.

The next morning the leaders of the crusade decided to only march until they found a good camping place beside the Rhone river. They would rest well and spend some time fishing, hunting, and looking for other necessities. They had only been on the move for a couple of hours when they located the perfect place on the east side of the river. There was a large field that had grown some sort of crop during the season but now was nothing more than a large flat plain of dirt and straw.

When everyone had found a place, the groups went into action.

The new crusaders from Lyon easily found a place to fit in with the others. Fishing and hunting turned out to produce very little so everyone returned to camp early.

Andre had unhitched the horse and had tied it to a tree with the wagon close by. The small band of friends always camped beside the wagon. A few blankets were tied to the wagon and then to tall sticks so that there could be some shade. Anna stayed in the shade and patched blankets and clothes while the others were out.

Phillip saw Anna working with a tunic and went over to talk to her. "Hello, Anna," he started. She looked up and smiled politely.

"Hello, Phillip, how are you?" she said.

"I'm fine. I've been wondering about your leg. How is it?"

"It's healing just fine. Tom doesn't think that there will be any long term problems because of it." Anna kept on sewing as she talked.

"I'm glad to hear that," said Phillip. "I had thought about getting a physician to look at it while I was in Lyon."

Anna stopped and looked up. "I appreciate that, Phillip," she said.

"Anna," began Phillip again, "please don't be angry with me for staying longer in Lyon."

Still looking at Phillip, Anna said sincerely, "Oh no, Phillip, I'm not angry with you at all."

"But you've been so quiet lately. I thought that you were angry with me."

"I was so scared, Phillip," she said with a tear. "I was so scared that you wouldn't return. You see, even when you didn't know that I was here, I knew you were here and I felt secure. Then you left. I was sure that you would stay with Mary in Lyon."

Phillip looked down and said humbly, "I'm sorry Anna."

"Don't be sorry," she continued. "It's my fault."

"How could it be your fault?"

"It just is," she said. "The night before we left Lyon I was especially afraid. I went out and did something that I hadn't done in a while. I prayed. When I had finished my prayer I remembered something that my mother had told me just after my father died. I remember being so frightened, and I'm sure that she was scared too. When I told her that I was scared, she told me that my father was a wonderful man, but the one who had been providing for us and protecting us for all the years was still alive. She told me that it was God." Anna looked at Phillip and smiled. "I'm embarrassed to say that I had almost forgotten that it is God who provides for us."

"Yes it is. Isn't it?" said Phillip thoughtfully. "Why have you kept away from me since I returned?"

"I don't know, Phillip," she said starting to sew again. "I'll be all right now." The conversation between them came to a natural stopping point so Phillip began to get up to see if he could help the others prepare the wagon for handing out the rest of the bread rations for the evening. He turned to leave when Ann spoke to him again. "Phillip?" He stopped and turned back. "What happened in Lyon and where's Mary? She was nice and I'm sorry that she didn't come back."

Phillip knew that someone would eventually ask, but he still didn't know how he'd respond. When he looked back at Anna without saying anything, she said, "It's all right Phillip. You don't have to say anything."

"You're wrong, Anna," he said rubbing back his hair. "I have a lot that I need to tell you." He sighed, "I have a lot that I need to tell all of you." Phillip decided right then that he would explain everything to his friends that night and ask their forgiveness. He felt better already.

That night when Phillip finally got everyone's attention he began explaining about Michelle. He told them how he knew who she was from the work that he'd done at the castle Velva, and then how he recognized her on the first day out of Paris when she rolled out of the bread sack. From there he told the spellbound listeners why he treated her the way that he did during the trip, and then why he really had to get her into Lyon. He did, however, leave out a lot of personal details.

No one made any comments during the recounting of the story. There was only an occasional, "I'll be," or "huh," or a nod of the head. He finished with the telling of the basic events that happened to him in the city of Lyon. He could not bring yet to tell them that he was ready, at one point, to abandon the crusade completely. He finished by telling them how, on the last day, when he heard the soldiers moving in the streets, he put on his old clothes and returned.

Finally Andre said, "Well if that don't beat all. Mary was nobility. I should have known."

Louis added, "You should have told us Phillip. We'd have helped you." Everyone else nodded in agreement.

Phillip tried to fight back his emotions of guilt. He hung his head and said, "I know that now. Can you forgive me? I am not a deceitful person. It's just that at first the deception seemed necessary. Later, when I knew that I could trust you, my close friends, I was to embarrassed to tell you the truth."

"Why are you telling us now?" asked Antoine.

" A couple of days ago I didn't think that I could," said Phillip, "but I knew that if I didn't tell you the truth now, that every time that we talked about Mary, Michelle I mean, and every time you asked me questions about Lyon, I would have to keep on making up stories."

"Does this mean that we all have to tell our secrets?" asked Madoc seriously.

"Of course not," said Anna.

Louis laughing said, "Madoc thinks this is some kind of group confessional meeting or something."

Phillip laughed. He needed to laugh a little to break up the tension inside him. "This has been more than just a secret, Madoc. It's something that has involved all of you and I should have told you the truth a long time ago."

"No harm done," said Antoine. "Just forget about it."

Anna knowing what this confession meant to Phillip said, "I forgive you Phillip."

Phillip smiled and said, "Thank you."

Then everyone else took turns saying, "I forgive you."

Phillip looked around smiling at everyone and again said a sincere, "Thank you."

The rest of the night the friends sat around re-telling stories about Michelle and laughing. "You know," said Andre, "I really miss the princess." Again everyone agreed. That night Phillip slept better than he had slept in weeks.

There was no breakfast given out the next morning so if a person didn't have any food saved he had to begin the next day's march without it.

It was a hard day. The ground was hard, the sun was hot, and the air was dry. The crusade had a difficult time staying together because one section or another was constantly having to stop.

When the front section finally reached the place where they would stop for the night, it was another hour before everybody else arrived. That night moans and groans were audible throughout the camp. Many had headaches and slight fevers because of the sun.

"We must stop for a couple of days," said Father Gilbert to Father David and Stephen.

"We just got started again," said Father David. "Besides, stopping here will not help the situation."

"Why can't we stop for a while?" asked Stephen.

Father David looked at Stephen and then at Father Gilbert and responded, "It's no good to stop here. There's no food in this valley and all of the farm houses and villages are shut up completely."

Father Gilbert looked at Father David and nodded. Stephen just looked at the ground and didn't say anything.

The next day the crusade got a late start, but it did get started. It was another miserable day. More and more fell sick because of hunger and heat. When the crusade finally found a place to camp, it was quite a distance from the river because a swampy lowland area acted as an impassable barrier between them and the Rhone.

Tom, who had been helping Anna with her leg, immediately went up front to talk to Father David and Father Gilbert. He addressed them formally and then began with, "It is dangerous to stop here. The water in this lowland area is rancid. Can't you smell it?"

Father Gilbert asked, "You mean that this will be a problem for us?"

"Yes," said the physician, "this water is not suitable for drinking or anything else. In fact it's dangerous just be close to it."

Stephen said, "But look. The road out leads even farther away from the river."

"Yes, I see that," began Tom, "but most of us still have sacks of water enough to last two days."

Father David, who had been listening to everything suddenly closed his eyes and began to pray in a chant. It caught everyone off guard. When Father David finished, he opened his eyes and calmly stated, "I know what must be done."

Within fifteen minutes Father David had called together some of the other priests. They stood at the edge of the swamp area and began to pray together. The rest of the crusaders were kneeling down. After the priests said many prayers over the swamp water, Stephen stepped forward with a branch that he had cut off of a nearby tree. When he threw the branch into the water the priests began to wave their crucifixes over the swamp and pray. Finally Father David called out, "And now the bitter waters called "mara" shall be sweet and shall be useful to all of God's children." At that very moment a strong breeze did blow the stench of the swamp away so that it smelled better.

It wasn't too long before the crusaders had set up camp and were going about their duties. Even though it was no use trying to fish, a number of boys who were handy with a slingshot knocked down a good number of birds to eat.

Hungry made a few trips into the shallow looking for something to hunt but didn't have any luck. The only animal life around the water, besides bugs, were multitudes of frogs and slugs. The only other life was the birds high in the trees and brush.

The mosquitoes made it hard to sleep that night and even at nighttime it was hot.

Phillip woke up a bit late the next day with a slight headache. He sat up on his blanket holding his head and squinting his eyes. After a brief look around, Phillip noticed that their horse was laying on the ground groaning. He jumped out of his blanket and shook Andre who was next to him. "Andre, get up. The horse doesn't look very good."

Andre slowly rolled over and looked at Phillip with blood shot eyes. Phillip noticed that there were beads of sweat on his forehead. "Andre," he said bending down, "are you all right?"

"I don't know," said Andre weakly. "I don't feel right, but I didn't sleep very good last night."

"Me either," said Phillip. "You go ahead and rest a little longer, I'm going to check on the horse." Phillip stood up dizzily.

He reached the horse and looked at it closely. The horse was sick, but Phillip didn't know anything about animals. "I've got to find someone who can look at the horse," he thought. There was one boy who usually looked after the horses when they were hurt. He decided to try to find the boy before the crusade got moving.

Making his way through the camp, Phillip noticed that there was a larger problem than just his horse. Many of the children were up and stumbling around while others just laid in their places groaning. He stopped looking for the boy and returned to his friends quickly.

Phillip was nearing his camp again when he heard a man's voice yelling out instructions. "Do not drink any of the water from this place. Use only water that you have saved. This water is bad water," the voice said. Even at a distance Phillip recognized the man yelling as Old Tom. Tom was moving throughout the entire camp yelling his message over and over.

"What does he mean?" asked Louis. "Almost all of us have already drunk some of the water."

"If its bad water, then why didn't they tell us before?" added Antoine.

Phillip heard everything that was being said. He had used some of the water from a clean looking pool to wash his body with last night after the long day's journey. He remembered now that he also drank a handful or two. "How could we have known that the water was bad?"

"Well Old Tom seems to know," said Antoine.

"Its pretty obvious now," said Louis. "Look around; everybody's sick. You don't have to be a doctor to figure out what the problem is."

"Yeah, look at the horses," said Phillip. Then turning his head and looking over his left shoulder he said, "I guess Hungry's sick too." There was Madoc kneeling down by his faithful friend as he lay on one side panting heavily. "Maybe it'll..."

The conversation was interrupted as Andre doubled up on his blanket holding his stomach. He moaned loudly. Everyone looked over. Anna was already beside him squatting down the best she could, trying to comfort him.

Phillip got up and slowly walked over to where Andre and Anna were. "He's pretty bad, isn't he?" he asked.

"Seems to be," said Anna wiping Andre's forehead with a rag. "I wonder if we could get Tom to look at him?"

"I want to see him right now!" said Father David looking fiercely at the young messenger. "He has no right saying those things." Father David paced angrily for a few seconds as Stephen and a few others looked on. "James, you and Charles go ask our good physician if he would be so kind as to talk with me?" The two boys left immediately.

About five minutes later, James, Charles, and Old Tom came walking up to where Father David and Stephen were. Father David started in on the older man without any greeting, "Why in the world are you going around getting everyone in a panic about this water thing?"

Tom stared at the priest in unbelief. "Isn't it obvious to you that the water is making everyone sick?"

"It isn't the water," said Father David glaring at Tom. Just then Father Gilbert walked up and stood back to listen.

"It must be the water," returned Tom pleadingly. "If we stop the usage of the water now, it may keep others from getting sick."

"I repeat," said Father David gritting his teeth, "It is not the water. The water has been blessed and purified. I know it, and the others know it. You seem to be the only one who wasn't present yesterday at the blessing."

"I was present Father," said Tom defending himself, "but, but, . . "

"But what?" demanded Father David. "But you don't believe that the Lord fulfilled his promise to make the water usable. Is that it?" Father David folded his arms on his chest and stared at Tom. Tom looked around now at all of the others. They were all looking at him, awaiting an answer.

Father Gilbert began to take a step forward when Father David shot a vicious stare at him as if to say, "Don't interfere!" Father Gilbert stepped back and said nothing.

Poor Tom could say nothing. He waited for Father David's next instructions.

"I am told that you are a sort of doctor," started Father David still looking at Tom. "Would you please do me a favor? It seems that a few of the crusaders are suffering from heat exhaustion or maybe from not quite enough nourishment. Will you do what you can for them?"

Without saying anything more, Tom left the meeting and went to see what he could do for his fellow crusaders.

When Tom was gone Father David told the people around him to spread the word to the rest of the crusaders that they would be breaking camp immediately. They all left to give out the message. Only Father Gilbert stayed.

"This crusade is not going anywhere," said Father Gilbert flatly to Father David and Stephen. "More than half of the horses are lying down sick and at least one out of every four of the children have stomach cramps and fevers."

Father David turned red faced with anger but couldn't say anything. Finally Stephen, looking alternately at the two priests, said, "This place has a curse on it. Look at us. Not only are people getting sick, but everyone is yelling and screaming at each other."

"You are probably right," said Father David putting his hand on Stephen's shoulder. "This place has a curse on it and we must get out of here."

"We can not move," said Father Gilbert. "It is physically impossible."

Father David put his right hand up to his chin and stroked his short beard a few times. A smile began to form on his face as he looked up. "We can move," he said, "we must move. We must inform everyone of the curse on this place. We must tell them that we must leave this accursed ground."

"Who would have dared put a curse on the crusade of God?" asked Stephen. "Maybe witches use this place."

"No," said David, "I think that Satan has planted someone right in amongst us, and I think I know who it is."

At first when the crusaders heard that they would be moving soon they couldn't believe it. Soon, however, the rumor of the area being cursed and everyone began to move. Some of the crusaders even began going through their own personal exorcising rituals. Many made large crosses out of branches and laid them on the ground around their sick friends. Others began praying special prayers.

Anna leaned over Andre and prayed many times over a period of two hours. Madoc made little crosses and put them around Hungry. He stroked his Hungry's black fur and repeated, "Please get better. Please get better."

Phillip, Louis, Antoine and about three others from their camp held their own special service. Phillip reached down and got two fistfuls of dirt. The others gathered some long branches. Phillip began chanting an exorcising prayer in Latin that he had learned. At certain points in the prayer Phillip would toss up parts of the dirt in his hand into the air and as he did that the others struck the ground soundly with their branches. The ritual lasted for about ten minutes.

All of the confusion served to strike great fear in the hearts of all. No one felt better after they had prayed. It was then that a loud clanging noise got everyone's attention. Messengers came through the camp shouting that all who could walk should join Stephen at the waters edge.

When a large number of crusaders were gathered at the appointed place, Stephen began speaking. "This place that God meant for good and safety has been turned into a place of fear and sickness by a curse. This is accused ground." Everyone nodded in agreement.

"God has revealed to us who has done this blasphemous thing," said Stephen looking to his right side. A group of large boys pushed and shoved through the crowd dragging Old Tom by the arms. There were two other boys following them with armloads of sticks and rags. All of the crusaders got on tiptoes in order to see.

Stephen waited until the boys had brought Tom right in front of him. "This man," said Stephen looking out at the crowd and pointing down at Tom, "has been found to be guilty of witchcraft." One boy stepped forward and threw down a number of bottles, pouches, an old book that was hand stitched at the seams, and herbs in front of Tom. Stephen said, "This man has been found with potions, divining instruments, and books of chants in his possession." The crowd started talking amongst themselves and pointing at the evidence.

"We are a holy crusade of the Most Holy God and because this crusade is very important to God it would be foolish of us to think that Satan would not try to stop us," said Stephen in his penetrating voice.

"The Bible orders that known witches and warlocks must die." With those words the crowd began to murmur even louder.

Old Tom, who had just been standing there with his head down, looked up at the crusaders around him. He began to speak but Father David, who was standing nearby shouted at him to be silent. "We will not allow you to bewitch us again with your demonic words," he said.

When Tom tried to speak again, Father David looked at one of the two boys that were holding him and the boy struck Tom in the jaw. The crusaders grew silent.

Stephen began to speak again. "Listen! I am sure that many of you have come to know the accused. You may be wondering how this one who has seemed to be a friend could be a tool of the devil. We were also shocked to find out the truth about him. However, this is not a new trick of the devil," said Stephen.

"We find that in everyone of God's most holy plans, that the devil has placed his servants in the midst in order to try to stop them. In the Garden of Eden the devil used one of God's own creatures, the serpent, to deceive Eve. We also know that amongst the twelve disciples of our Lord Jesus, that Judas Iscariot was carefully placed in order to stop the Lord's plan of salvation." Stephen paused for effect and looked around, "However," he began shouted loudly, "God will not be stopped! God will be victorious! ...Will we?"

Many voices shouted out, "No!"

"No, we can't be stopped! We refuse to be stopped! We will go on!" shouted Stephen. Stephen then paused and took a deep breath. "We must leave this place immediately, but first we must do God's will and stop this man who wanted to stop us."

Stephen jumped down from the wagon he was standing in. The two boys who were holding Tom lifted him up into the wagon and one of the boys tied him up in the wagon and place a blindfold over his eyes. Other boys around started putting sticks and dry grass under the wagon.

From the side entered another boy carrying a large piece of a broken clay pot that had some red hot coals on it. The boy stopped as he reached the wagon and looked over at Father David. Father David motioned to him to put the coals on the pile under the wagon. As the fire began, Father David brought out his large crucifix and began to pray out loud for the soul of the accused.

Tom, who was still dazed, cried out weakly, "Please no! Please no!" Finally the smoke got so heavy that the condemned man could hardly be seen. His choking cries died out and only the loud crackling of the fire could be heard as it consumed the wagon.

When the fire died down a little, about ten boys started throwing water on it with pots. All of the other crusaders slowly went back to their campsites and did their best to get themselves and their sick companions ready to move.

The whole rest of the day was spent only moving a small distance away. Out of an original nineteen wagons there were only eight left. Half of the horses that pulled the wagons were dead or dying. Some of the sick were piled into the few remaining wagons while others were carried on stretchers. All along the way fresh graves marked the route where the crusade marched.

When the crusade finally found a place to stop, it was right next to the river at a bend. The individual groups had to reorganize because of all the sick. All duties except for finding food and water were canceled.

Phillip walked into the campsite that Antoine had picked dragging Andre behind him on a stretcher. Right behind Phillip was Anna on her crutches followed by Louis who was dragging a smaller stretcher that held Hungry. The others had already begun to set up camp.

When they had found where they would stay, the small group of friends did the minimum possible before they sat down for a long rest. All of them had taken turns carrying Andre even though many of them didn't feel very well either.

A few complained a bit at having to take turns pulling Hungry along also but they all had agreed beforehand that it was right. They also knew that Madoc would be lost without the dog and would never forgive them if they would've left him to die. Madoc took as many turns as he could carrying Hungry but there was no way that he could pull the stretcher all of the time and keep up.

That night there was no food so almost everyone went to sleep very tired and very hungry...again.

17

RIVER BEND

The next day proved that the spot that the crusade had picked to camp at was a good one. The water was good and the fishing was decent. The children were so hungry that many of the fish were eaten before they were even fully cooked or cleaned. Other children who didn't fish also had some luck in finding some vegetation to eat. Most of the weak crusaders were able to regain some strength as they ate and rested...but not all of them.

Andre was getting weaker and weaker no matter what his friends did to help him. By early afternoon Andre doubled up with stomach pains again and then could not control his bowels. After the sick young man soiled himself, his face went pale and motionless. His friends stood around watching helplessly not knowing what to do. Anna squatted down beside the body of Andre and put her hand just above his mouth to see if she could feel him breathing. When she pulled her hand away she looked up at everyone that was gathered around, and with tear filled eyes shook her head from side to side.

Phillip, Antoine, and Louis took the body of Andre down to the river and washed it in the shallows. They put a clean robe on him and combed back his wet brown hair. Father Gilbert was there as the friends gathered around a hole that they had dug for the burial. They all prayed for their dead friend and then gently lowered the blanket-covered body down into the cool earth.

When the grave was filled in, Father Gilbert walked solemnly to the next little graveside ceremony some 30 yards away, and then he went to the next, and then the next. Before the day had ended 43 fresh mounds of dirt marked with 43 crosses lined the outskirts of the campsite.

As the sun came up the next day, Madoc was awakened by the wet nose of Hungry nudging him behind the ear. Madoc smiled and put his hand up to pet the dog that was standing over him. "Good boy," he said.

Phillip rolled over on his blanket and saw Anna limping into camp. "Where have you been this morning?" he asked rubbing his eyes.

"I was out thinking," she said, "and praying."

"You look like you are limping a lot worse today," he said looking at her leg. "Is it getting worse?"

"No, it's not so bad," said Anna coming right up close to where Phillip was laying. "It's just sore from walking on it so much yesterday. I'm sure that it'll keep getting better. Old Tom said that..." Anna covered her face as the thought of what happened to the kind doctor came flooding back to her.

"Oh, Phillip," she cried softly. "I don't think I can take it anymore."

Phillip sat up and looked around to see if anyone else was watching what was going on. Nobody was. Crying was so common these days that nobody thought anything about it. Phillip then put his sandals on quickly and stood up. "Come on Anna. We can talk closer to the river." He led the way s the hobbling girl followed close behind.

When they were just outside of hearing range, Phillip turned to Anna. She was shaking and crying still. "Anna, I have seen how difficult the last few days have been on you. We are all grieving over Andre," said Phillip. "The whole thing about Tom was confusing and scary." Anna began to cry again.

Phillip continued looking firmly at Anna, "We are too close to turn back now. We have come to far and been through too much to falter." Slouching over her crutches, Anna remained with her tear filled eyes fixed on the ground in front of her. Phillip knew that he wasn't getting through.

Just then Madoc came walking up with Hungry beside him. "Look Anna, Hungry's better." Anna looked down at little Madoc and beside him was his faithful companion standing there panting. What a sight they were. Madoc was pale, thin, and dirty from the bottom of his bare feet to the top of his filthy matted hair. Poor Hungry was so thin that he looked like a skeleton walking around with a thin layer of dirty black skin drooping off of him.

Anna wiped her wet cheeks with her sleeve and smiled. "Madoc," she said, "go back to camp and look in my bag. You will find my pouch of soap chips in it." Madoc's smile disappeared. Anna stood up as straight as she could, and trying to sound as motherly as possible said, "Now go on and do as I ask. Both you and that dog of yours are way over due for a good bath."

Madoc turned on his heels and started walking back to camp. He wasn't in any hurry. Hungry followed.

Anna looked at Phillip and smiled slightly. Phillip nodded, smiled back, and then walked back to camp alone.

After three full days camped at the new site by the river, Father David was eager to get the crusade moving again. His greatest fear was being realized. The sick, injured, malnutritioned, and their friends were beginning to set up more permanent dwellings. It was obvious that they were planning on staying for a while.

"I don't see what's wrong with staying here for a while until we can get our strength back," said Stephen looking up at Father David from his sitting place.

"Not only do they need to stay for a while longer," said Father Gilbert to both Father David and Stephen, "but I am quite certain that they will refuse to leave."

Trying not to raise his voice so loudly that others could hear, Father David responded, "If we don't leave now, we'll never leave." He paused and looked sternly at the other two leaders. "If we lower the banner now, we're lost for sure."

Just at that moment the sound of horses hooves beating the ground at a good pace could be heard coming towards them. In a few moments three men rode in and pulled their horses up to an abrupt halt. Stephen, Father Gilbert, and Father David walked over to where the men had stopped.

"We have come with news from Lord Beaumont," one of the men shouted out as he looked around trying to find someone who looked to be in charge. When he spotted the two priests and the young boy coming towards them, he smiled and said with a loud voice, "Good news to you, servants of the Church. Our lord, Sir Beaumont, has been watching your struggle these past days as you have been passing over his land."

When Stephen and the priests arrived, the messenger continued on shouting out his news so that the many crusaders that were beginning to close in could hear. "Our good master is a God fearing man and a patriot of his mother France." The messenger then waited a few moments as everyone strained to hear better. "You all are invited to stay here for as long as you need." Father David's mouth dropped open.

"Also," continued the young man, "in a few minutes ten wagons will arrive with bread, fruit, and some vegetables." With that, a loud cheer went up all at once from the crusaders. The others who had not been present up to that point rushed in to hear what all of the excitement was about. Father Gilbert fell to his knees thanking God in prayer. Others did likewise.

Father David walked away muttering, "Disaster! Disaster!" Stephen and the other children continued to shout with joy.

Father Gilbert stood back up and gave each one of the messengers a special blessing before they departed.

Three days after the visit of Lord Beaumont's messengers, the crusade was noticeably stronger and healthier. In the camp some laughter could be heard as children joked and teased. Some children were playing games and singing. Father Gilbert could not help but be overjoyed inside as he watched the children acting like children for the first time since the beginning of the crusade.

"Father Gilbert," said a young man tapping the priest on the shoulder, "Father David said that he would like to talk to you." The smile that was on Father Gilbert's face immediately disappeared and he sighed deeply.

"All right," he said kindly, "tell Father David that I'll be there in a few minutes."

When Father Gilbert finally showed up, he and Father David acknowledged each other and began to walk out of camp together. "You cannot avoid me any longer Father Gilbert," said David. "You know, as well as I, that it is time to depart."

Still walking slowly, Father Gilbert didn't even look up at his companion. "I don't know what I know anymore David," he said.

Father David turned a bit red but spoke softly, "What exactly is it then that you do know?"

Gilbert stopped and looked sincerely at his fellow priest, "The reality that thousands of children have left our crusade because they were starving and sick, that hundreds have died for all kinds of reasons, and that all have suffered tremendously...has become more than I can stomach. Can you tell me David, that it doesn't make you doubt?"

Father David stared straight ahead, "No, I don't doubt." Looking at Gilbert he continued, "If we arrive at the Holy Land with only Gideon's 300, I will not doubt."

A look of disbelief came over Father Gilbert's face. "But the children...?" he began pleadingly.

"They are not 'just' children! They are God's hands and God's feet," was the response that David gave. There was a long silence as the two priests turned around and headed back towards camp.

When they reached a small hill that allowed them to overlook the crusade, they stopped. Without looking at Father David, Gilbert said, "I just can't ask them to go on any farther," and then he walked down the hill alone.

The rest of the day Father David spent with Stephen. At night, the two of them were left alone to talk.

Deep into the night the camp was awakened by a horrible scream. Many jumped immediately to their feet to see what the cause was. It was the boy leader, Stephen himself. Many tried to crowd in to see if he was all right but were soon dismissed by the smiling Father David.

When Father Gilbert heard the screaming, he recognized it

immediately and sprang to his feet. He had been sleeping at the far side of the camp so it took him a minute to get to the front where the leaders of the crusade stayed. As he got close three stout young men cut him off. They were Father David's "errand boys", and they were not going to allow him to pass.

Father Gilbert looked hard and long at them. Finally one of the boys spoke up, "Father David told us to tell you, Father, that you did-n't have to worry. He is taking care of things."

The young priest stood in shock. Not because of what had just happened, but because everything was becoming clear to him. He turned around and began to walk towards the river in order to think.

He was dumbfounded as he thought back at all of the events that had taken place in the past three months. He began to see all of the people around Father David as simple pawns, being manipulated at his will. Worst of all was that he himself had been a major player. All of this time he had thought of himself as a great help and blessing for the chil-dren, and now he realized that even his benevolence was being used as a tool to keep the crusade going.

Father Gilbert walked up to the water's edge and sat down. As he listened to the swift current twisting its way around the bend, a new thought struck him. Not only did Father David manipulate everything and everyone, but those that he couldn't manipulate always seemed to disappear.

Just then, Father Gilbert heard the sound of footsteps coming closer. A cold chill ran through his body as he turned to see who was coming.

The next morning Stephen was up early firing away with a power-ful message. Father David watched anxiously as small groups of cru-saders slowly made their way to where the preaching was going on. Many, however, didn't come to listen.

After about a half hour of preaching, Stephen stopped and Father David stepped up on the back of the wagon. "Please spread the word that we will be having communion shortly." Twenty minutes later most of the crusaders had shown up to partake.

As the bread was being readied, Stephen got back up on the wagon and began to preach again. After another half hour, it seemed that the crusaders were finally beginning to listen. The communion, which consisted of bread and water, was quickly dispersed.

Almost before the children had finished eating their bread, Stephen was back up on the wagon. "Now as we remember the great work that Christ did for us on the cross, we should remember what our great work is for him here and now. As Christ, even though tempted by Satan to abandon his sacrificial work, renewed his vow to God in the Garden of Gethsemane, it is time for us to renew our vows to God here. It is time to march on to the Holy Land. Tomorrow morning we march." Stephen paused a moment and looked around slowly. Then he raised his hand in the air and shouted, "For God and the Church."

Finally, the crowd responded with a half-hearted, "For God and the Church." When they dispersed back to their camps there was no joy in the faces of the crusaders. Hardly anyone talked as they carried out their daily chores. The thought of leaving this place was not welcomed. The land at the river bend didn't provide the crusaders with much extra, but there was always enough. The food brought by lord Beaumont's men was running out, but there was fish in the river, and some edible vegetation to be found.

Later, Louis, Antoine, and two other boys sat around a low fire. They began to discuss the upcoming departure, while Phillip, Anna, and Madoc listened from a couple of yards behind. Louis, who was poking at the fire with a stick, began, "I suppose now is as good a time as any to get back on track." There was a short pause as the four boys stared, hypnotically, at the small flickering flames.

"I don't know," began a boy named Walter. "I could stand it another week or two here myself."

"Yes," chimed in a tall boy who sat to Walter's right, "I feel like I'm just starting to get my strength back. I don't know if I can start again so soon."

"We don't have much of a choice about it really," said Antoine. "They say that the ocean is only a week from here anyway."

"Is that all that it is to Marseilles?" asked Walter.

"That's what they say," repeated Antoine.

"A whole week?" said the other boy. "A person could die in a week."

"I guess a week's not too bad considering all that we've already been through," said Louis. Then looking up at the other three he added, "And a vow is a vow."

"Maybe so, but you can't fill your stomach with a vow," replied Walter. "If we can't find food along the way, that week may be an eternity."

Phillip, who had been sitting on a stump nearby, got up and walked out into the night. A number of yards out but still within listening range of the fireside conversation, Phillip dropped his head and prayed silently. "Dear Mother Mary, have mercy on us. You are our mother, and we are your children. We need your guidance to make it the rest of the way. Show us what we must do to make the journey."

18

TO THE SEA

The next morning, during the preparation time it became obvious that almost half of the crusade was not planning on continuing. In the past when crusaders decided not to continue, they waited at the back of the procession and pretended like they were going to go with the others, but when they had distanced themselves a good ways behind, they began to walk back the other direction. This time, however, those that had decided to abandon the crusade openly and defiantly made their intentions clear by simply doing nothing.

The front of the procession started off at a strong pace. As the last of the crusade began moving, Anna looked back at the thousands of children and young adults that were staying behind. A handful of them were still lying sick on their beds, while others solemnly watched the crusade move out. They had come so far and been through so much in the past weeks, and now the crusade was going on without them. Anna hadn't said anything, but even though the deserting crusaders looked unhappy and pathetic, she wished that she was among them.

Phillip was looking the other direction when the crusade began moving. Up on the hills, mounted on horseback, was a small company of lord Beaumont's men watching them leave. Among them was the enthusiastic young officer who had greeted them with the news of the forthcoming food and help. How gracious they had been. Phillip wondered how gracious they would be when they found that almost half of the crusade enjoyed their hospitality so much that they decided to stay.

197

Phillip had to at least admit to himself that he had considered
staying also. He even went so far as to look for Father Gilbert in
order to confess his doubts and fears and then ask him for advice.
When he couldn't find the kindly priest that he had come to trust,
he took it as a sign that the Lord wanted him to not ask any questions and just follow along.

Phillip was reminded of his studies back at the Seminary. Father
Timothy had told him to put all of his theological doubts and fears out
of his mind and conform himself to the teaching of the Church. "I
guess that there are times when one must close his mind and heart and
just follow," he said to himself. "After all, isn't it in Jeremiah 17 that
says that the heart of man is desperately wicked?"

Again, Phillip glanced up at the soldiers on the hillside and sighed.
"If every lord and village would be as open and helpful as these, we
would not have any problems reaching the sea shore," he thought.
Suddenly an idea sprang to his mind.

"Anna," he said looking over his right shoulder, "I will be back in a
couple of hours. I must talk to Stephen, Father David, and Father
Gilbert." Phillip started weaving his way through the crowd toward the
front. Louis and Antoine exchanged puzzled looks and kept walking.

Phillip's plan was working very well. Even though not all of the villages along the way responded positively to the petition made for help,
enough responded so that the crusaders did not starve.

When Father David first heard of the plan he rejected it and sent
Phillip back disappointed, but later in the day one of the priests' errand
boys came and informed Phillip that Father David would like to talk to
him further about his idea. Father David took Phillip aside after the
day's march and they talked about how they might go about carrying
out the plan.

Enthusiastically, Phillip laid out his plan. They would send a small
group of the most diplomatically pleasing crusaders a day ahead of the
rest and as representatives, they would petition every village that they
came upon to help them complete their mission by sharing a small
amount of their food supply.

As Father David listened, he was taken back by the intelligence of the youth in front of him, but he dared not reveal his thoughts.

It seemed to Phillip that Father David listened with an almost disinterested air about him. He would have been discouraged by the spiritual leader's attitude, but when he finished talking, Father David began to nod. "It's a good plan, young Phillip. God has revealed it to you. This evening I will choose five others to go with you so that you can leave tomorrow early in the morning."

Phillip was stunned into silence for a few seconds before he could respond. "I 'm not sure, Father, that I am the best choice to do this job. Surely there are others with more experience in this type of thing."

"Don't be ridiculous. Of course you're the right person to do this job!" said the priest bluntly. "Now go and inform your group leader that you will be leaving them." Phillip was about to leave when he finally got up enough courage to ask, "Father?"

"Yes,"

"Did Father Gilbert stay behind at the river bend?"

A sad look came into Father David's face and he responded simply, "Yes he did." Then the priest walked off.

Even though the crusade was moving at a pretty good pace now, the promised week turned into two-and-a-half weeks. However, spirits were getting higher as the news spread that they would finally arrive at the seashore in just two days. Phillip and the other "ambassadors" rejoined the camp after being separated from the main group the whole time. They were coming closer to the sea and were just about to cut off from the Rhone River and head East towards Marseilles.

When Anna and the others saw him coming into their camp that afternoon they all rushed to meet him with hardy handshakes and kisses on the cheek. All his old friends treated him like royalty, and they almost didn't get any of their chores done, because they were all so busy telling each other stories about what had happened over the past few weeks.

Phillip couldn't help but notice how much better everybody looked than they had when he had left them. They looked healthier and in much better spirits. Anna still had a bit of a limp but it was almost unnoticeable. The others who had been still weak from sickness looked as if they had recovered completely. Even Hungry looked perkier than normal. It was obvious that the fact that they were just about to arrive at Marseilles had worked an emotional, physical, and spiritual healing in them all. Their dream that had turned into a nightmare was turning into a dream again.

The next two days went by quickly. The crusaders were more efficient than ever in completing their daily tasks. They were friendlier with each other also. Many individuals, who had begun to be defensive, lightened up a bit and small groups that had become exclusive began to open back up again. They all had the common feeling of completing an immense goal.

Phillip spent most of his time with Anna. He realized that he never tired of being with her. She was so much different than anyone else he knew. Most of Phillip's other friends could only carry on conversations about superficial things like how to handle a horse, or what they wanted to own when they arrived in the Holy Land.

Anna always looked at the things of life from an inward-outward viewpoint. She saw the qualities of the heart as the fountain of all value in life. When she talked about her home in Paris, she talked about the joy, laughter, sadness, and the feelings that had been a part of her life there, instead of the color of the paint on the walls or of the quality of the furniture. However, the conversation that most captivated Phillip was when Anna would talk about God and His characteristics. Sometimes Phillip would just listen, as she would talk about her Lord and how she experienced Him in her life.

When Anna had talked about spiritual things before, Phillip would always try to insert different theological points that he had picked up in his studies, so that she would know that he was not ignorant on the subject. Yet, it always seemed to him that when he spoke about theology that that was exactly what it sounded like. When Anna spoke about the same things, they sounded much more simple and yet so much more real.

On the second day, the crusade stopped and set up camp early in the afternoon. Part of Stephen and father David's plan was to march triumphantly to the shore the next morning. Antoine had said that he wouldn't be able to sleep at all that night, knowing that he could walk to the beach by Marseilles in less than two hours. The general feeling around all of the campfires that night was giddy and cheerful. The priests were extra busy going around talking to the campers and blessing various ones.

That evening before supper, Anna asked Phillip to go to the top of the hill with her and Madoc, so that they could pray together. Phillip felt a bit uncomfortable but agreed. When they got to the top of the hill, Anna and Madoc kneeled down immediately and readied themselves. Phillip thought to himself how natural they looked. He always felt so uncomfortable and rigid when he prayed.

Phillip kneeled down beside his friends and began. He prayed a beautiful prayer that he had memorized almost three years before. After finishing, Phillip was about to get up when Anna began to pray. Her prayer was not memorized and not eloquent at all, but spoke of the basic needs of the crusaders along with giving thanks to the Lord. When she finished, Madoc began a simple prayer also. Phillip could hardly concentrate on the words he spoke at first, because he was so shocked that the little boy who would hardly speak would open his mouth and pray out loud. When Phillip began to focus on the words of the little boy beside him, it was as if the little beggar was transformed into a little prince. Even though his words were still spoken as an uneducated child might speak, the strength and confidence in the prayer moved him.

When they had all prayed, Phillip stood up and looked anew at Anna and Madoc. When Anna had asked him to come and pray with them, he thought that she wanted him to come and pray for them. Now he realized that they were not asking him to come and bless them but instead to come and be a part of something very special with them.

"Where did you learn to pray?" asked Phillip to Madoc.

Madoc answered, "Anna and me, we pray together every day. I learned from her."

Phillip's mind wandered back to when they lived in Paris. He remembered how highly he thought of Madam Christina and how beautiful she was. He could recall how much different she was from most other people that he knew. She was special. Now, as he looked at Anna he saw the same beauty in her and also recognized the fact that the beauty he saw was something that came from deep within them. The eyes of Christina and Anna were like windows that allowed you to look inside their souls, and without shame or fear. It was as if they were inviting you to look in, because there was something inside that they wanted you to find.

"Phillip, are you all right?" asked Anna. Phillip snapped out of the temporary trance he was in.

"Can we go back now?" asked Madoc a bit impatiently. He didn't like the way that Phillip was looking at Anna. He liked Phillip, but he liked him farther away from Anna.

The next morning everyone was up before the sun had begun to rise. Even though it was almost completely dark, the young crusaders easily did their memorized morning chores and excitedly readied themselves for the day's journey.

Phillip was waiting with the rest for the order to move when one of Father David's messengers showed up to tell him that the priest had requested him to meet with him. A bit reluctantly, Phillip put his things in the care of Louis and quickly followed after the messenger.

When Phillip got to the front of the crusade, he recognized a small group of young men that stood around Stephen and Father David as the same group that had been used as ambassadors to the villages. Phillip guessed correctly that they would be sent out one last time to help prepare the way for the crusade's arrival at the seashore.

Phillip and the others moved out right away. They were to be the eyes of the crusade and would try to see what kind of reception they would receive on their arrival at the shore by the city of Marseilles. Father David said that he was sure that if the all of the villages and towns along the route knew of their coming way in advance, then the great commercial city of Southern France would also be well informed. In fact, they had already passed many travelers on their way to the city, and there had been a steady stream of them as they got closer and closer.

19

MARSEILLES

Traveling for the small band was easy in the flat lowlands that led from the Rhone valley towards Marseilles. Almost from the outset of the journey they could see the Mediterranean Sea at a distance to their right, and as they got closer they could smell the summer sea air thick and humid. When the roads became wider and bit busier with traffic they knew they were drawing near. Finally the city itself came into view.

When the young men topped a small hill, they suddenly stopped at once as if they had been ordered to do so. There it was, the city and the seaport in plain view. The thriving city wrapped itself around the large rectangular bay area. It was splendid!

For all French who lived in the interior, Marseilles was like another country. Phillip had heard stories all of his life about the city's splendor and mystery. It was France's "gateway" to the rest of the world. All of the new and expensive materials and other treasures that came from the East and from parts of Northern Africa arrived in Marseilles before it was caravanned to other parts of the country.

Phillip also remembered that many of the priests had talked about the city like it was a pagan temple complete with all of the trappings of sin and idolatry. Peoples from many parts of the world lived there and brought with them their different languages, their different clothes, and their different religions. The cultured and religiously pious were said to shun the city like the Plague and yet many of the business dealings of the

Church and of many of the lords from all over the country depended heavily on their investments in the shipping industries.

It was also a problem to the Catholic Church in that there were a few strong Christian sects that thrived in Marseilles and other of the southern cities. One of these groups, the Albegenses was so prominent that the bishop of Marseilles said, "We are being over run and run out by them."

"How interesting that God would choose such a city as this to be the site of one of His greatest miracles," said Phillip aloud as he stood there staring. The others didn't say anything. Silently they began again towards the city.

Walking into Marseilles was completely different than walking into any of the other villages they had visited over the past weeks. In the other villages the band of boys was immediately recognized and brought before one of the leaders of that particular area. Here in the big city, nobody even gave them a second glance. Fortunately Father David had instructed them, before they left, to ask where the Church was located and to go directly to the bishop.

They boys only had to wait a few minutes before the bishop's secretary announced to them that the bishop would see them right away. He didn't wait for the boys to be shown into his reception hall but walked, instead, into the waiting vestibule to meet them. "Welcome young men," he said eyeing them over and smiling.

"Thank you Bishop," the boys all said respectfully.

"I must admit that you have caught me a bit off guard," said the bishop still smiling. "We have been expecting you and in fact were going to go out to meet you later this morning. Have you young men been sent out ahead?" asked the church official, guessing at the reason for their being there.

Phillip had been the spokesman for the group most of the time that they had been out before and so naturally spoke up first. "Yes, your Highness, we are here to inform you that we have arrived," he said.

"Of course you have," said the bishop. "We have been expecting you for quite some time now. In fact I was going out personally to meet with you. I even sent a group of servants of the Church to go out ahead of me and report to me as soon as the crusade was in sight."

The bishop looked over at his secretary and motioned over to him. "I want everyone ready to go in thirty minutes," he said. The secretary left the room immediately and the bishop invited the boys into his reception chambers where he talked to them for the full thirty minutes.

When the welcoming committee was ready to go, there were about forty priests, monks, and other Church servants. By the time the procession reached the outskirts of the city there were more than two thousand people following along. A short distance from the city limits everyone stopped and waited for the arrival of the crusade. More and more people came out to join them as they heard that the crusade would be coming in. By the time the news came that the rest of the crusade was about to arrive, the mass of people had grown to twenty or thirty thousand people.

Phillip and the other crusade ambassadors were in front of everyone at the side of the bishop of Marseilles, he in his fresh clean flowing robes and they, as a stark contrast, in their heavily worn but clean smocks. Yet there was a difference with the bishop here from other high Church officials that Phillip knew. The difference was not in the man himself but in the way that the people treated him. They showed him respect and many showed reverence, but the people and officials of the city obviously did not hold him up, as did officials of other cities. Most of the high city officials and other important persons rode together in one group while the bishop and his people rode separately.

Suddenly a horse rider came galloping up to the side of one of the high city officials that had come out to watch and announced, "They are only a short distance down the way, Monsieur." The finely dressed man nodded.

While the crusade was still out of sight, a number of children and youth who couldn't contain their excitement any longer ran down the road towards them. Only a few minutes more passed before the crusade could be seen and heard.

Although there were many people crowded around the crusade and many others tagging along, it was not difficult to identify the real crusaders. They looked different. It was true that their clothes were tattered and torn, but more than that, there was something different in the way they carried themselves. Although almost all of them were young people and children, they had a look of seriousness in their eyes that one usually found in grown men and women who had experienced much of life already.

Phillip felt a great swelling of pride when the crowd of now many thousands cheered in unison as the crusaders reached them. The boy prophet, Stephen, was standing in the lead wagon trying to keep his balance as the tired horse slowly pulled it along the bumpy road. Held high in the air with his right hand was the scroll that contained the letter from "the Lord." Father David and others walked humbly beside the wagon of the boy that would be the instrument of God to lead the crusade the rest of the way over dry ground through the parted Mediterranean Sea.

The crowd continued to cheer until almost all of the fifty-five hundred crusaders had arrived. When Stephen's wagon came to a stop Father David climbed up into the back with the boy. Phillip then noticed that the high city official and the bishop stared over at one another from the distance that was between them. Not a look of courteousness but more of a look of cynicism. The official, who was Rufus the vice-governor of the city, and the bishop, began to converge on the boy prophet at the same time from their prospective places.

Stephen was smiling and trying to speak, but could not be heard over the noise of the crowd. Shortly, the vice-governor arrived with his group that included a handful of men, some young and old, from the aristocracy. He raised his hand as a signal that he wanted to speak and the people around grew slowly silent. "I am Rufus, vice-governor of our great city," he said motioning his hand in the direction of Marseilles. "We know of you and your following, and the governor has consented to allow you to stay out here by our shore."

Stephen looked at Father David and then back at the vice-governor. "Thank you monsieur, we will only be here a short time. After only a few days of rest, we will be about God's marvelous business," said the boy raising the scroll into the air and bringing his voice to a high-excited pitch. Many that were close enough to hear, cheered.

Rufus smiled and replied under his breath, but loud enough to be heard, "Let's hope so." Then as he glanced over his left shoulder and saw the bishop getting close, he nodded to his men and they turned their horses and began making their way back out of the crowd.

When the bishop arrived, he was only slightly more cordial. Stephen, Father David, and the rest nodded in respect of the Church official. Stephen spoke out first, "We have come on business of God and of the Church," he pronounced. Then he looked to the side and caught a slight glare from Father David, so he became quiet.

"Yes, so we have heard," replied the bishop looking at Stephen. Then turning his gaze to Father David he said, "I have been asked to make you as comfortable as possible while you are here Father."

"That is gracious of your, Holiness," said Father David nodding again. "Our crusaders will be thankful for any assistance that you can provide."

The bishop then rose up on his saddle and strained to look back at the entire crusade, "I must admit that there are many less of you than we had heard," he said.

Stephen again spoke up and said boastingly, "We started with around thirty thousand, Bishop." Again Father David shot a stern look at the boy.

The Church official then looked at the two leaders in the wagon and asked with a smirk on his face, "Have you encountered problems along the way then?"

Phillip, who stood beside the bishop's horse, listened sadly to the volley of words, because he knew that the bishop had heard from them all about the crusade and it's problems and was simply using the information to mock the two leaders. He realized that their "triumphal entry" was not so triumphal in the eyes of the city and Church leaders. They were only being tolerated, much as one would tolerate an unwanted relative who had come to visit.

A few more words were shared between the two parties, and then the bishop turned on his horse and he and his entourage left in much the same manner as the vice-governor. Phillip looked up into the eyes of Stephen who looked a bit confused and then into the eyes of Father

David who had not lost any of his resolve. Father David then looked down and caught Phillip's gaze. His expression did not change. Then the priest turned on his heels and yelled out so that everyone could hear, "We set up camp here. This afternoon Stephen will preach."

At hearing this, the crusaders began to try to work their way through the crowd in order to locate a good spot to set up their campsites. The crowd from the city began to murmur amongst themselves about the fact that the prophet boy was going to preach and if they were going to come back to hear the message or not.

During the day, many of the people of the city returned to their homes and then came back out individually to give out presents of food, clothes, sandals, and other things to some of the crusaders. Many of the cities people stayed out with the crusaders throughout the day in order to watch them. Some entered into conversations with various of the crusaders because they could not contain their curiosity any longer, while most just stayed at a distance watching them go through their daily routines as if they were heathens going through some pagan ritual.

Phillip made his way to the campsite of his friends where he found them to be in the same mood as himself. Somehow they had all fooled themselves into thinking that the arrival at Marseilles would be victorious and grand and that the people would finally realize that they were a true crusade of God. They had pictured themselves being ushered in to the city as heroes of the Faith, but instead they were being treated as freaks brought in by an Asian caravan.

Phillip found himself wishing that Father Gilbert were there. He could picture the kindly priest passing through their camp. "Don't worry," he would say putting his hand on your shoulder. "God's very angels have cheered at our arrival and it is they who will lead us into Jerusalem in the end." Phillip thought about telling those words to his friends as they sat around long faced, but he didn't know if he believed it himself.

Later that afternoon a tremendous crowd had gathered to hear Stephen preach his message. The people of the city gathered on one side of the open area while the children crusaders were gathered together on the other side. In the crowd of people from Marseilles, there were almost no children present, and there was an air about them that was different from any other place that they had been in. It felt to Phillip like the citizens that had come to watch were there, not as hearers but as judges. He could see it in their faces and in their manner.

Phillip remembered back a few years ago at St. Denise's when one of the priests of the Seminary (he remembered that his name was Father Edward) came under scrutiny for his teaching. He was a very educated priest and Phillip had always considered him to be a great man of personal faith. He was too young at the time to have any of his classes, but he remembered the older students raving about how wonderful his classes were. He had looked forward to being in his classes also.

He remembered clearly the day when Father Edward was to give the mass for the entire school. Instead of staying with the normally programmed prayers and the memorized Latin wording, he began to preach spontaneously. At first Phillip was caught off guard, but after a minute or so, he found himself drinking in the message as if he had before been walking in a desert without a container of water and now had found an oasis. He couldn't remember the message, but he did remember that it made him think about Christ and forget about the ceremony. Normally during the Mass, Phillip would look at the beautiful utensils used and the fine robes of the servants, but for once he forgot all of the pomp and thought about the Savior himself.

Phillip remembered briefly looking around at the other students and seeing them entranced by the message and the messenger. Then he looked back at the other priests, teachers, and Church officials. It was that look that the Church and Seminary leaders had in their eyes that reminded him of how the citizens of Marseilles looked now. It was a cold, hard look, as if the doors to their souls were being held firmly shut by some inward force. It was a force that Phillip did not entirely understand, but he had seen, since that time, in other adults of various walks of life. It seemed to come from a heart that had long ago formed its views on life and anything or anybody who was of a different view, was immediately suspect to scrutiny and judgment based upon that personal view.

Phillip remembered that it was not more than a few weeks after Father Edward gave the mass that he was sent to another post.

That afternoon by the Mediterranean Sea turned out to be abnormally hot and humid and the slight breeze that existed only served to bring a foul odor that came from a nearby fishery. When Stephen began to preach, the people did not stop talking amongst themselves, so he ended up having to yell out his message. After only a few minutes, it was obvious that something was happening that Phillip had not observed before in all of the times he had listened to Stephen preach. The message was going flat.

People were getting more and more fidgety as Stephen tried, without success, to gain some momentum. The yelling and raving became annoying and the people on the fringes of the crowd began to leave. At one point Stephen paused and looked down at Father David pleadingly, but the priest only looked straight ahead, not giving any guidance to the boy as to what he might do.

Almost in tears Stephen finished his message and hopped down out of the wagon before Father David had even climbed in. Father David quickly made some closing remarks and he too climbed down from the wagon letting the crowd disperse by themselves.

20

MOMENT OF TRUTH

A thick, black cloud of depression and confusion was settling on the crusade, and Father David decided right then that they could not wait for a week in order to perform the miracle of the parting of the sea. He talked with a very discouraged Stephen that night and convinced him that the next day at noon would be the moment. He then sent messengers to the individual campsites in order to inform the other crusaders of their decision.

The news of the next day's events affected everyone differently. Phillip tried to convince himself that the intense feeling that he had inside that the miracle would never really take place was a sign of his own weakness but that he should try to encourage the others anyway. He tried to get the others to talk about it but it was difficult.

"What are you going to do, Louis, as you are walking through the great sea with walls of water on each side?" he started.

Louis said, "Truthfully, I hadn't thought about that part of it so much. I guess I'll walk quickly and pray constantly." The others chuckled a bit. The conversation was beginning to have the effect that Phillip was hoping for.

Antoine smiled and said, "One thing is good about it. When we are hungry, we will be able to reach right into the water and pluck out any fish we want." Then he got a puzzled look on his face. "I guess that means we will have to load up some wood and dried grass to cook with, cause I'm sure we won't find any on the sea floor."

"True enough," said Phillip smiling.

"How long will the journey through the sea take?" asked Madoc.

Everyone took a moment to look at each other with questioning eyes. "I don't know," said Phillip looking at the thin boy. "Maybe God will be merciful and speed up our journey. They say that the sea is very large."

"I wonder how Hungry will act when we go through the sea? I think it might scare 'em," said Madoc.

"You ask a lot of questions," said another boy sitting close by. Madoc shrugged and reached down to pet Hungry, who was laying down by his side.

Anna reached over and put her hand on Madoc's head and stroked his dust filled hair. "I guess there's a lot we still don't know isn't there," she said gently. "I think that tomorrow will bring its own answers."

Not wanting the mood to get serious again, Phillip said, "It's true that tomorrow will show us what really is, but today we can still dream. I think dreams are a good thing."

"I'm really scared," said Stephen to Father David when they walked by the shore of the sea. The clear moonlit sky shown down on the two lone figures walking by the calm waters. "I haven't gotten any new revelations from the spirit in a long time. I can't remember my dreams anymore. What's happening?"

Father David felt uncomfortable also. First of all, he hadn't gotten any new messages from the spirit either, and second of all, he didn't know how to comfort Stephen. He knew that if he couldn't do something to make him feel better, the whole venture would be in jeopardy. "We haven't been abandoned Son," he began. "You saw the revelations and felt the moving of the spirit. Do your feelings now change that fact? Do your feelings make the letter unreal?"

Stephen bowed his head and muttered, "No. I know that it doesn't but I'm afraid anyway. You saw the people today. They were laughing at us."

"They won't laugh after tomorrow," said David.

Stephen seemed to ignore the answer. "Why tomorrow?" he asked.

"Because we can't wait any longer. We've got to go ahead now."

"I don't feel ready. What if God doesn't want me to do it yet?"

"He does," replied the priest firmly.

The next day the crusaders got up early and were informed that they should get ready to move ahead. Banners were raised, camps were picked up, and by noon the entire crusade was waiting close to the waters edge. It seemed that the entire city came out for the spectacle. Many stores must have been closed and many factories shut down for the big event. The richer people had brought out chairs and had servants reserve the best spots for viewing the great event. It was the big event of the century for these people, and though almost no one believed that it would actually happen, everyone wanted to be in on it.

Close to the shore out in the bay were many small fishing boats with other watchers. A number of the fishermen who got up before dawn to throw out nets and hook lines were passing up their afternoon naps in order to watch from their special viewpoint.

Dispersed throughout the crowd on the shore were hundreds and maybe thousands of sick and dying people. Many hovered in groups together as they were rejected by the general society. They hoped that if the miracle were true that they would also receive healing by proxy.

Young businessmen didn't miss the opportunity to set up carts of food and other wares for the crowd to buy while they were waiting. Some had quickly fashioned small wooden crosses or other religious trinkets to sell to those who were hoping for the best.

Suddenly the crowd drew quiet as a small procession of the priests from the crusade walked orderly in a rectangle towards the shore of the sea. In the middle of the priests was the boy prophet holding his sacred letter and looking very serious. As if driven by some hidden beat the procession marched in unison closer and closer to its destination. The people watched with quiet respect.

When the front of the procession reached the shore they stopped and allowed the other priests to join them. Stephen waited a few steps behind. The priests all prayed individual prayers at the same time, kissing the crucifixes that hung around their necks, and then bending and touching the water with it. After a few minutes the priests stepped back and all eyes were on Stephen.

As Stephen took the final steps that led to the shore, all eyes were attentive and all mouths closed. Only the waves as they continued to beat calmly against the shore and the sea gulls that playfully squawked at each other as they dipped and dove above the crowd, didn't seem to understand the importance of the next moment.

Father David waited back with the other priests as the boy prophet reached the waters' edge and stopped. Raising his hands and head up to the sky, Stephen closed his eyes and began to speak to his Maker in a loud confident voice, "The hour has come, Lord. Make a way for us through these waters to your Holy City!" The boy's high-pitched voice rang out the petition so that all on land and sea heard clearly. In a moment the sound of the boy's petition was swallowed up by the unchanging steady rhythmic sound of the waves that continued on in the course that was laid out for them from the beginning of time.

After a few minutes of silent expectation, a murmur arose from the crowds. The crowd was silenced again, however, when the prophet shouted out his request once more. Again, there was no change in the sea. Now began a louder murmur from the crowd accompanied by some laughter.

Without looking back, Stephen walked into the sea up to his waist and with his letter held high once more shouted, "Lord, divide this sea so that we might walk across on dry ground." This time, without even waiting the crowd began to laugh out loud. The crusaders unconsciously began to huddle closer one to another. As the crowd began to mock openly, Stephen unflinchingly stared straight ahead out to sea.

Two well-dressed merchants were among the audience.

"Hugh," said William, suddenly stopping laughing, "My friend, I see a possible opportunity here."

His well-dressed friend looked over at him, still chuckling, and responded, "What on earth could you be thinking about."

William said smiling, "Come, let's talk some place else."

After the bishop had mounted his horse and had begun his solemn march back to the city, others in the crowd also left. Laughter and insults filled the air.

As the crusaders huddled in closer to one another, the crowd began to distance themselves from them until there was a buffer zone between them of about 20 feet. That distance slowly grew wider and wider as if there was sudden news that the crusaders were carrying some sort of contagious disease.

Phillip tried to keep Anna from falling as she began to feel light headed. Other crusaders had already passed out. The rag-tag group of children that had recently marched triumphantly up to the city just a day earlier now kept huddling closer and closer together as if they had suddenly realized that they had no clothes on and were trying to hide the shame of their nakedness. There was no sound made by the crusaders. All eyes fixed themselves on Stephen. In twenty short minutes an eternity had passed.

Without notice there was a sudden swelling of the waves and the boy prophet was being tossed around as he tried desperately to keep his balance. The crowd from the city laughed wildly at the scene of the soaking boy trying to keep his precious letter from getting wet.

Finally, an older priest who had accompanied the crusade from the beginning looked over at Father David and nodded at him pleadingly. The priest that had spearheaded the whole crusade and had moved it forward every step of the way was now as rigid and as expressionless as one of the statues that adorned the great cathedrals. Receiving no sign from Father David, the older priest could not contain himself any longer and ran out to retrieve Stephen. Fighting through the waves Father Dominic reached Stephen. Stephen felt the arm of the priest around him and he dreamily turned his head towards him and gave him a desperate look. He then surrendered to the priests firm tugging. The two were met at the water's edge by a few other crusaders who helped carry Stephen farther into shore until they found a good spot to set him down. With this, the rest of the crowd from the city filed out as if they had just seen the conclusion of a concert at the coliseum.

"All right," said Hugh to his corpulent friend as they both were now seated in their favorite table at the Water's Edge Inn. "What is this opportunity of yours?"

William scooted his chair back from the table as to give his stomach more room and smiled over at Hugh, "We are business men, right?"

"The best," grinned Hugh. "So what of it?"

"You know, as well as I, that desperate situations make for good business opportunities, right?"

"I still don't follow."

"The crusade, you idiot. The crusade," said William leaning over table. Hugh looked puzzled. "Who's more desperate than that group of youngsters out there?" continued William.

Hugh thought for a moment and then finally said in frustration, "Call me dumb if you will, but I still don't get it. What possible business could we transact with a bunch of half-starved beggar children that have lost their..." Suddenly Hugh stopped and looked seriously over at William. "You mean..."

William leaned back in his chair triumphantly and said, "Exactly."

All form of organization had gone out of the crusaders. There were no groups, only individuals. Many of the youth just wandered around the seashore aimlessly.

A few hours after the event at the seashore, Phillip found himself sitting on a rock looking out at the sea. What had he been doing for the past few hours? He couldn't remember. He looked around and didn't see any of his friends. He had to find them.

Phillip found Louis standing by the shore throwing stones and shells into the tide. "Come on Louis, let's go find everyone else."

"That's fine, Phillip," said Louis, and he fell into step behind him.

Anna was sitting down with Madoc's head resting in her lap as she stroked his hair and sang softly. Hungry lay at the feet of Anna and Madoc and moaned deeply as Madoc reached over and patted him on the head.

Phillip and the 14 others that he had rounded up found Anna and Madoc sitting like that about 50 feet from the shore on a patch of grass.

Phillip looked at the small group and began passing out assignments. Soon other crusaders began to show up. Phillip gave them orders also. Some would look for food. Others would go back to the river and get water. Within an hour, Phillip's fourteen had grown to around two hundred, and by the time the sun set there were probably five to six hundred waiting for instructions.

No one talked about what they might do tomorrow, as for now these "lost sheep" were content to know what to do right now.

That night there was a lot of sharing, because in the confusion of things many had lost track of their personal items. Almost all of the crusaders went to sleep early not wanting the day to be any longer than it already had been.

Phillip was one of the last to go to sleep. He had found escape from his torturous thoughts by keeping everyone else busy. Now when he finally lay down to sleep, his mind replayed the day's events over and over and over again. The images came faster and faster until his mind was spinning. When he woke up the next day he was not sure if he had fallen asleep or passed out.

William and Hugh found Stephen and Father David at mid-morning. They were sleeping in the center of a large group of the crusaders who still clung to them as their only hope even when there was no real reason to hope.

William and Hugh finally convinced the boy and the priest to follow them to the city so that they could talk.

Anna arose from sleep early in the morning and walked alongside the sea with a playful Hungry. She ambled on at least a few hundred yards before turning to walk back. The sun had arisen and she could see how the crusaders were splintered off in groups. The larger group, which consisted of a couple thousand, still hung together near to where most of the wagons were. One other large group of about five hundred were located only a few hundred yards from the main group, and then there were many smaller bands spread out randomly along the shore.

"Hungry," said Anna inspecting the condition of the crusade, "I may be wrong, but it appears that there are many who are not here any more."

"Lord, what will become of us?" she whispered in prayer. "Please guide us...please guide me." She continued on, getting closer to where the camps where, "Have we failed you Lord?" she asked prayerfully. Anna's mind began to think about all of her friends that were on the crusade. Poor Madoc; there was no going back for him. And Phillip; there was almost no returning for him either. Saint Denis would probably never take him back now.

Suddenly she stopped and let herself think about her mother. There was no doubt that if she could get back, her mother would welcome her home, but...no, no buts. Her mother would take her back with arms wide opened. She would be forgiven. "Yes, but can I ever forgive myself," she thought as tears began to well up in her eyes.

Finally, she was distracted from her thoughts by Hungry who had decided that it was great fun to chase the waves into the sea and then run from them as they rolled back up on the shore. One time she even laughed aloud as Hungry misjudged one of the returning waves and got totally soaked. She stopped laughing when Hungry shook himself off right beside her. "Hungry," she scolded while wiping the water off of her face and looking at her sprinkled clothes, "look what you've done." Then she smiled and the two of them kept walking back along the shore, Hungry content now just to bark at the waves that came up too close.

Father David and Stephen followed the two wealthy merchants to their office in the city. As they stepped through the door of the office building a feeling of uneasiness came over the priest and the young servant. They stared face to face with dozens of fierce looking pagan statues and idols that decorated the inside of the large entrance hall. Hugh looked back and smiled at their obvious disgust. "Don't worry father. Those are just trinkets that we've picked up from some of the countries that we trade in. Our office is this way."

The once "spiritually" proud priest now humbly followed the direction of the merchant. For three months he had been a great leader of a crusade, forced to sleep outside under the stars as he traveled towards his destiny. Now he felt insignificant as he was led back into a world in were money and power reigned.

The whole night before, David had been trying in desperation to contact the guiding spirit that had been with them from the beginning. Why had it deserted them? He had begun to envision himself as a roving priest ridiculed from any normal position. And yet...this morning as the two strangers from the city came to talk to them, he felt a stirring inside of him.

Stephen was still in a state of dumbfoundedness. He only came along with Father David because of the insistence of the two men. He did not want to be here. He didn't want to be anywhere. He let his mind wander back, as had happened much in the past day, reminiscing about how his life was in the country—peaceful. Then he had then been called out to speak before bishops and the king, challenging them all. Now he wished that none of it had ever happened. He longed to put in a hard day of work in the fields by his house and then eat at the same table with his mother and brothers.

"This way," said Hugh as he motioned the two to follow his large friend into his office.

"Its tremendous! Its a miracle!" a friend of Phillip's yelled, running toward them. "It's on again," he said loudly as he stood before Phillip and the others.

A puzzled Phillip didn't have time to ask what the excited messenger was talking about before he began to explain. "The crusade! we're going!" Phillip and the others still had a puzzled look on their faces. "We're going in ships," said the young man that had accompanied Phillip to ask for food during the last weeks of the crusade.

"On ships?" asked Phillip. "I don't understand."

"That's right! Its all been arranged, Phillip. We just heard about it a few minutes ago. God has led two local merchants to lend us their ships to take us."

Phillip looked around at the scared faces of his friends and then replied, "That doesn't make any sense."

"Sure it does," said the enthusiastic messenger. "Father David says that the Lord was testing us before, or something like that. Anyway, there's a big meeting about it for all of the crusaders in a half-hour."

"No Phillip, we can't go," said Antoine who put his hand on Phillip's shoulder and looked him straight in the eye. Phillip saw the fear. Phillip looked around. The others had the same panicky look in their eyes and they were all looking at him. They had had enough. They were done. Many of these young people had come this far because of him and now his conscience was screaming out at him to stop it.

"No," said Phillip bluntly. The countenance of the young messenger who stood before him dropped. "We are not going on any farther," said Phillip. "We will not be there at the meeting."

As the drooped shouldered young man made his way out of the crowd that had pressed in to hear, Antoine grabbed both shoulders of Phillip and hugged him tightly, crying in convulsions. A few muffled cheers went up but mostly the circle of friends drew closer and cried together. It was over for them. The nightmare had ended and somehow they were sure that they would all soon be going home.

It was not long before Phillip could hear the high-pitched voice of Stephen piercing the air. He could not understand the words that were being said from the distance but occasional cheers from the crowd assured him that the messenger was right. They planned to go on. Phillip could not help but feel remorseful about not joining even though he had not changed his mind.

As the sermon went on, some of the young people from Phillip's group were drawn over to listen more closely. It was like the first days in Paris when the voice of the boy prophet drew people to him like the pied piper. Now, in the night air, the enchanted voice rang out again but not all followed this time.

Phillip's friends formed a circle around a fire that produced only a small flickering flame and tried to make idle conversation but the distant voice would rise to a screeching peak and disturb any fluidity of thought. Anna stood up to straighten out her dress and looked around to see the campfires of the others who chose not to attend the meeting. Children were huddled close together. At first glance one might think that it was the chilly sea air that pulled them together but Anna knew better. When she sat down she drew Madoc close to her.

"Not enough!" raved William, "not enough!"

"What are you talking about?" said the portly man's partner as they sat drinking spirits in their favorite pub. "The priest said that there were at least 1,500."

"Can't you add? Seven ships, 250 a ship, that's 1,750. We need another 250 at least. And who knows. With children, we might be able to pack more on," said William with greed in his eyes.

After a brief pause to think, Hugh said calmly, "Why don't we just send one of the ships to Constantinople? We have a warehouse full of goods that we are holding until after we're done with this venture anyway."

"No good. Those trades in Constantinople won't bring one third of what we'll get for a ship full of children." William leaned in close and looked seriously in the eyes of his friend, "Besides, if the governor gets wise to us on this one, we'll be done for. I tell you, we get all of the money we can, and get ready to move from Marseilles as soon as possible."

"Are you crazy?" retorted Hugh, "and leave everything?"

"You just don't see, do you? This shipment will make us rich. We can take our ships and set up business anywhere in the world. Our office and warehouse here are nothing. Our investors are wealthy people. They can take a bit of a loss." William paused and sat back in his chair. "Besides, if the governor never finds out, we can go on with business as usual."

Finally Hugh sighed as if to surrender and said, "All right then, how do we get another ship full of kids?"

Early the next morning Phillip decided to start finding out a way to help his friends survive until they could start back up the Rhone River towards home. Taking Antoine and Louis with him, he headed to the one person that he could think of that might help, the bishop.

The streets of Marseilles were busy with everyday traffic. The past few years had seen great progress in commerce and trade and the benefits were obvious. The shops, factories, docks, warehouses were all alive. Even Paris didn't enjoy the success that this great port city was seeing.

The bishop was not eager to see the three former crusaders but after making them wait an unusually long time, he saw them in. The bishop recognized Phillip and began talking to him before he even had a chance to introduce himself in the proper way. "My secretary says that you wish to speak to me young man. Are you not the same young man that came to me when your group first arrived?"

"Yes, Bishop, I am," responded Phillip. Antoine and Louis kept silent. "And Bishop, I am sorry for interrupting you."

The bishop paused a minute and said impatiently, "Well, what is it that you wish to say?"

"Bishop, I am not here about the crusade," started Phillip. The Bishop raised an eyebrow. Phillip then went on, "A number of us wish to return home to Paris, and not go on with the crusade."

"What crusade?" snapped the bishop waving his arms in the air towards the ocean. "Not only is this not a crusade, but it never has been a crusade. I would hope that the whole lot of you would be planning your return home immediately." Without allowing Phillip to respond, the bishop went on a tirade about how much harm to the Church, the whole crusade had been and how much it fed the fires of the enemy.

Phillip respectfully and shamefully listened to the Church official rant on, but quickly got the idea that he did not know about the new events that were transpiring with Stephen, Father David, and the crusade. Finally when the red faced bishop stopped to hear a response, Phillip reluctantly told the him about how the main part of the crusade was planning on going on with their mission by ship. The news stunned the bishop into silence.

When the bishop finally regained his composure, he simply said, "Out! I have heard enough! I wash my hands of this whole business and the Church washes its hands also." Phillip tried to explain how they were not with the crusade any longer but the bishop had already reached for the little hand bell on his desk that summoned his secretary. "Please show these young men out," he told his secretary.

Within a minute, Phillip, Antoine, and Louis found themselves outside the doors of the Cathedral and very much alone.

"Now what do we do?" asked Louis. There was no response.

Now, as the boys passed back through the city on the way back to the seashore it had lost its wonder. It seemed big and hard.

As they reached a large square in the city the boys passed the main government building. The ancient Roman architecture caught the eye of the distraught friends and they couldn't help but look up at it as they went by. "What about the governor?" asked Antoine. "Do you think he might help us?"

Phillip didn't even slow down to answer, "Not very likely." The other two boys slowed down until Phillip was forced to stop and look back at them. They then stopped completely. "It won't do any good," repeated Phillip but Antoine and Louis didn't move.

Phillip tried to argue but within 10 minutes he found himself climbing the stairs that led to the great double doors of the building. The doors were open and there was a slight but steady stream of people walking in and out. Ignoring the stares, the rag-tag looking boys entered.

Inside was a maze of offices and waiting rooms, but somehow the three found themselves standing before the office of the secretary of the governor. There wasn't anyone in the waiting room. "Nobody's going to be here," said Phillip to the others.

"You might as well knock," said Louis. Phillip stepped up and knocked softly, then after just a few seconds, he turned to walk away, but the door began to open.

A very well dressed official cracked open the door and peered out at the boys. After looking at them for a few seconds he asked, "How did you get in here?"

"Some people told us that the governors office was this way, so we just came," said Louis.

"Where's the attendant?" asked the man.

"We didn't see anybody, Monsieur," responded Louis. Then he

added, "We need to talk to the governor."

The man chuckled, "You don't just see the governor. He is a very busy man and he is very hard to get a hold of."

"Could we wait here for him then?" tried Louis.

Again the man chuckled kindly, "You must have an appointment and the governor is booked up for at least three weeks. Why don't you boys tell your problem to your fathers and I'm sure that they will be able to help you out."

Phillip thought to himself, "That's how it's supposed to be, isn't it. How nice it would be to have a father that took care of all my problems." He realized that he had never had what one might call a "normal" childhood. He thought about all of the children on the crusade that were "normal" children just three months ago, but now they were like him. Their childhood was gone. They were not like other kids anymore. They had to act like adults now to survive.

"Monsieur," started Phillip, looking sternly at the man at the door, "this is no normal matter. It is urgent that we speak with the governor or many people may lose their lives within the next few days."

The expression on the man's face changed and he looked long and solemnly into Phillip's unflinching eyes. Then the man turned as the door he was holding partially shut was being pulled opened by another man that was inside. Phillip immediately recognized the man as the vice-governor who had come out to welcome the crusade on the day that they had arrived at the city.

"It's all right Paul," the vice-governor said to the first man, "we haven't started our meeting yet. Let's hear what the young men have to say." Paul motioned the boys into the office. Standing at the far side of the room a gray haired man with a strong face watched as they entered.

"If I guess correctly governor," said the vice-governor to the elderly gentleman, "these are young representatives of our friends at the sea." The governor exchanged his stern look for a kind smile.

"Rufus, offer the young men a seat," said the governor. The vice-governor pointed to a few chairs that were situated opposite of the governor. The young men obeyed and sat silently while the governor looked them over. "Have you been sent to ask for something?"

"Governor," began Phillip, "we have not come in behalf of the crusade." The governor gave him a questioning look but said nothing. Phillip continued, "There are approximately 400 - 450 of us who feel that going on with the crusade is not what we should do. We would like to return to our homes but need supplies to get us started on our trip back." The governor shot a puzzled look over to Rufus who only shrugged his shoulders.

The governor leaned back in his chair and said, "I'm sorry young man. I think that there is some confusion as to what is going on with your group at the shore. I haven't heard much in the past few days about your situation. Would you mind filling me in?"

Phillip suddenly remembered how the bishop was surprised by the news of the crusade and realized that people didn't know. Since he figured that everyone knew about the failure of the sea to open, he began telling the governor about the events that had transpired since that time. The governor sat silently listening to the story of the disillusionment of the crusade and the split up. When he got to the part about the crusade being offered ships, Rufus pounded his fist on a table in front of him, interrupted Phillip and said to the governor, "Son-of-a...I'll give you one guess as to who offered them those ships."

The governor nodded at Rufus in agreement but turned back to Phillip and allowed him to finish his story. "We almost feel like we are abandoning our calling to finish the crusade but we have seen so many contradictions and heard so many false promises that we can not go on deceiving ourselves." Then Phillip ended with a final plea, "Will you please help us to finish our journey? The journey home?"

The governor responded by saying compassionately, "You have been through a lot haven't you? And so young...all of you." He smiled and added, "I'm very glad that you came."

"You know," said the governor, "Joseph was about your age when his brothers sold him into slavery. He went through a lot that a normal person shouldn't have to go through, but he became a great man because of it." The governor then laughed, "Ha, when I was your age I was flirting with girls, playing around with my studies, arguing with my parents about things I knew nothing about, and generally just being a big pain in the neck."

The governor breathed in deeply and looked in the eyes of each of the boys and said, "I admire you. But not because you left your homes and came on this devilish crusade. I admire you because you got out and refuse to go back. Don't ever feel guilty about it. Would you feel guilty if you vowed to kill all Spaniards in the name of God but later figured out that God didn't want all Spaniards killed and so broke that vow?" The boys didn't respond. "Well, would you?" asked the governor. The boys shook their heads.

"Listen boys, an ungodly vow is a foolish thing to make, but even more foolish to keep. Don't feel too badly though," said the governor, "Even old fools make bad promises. Fortunately God is good and forgiving." He thought for a moment before continuing. "Yes, I will try to find a way to help you and your friends who want to go home."

The boys were still speechless when the governor stood up as a signal for them to do the same. He reached to his side and pulled out his money pouch. He started to reach into his pouch to pull out some money, but when he stopped to look at the boys again, he just handed over the whole thing. "Here, take this for now," he said. "I will be out in a couple of days with some friends to talk to you some more about how we can get you going back in the right direction."

Phillip accepted the gift, "Thank you Governor. This is much more than we expected. You are very gracious."

"God is gracious, Son. I just do what I can." The boys were then shown out by the man they had met at the door and didn't say a word to each other until they had exited the building.

When the boys were gone from the room, the governor turned to Rufus with a serious look on his face and said, "I want you to get me some immediate information on this story about the crusade going over by ship, and if it is our two enterprising merchant friends and if they are trying to pull off some odd deal, I want the council called in immediately."

"I guarantee it is them," said Rufus back. "The last few days they have been busily unpacking their freshly loaded cargo and putting it back in its warehouses. They have seven empty ships waiting out in the harbor, ready to load. Now we know what they are going to load, but we don't know why. At least the real reason why."

"Cancel our meetings for the day," said the governor to his secretary. "Rufus," he said turning back to the vice-governor, "if I know William the Pig and Hugh the Iron, there are many more lives at stake than just the ones that these young men were worried about. I would say that the whole lot of them are in serious danger."

"Why is it so important that they come?" asked Father David. "We have the faithful remnant with whom God would use to finish His crusade."

William was now leaning forward with his elbows resting on his desk, losing his patience. "Father, I have tried to explain to you that we have seven ships. Now I figure that if God has provided seven, ships then he also wants to fill them."

The priest had regained much of his pride and self-confidence and William and Hugh were finding it more and more difficult to manipulate him. Father David answered, "They look to a young man named Phillip as their leader. He has refused to go on, and as long as he refuses, it is hopeless to even try. Maybe, if you give me a week to talk with him, I could encourage him join us again."

"A week!" responded Hugh, who had allowed his partner to do most of the talking up to this point. "We're ready to sail tomorrow." Then leaning down at William he repeated emphatically, "We must sail tomorrow."

Father David, noticing that there was something going on between the two that he wasn't in on, asked, "Why must we sail tomorrow?"

William smiled back and simply said, "Currents and winds. The currents and winds are much more favorable right now, but we are getting close to storm season. The sooner we leave, the better."

The priest thought for a moment and then shook his head, "I don't believe I can convince this young man by tomorrow. It may be a good idea to at least wait a few days"

Hugh looked hard at William. William then looked to the priest and said, "Maybe there is another way to persuade the young man."

21

PARTINGS

Madoc and Hungry were becoming professional beach-combers. After the decision was made to separate from the crusade, life had actually become enjoyable again for Madoc and he spent most of his time with his dog going up and down the vast shore exploring. He knew that everyone was talking about going back to their homes, but he wasn't too thrilled with that prospect. Life here was good. Even if he had to go back to begging, he figured that he would better off here.

Anna had talked more about her home in Paris to Madoc over the past few days than she had during the entire journey up to this point. He was sure that she would return...and that he would not.

Anna hummed old songs that her father and mother had taught her as she patched clothes and did general chores for the others. She couldn't help but envisioning herself walking up to her old house in Paris, knocking on the door, and then throwing herself in the awaiting arms of her mother. "What a reunion that will be," she thought.

"Marie," she said turning to a young girl that was working beside her, "do you want to learn a song that my dad taught me?"

"Certainly, why not," responded the little girl. The two of them spent the next hour singing and working.

Phillip, Antoine, Louis, and about a dozen others were sitting around talking about the miraculous events that had transpired during the day. They hadn't told anybody yet where they got the food that they had brought with them from the city, nor about the governor's promise to help them. They had learned that it was better to not hope for too much. However, they couldn't help but begin to tell the others about the conversation that they had with the city officials.

"The governor must have had some theological training," said Louis. "It is obvious that he knows something about the Bible."

"It is interesting, though," said Phillip, "I kind a got the impression from the bishop that he didn't get along with the governor."

"Well it's not like the city officials and Church officials in Paris fight all of the time, but they have their share of squabbles," noted Louis.

Everyone nodded in agreement, "That's true."

"The way I see it," started Antoine, "this time their squabbling is a blessing for us. I didn't think that the bishop was going to be too helpful." Again, everyone nodded.

"You mean," said one of the other boys, "That the governor is going to help us?"

Phillip, Antoine, and Louis looked at each other. "He gave us the money for food today, and he promised to help us some more later," said Phillip. Then he cautioned, "But we don't know what they actually mean by that."

At that moment another young man entered into the circle and looked at Phillip, "Phillip, Father David would speak with you."

The other boys looked at Phillip with questioning looks. Phillip responded to the boys' looks by shrugging his shoulders and saying, "I don't know." He then stood up and obediently followed the messenger.

Just before dusk Madoc went out with Hungry to try to find something extra for supper. Lately he had been surprising his friends with fish that they had found caught in tide pools and he liked the attention that he was getting. So he carried off his little home made spear to see if his luck would hold out. Usually at this time the tide was low and it was perfect for looking for the fish.

As they got closer to the pools Hungry ran out ahead in anticipation as to where they were going. Hungry started barking and snapping at something in a pool that had a diameter of only about five feet, and even from a distance Madoc could see that whatever it was, was splashing around a lot. Hoping for the best, Madoc picked up his pace, his feet leaving sandal shaped indentations in the sand as he ran.

Madoc found himself staring down at a very big, very active fish of some sort. Somebody would know if it was good to eat or not. It looked good anyway.

"Hungry, stop it!" he yelled as the dog almost knocked him into the pool. "Calm down boy. We'll get it." He wasn't so sure.

After a number of attempts to jab the prize, his spear just glancing off of the thick scales, Madoc sat down on the wet sand in exhaustion, looking at it. Hungry kept barking at the fish but seemed to have no intention of trying to grab it.

For all of the noise that Hungry was making, Madoc didn't notice the group of boys approaching. "What's going on?" one of the boys asked Madoc. Madoc whipped around in surprise to see a group of six boys standing over him.

"We caught a fish," said Madoc to the boys.

"Don't look like you caught 'em yet," said one stout dark haired boy. "And that mutt dog of yours ain't gonna help. All's he's good for is stealin' food,"

The boy had looked familiar but now Madoc recognized him as the same boy that gave them trouble before.

"Gimme that," said the boy snatching the spear out of Madoc's hand. Madoc didn't try to stop him. The dark-haired boy motioned to the other boys to surround the pool. A few of them had clubs.

Hungry was still so absorbed by the fish that he hadn't really taken notice of the presence of the boys. "Get that mutt out of here. He's scarin' the fish," snapped the boy.

The boy closest to Hungry poked him with his club and said, "Scat dog!" Hungry snapped at the club and went back to pestering the fish.

"Hey boy, get rid of the dog before I get rid of him for you," said the dark-haired boy to Madoc. Before Madoc had a chance to call out to

Hungry, the boy who had poked Hungry before poked at him harder. Hungry reacted by snatching the club out of his hand. The startled boy fell into the pool. Madoc couldn't help but chuckle, as did some of the other boys. The leader of the group didn't laugh, however.

"That does it!" said the leader throwing the fishing spear angrily at Hungry. The boy was as surprised as everyone else when the spear struck the dog in the back, taking off a chunk of skin. Hungry was stunned only for a split second before he bore his teeth and lunged.

Terrified, the boy fell backwards and screamed for help. The other boys arrived swinging their clubs as Hungry was already on top of their leader.

"No!" screamed Madoc leaping to his feet and running at the group, "No!" He plowed into the back of one of the other boys that had begun to beat Hungry with a club. The boy fell forward knocking another one down as he fell, but soon he was back on his feet and looking at Madoc angrily.

The gentle waves of the rising tide woke Madoc up as the cool water splashed against his body. It was very dark all around. Madoc struggled to sit up, and found that his head was pounding with pain.

Suddenly the events of the day rushed back to him. "Hungry!" he yelled as he tried to rise. Madoc had just gotten to his feet when he fell down dizzily. "Hungry!" he yelled out as he lay on the sand.

Madoc heard a faint whimpering nearby. "Hungry!" he called out trying to get to his knees. The pain in his head was almost intolerable and he fell on his face again. Again he heard the whimpering. Madoc slowly crawled on his belly in the wet sand. Though he could not see because of the blackness of the night the heavy breathing of Hungry lead Madoc to him.

The boy crawled up to the broken body of his dearest friend and curled up next to him. Putting his head next to Hungry's he whispered in his ear, "I'm here, Boy." Hungry responded by rolling his head over and whimpering. Madoc's mind took him back to the day when he had heard the whimpering of a half-dead puppy coming from the riverbank in Paris. How that puppy had changed his life—given him life.

Madoc put his arm under Hungry's head so that he would have something softer to lie on. Hungry groaned deeply and licked Madoc's arm. He took one last breath, groaned again, and then breathed no more. Madoc pulled Hungry's body close and cried himself to sleep.

Anna, Antoine, and a few others found Madoc and Hungry lying near the shore later that night. At first Anna wouldn't let anyone else carry Madoc. She wanted to be holding him if he awoke, so she tried carrying him herself. That only lasted a short while. Her bad leg throbbed with pain after carrying her little friend a few hundred yards. One of the others helped her when she couldn't go on any more. Antoine and another boy stayed back and buried the body of Hungry.

Anna stayed up the rest of the night with the delirious Madoc, and when Madoc was asleep, she would shoot a worried look over at the empty bedroll of Phillip. "Lord, what is going on?" she whispered in prayer.

Bright and early the next morning, the split off group from the crusade received an unexpected visitor. Stephen, the boy prophet, appeared with two other boys at his side. "I would speak with you," he called out. He repeated himself several times as most of the group gathered around to listen, then he stood on the highest spot that he could find so that he could address the listeners.

When Stephen began to call everyone together, Anna raised her weary head but didn't move from her spot beside Madoc. Louis, Antoine, and the others close by looked over at Phillip's empty bedroll once more and then stood up. They glanced over at Anna and she smiled and nodded to them, as to say that it was fine to go listen, but that she was going stay with Madoc.

"Crusaders, listen to me," began Stephen. The crowd shifted uneasily. "I know that you have lost your faith. I too had almost lost my faith, but God was gracious enough to forgive me and allow me to go on. We must go on for God!" Stephen paused and looked around. The children were listening but they weren't sold yet. He then decided against a long speech and went right for their hearts.

"Phillip is going on with us," he called out. The response was exactly what he had expected. A mass of puzzled looks and gasps of unbelief rose from the group.

"What?!" called out some..."Impossible!" called out others, while many just sighed heavily.

Stephen allowed the words to have their full impact before going on. "Last night Phillip talked with us for quite some time. Finally he fell on his knees in repentance and swore an oath not to fail the Church and Her God again."

From the stunned crowd different individuals began to call out, "Where's Phillip? We want to talk to Phillip!"

"Phillip would be here, but as a gesture of his repentance and as an affirmation of his faith, he chose to be the first one to board the first ship this morning," called out Stephen.

"This morning?" called out Louis from behind the crowd.

"That's right. We are beginning to board right now," called out Stephen, articulating clearly every word. A roar of noise now shot up from the group. Stephen yelled out loudly, "Phillip's only request to me was that I come here this morning and give everyone of you the same opportunity to return to God that he had." Now raising his voice to that familiar high-pitched frenzy, he gave his final invitation, "Who...Will Go On...For God...And For The Church?!!"

At that moment around half of the listeners dropped to their knees and put their faces in their hands in shame and repentance. In seconds the chant began, "For God and the Church!" Children began to run back and get their things and then run towards the docks towards the ships. Others angrily grabbed their things and split up.

When Antoine and Louis reached Anna and Madoc it was obvious that she had heard everything. She sat on the ground with Madoc's head in her lap rocking back and forth as she cried.

"It's a lie!" Louis exclaimed angrily pounding his fist into his hand.

"I can't believe it," said Antoine staring out at the sea. "It doesn't make since."

Still rocking back and forth, Anna tried to sing a cradlesong through her tears, "Don't cry my ba-by. Daddy's strong a-rms will hold you so tight. Mommy's sweet he-art will love you just right. Don't you cry my ba-by."

"When will the others get here, Paul?" said the governor to his secretary as he marched hurriedly into the waiting room outside of the conference hall.

"Most of them are already inside waiting," said the secretary.

"Good," said the governor walking towards the large wooden double doors. He could hear the noise of heated discussion going on even before he reached them. "Let's get to it then," said the head official as he reached for the knob.

The others in the counsel turned from their conversations and stood silent as the elderly statesman opened the door and walked to the head of the table. Everyone knew what the emergency meeting was about. "Rufus," said the governor looking straight at the vice-governor who was seated to his right, "Fill us in." The governor then took a seat signaling the others to do the same.

Rufus remained standing. "As we already know, William the Pig and Hugh the Iron are "offering" their ships to the crusade. They maintain that they have been sent by God to allow the crusaders to use their ships to take them to the Holy Land so that they can complete their mission," said Rufus cynically. "They have somehow convinced most of their creditors to go along with their idea and those that they haven't convinced, they have bought off."

"What are you trying to say, exactly?" asked one of the council members. "I mean, you obviously don't believe their story or we wouldn't be here."

"Besides," said another before Rufus could answer, "what does all of this have to do with Marseilles?"

The governor raised his hand to silence everyone. "Now Rufus, tell us what you are driving at."

Rufus, still standing, took in a deep breath and began, "I have information that this whole story of William and of Hugh has been made up and that their real intentions are to sell the children in Northern Africa."

An immediate uproar arose from everyone in the room. The governor rose from his chair, and again, motioned everyone to be silent. "Everyone will get his chance to speak, but not at once. Thibald," he said looking all the way down the table to the most senior of the council members, "what do you think?"

The very aged gentleman rose and begin to speak in a weak voice, "As all of you know, I try to be analytical about these things, and I can't for the life of me see what the big emergency was that dragged us out of our daily events to listen to this today. Even William the Pig and Hugh the Iron deserve some credit. Hugh's father was a good friend of mine and loyal to the Church. I can't imagine his son going off and doing something that would destroy his good name. With all due respect, vice-governor, this white slavery phobia is getting out of hand. I've heard tails about children being stolen and sold to the Moors all of my life but I've rarely ever seen any real confirmation of this. Now you tell us that a couple of merchants from our great city are going to perpetrate the sell of a thousand or so?" Thibald looked at the governor and then sat down.

"Over two thousand children," corrected Rufus respectfully. "And the emergency is that we just received notice about the children being loaded into the ships as we speak. If we are to act, we must act now." Rufus sat back down.

"Simon," said the governor, "do you have something to add?"

Simon rose and nodded to the governor, "Yes, thank you. The vice-governor asked me, two days ago, to help him with an emergency project. When he informed me that it had to do with this crazy children's crusade thing, I told him that I wasn't that interested and that I thought that he was just wasting his time. He then told me of his suspicions about William and Hugh. Let's face it gentlemen, these two merchants have been the center of no less than three inquiries over the past two years alone. I suspended my own personal affairs and agreed to help him. Such a thing as this, if true, would be a black mark against Marseilles to the whole Christian world."

"Wait a minute," said another council member interrupting Simon. The governor began to call him down but he went on, "Please, governor, I must point out a very great flaw in this investigation already."

The governor looked over at Simon, "Let's hear what Reynald has to say and then you may continue." Simon nodded and sat down.

"Thank you," said Reynald. "I see two things here that I don't like already. One is that the vice-governor went into this so-called "investigation" with prejudices against William and Hugh. It appears that he already had them tried and condemned before he ever started." Rufus sat back in his chair listening with his arms folded. He knew that Reynald would be his one big obstacle. He was sure that Reynald was on William and Hugh's payroll even though he would never voice that opinion. Reynald seemed to have the inside track on William and Hugh and seemed to always have an excuse for their under handed business dealings.

Reynald went on, "Secondly, this being a crusade, our non-Catholic vice-governor would naturally try to stop it."

Rufus and four other members immediately jumped to their feet. Rufus was not expecting this ploy and pointed a shaking finger at Reynald, "My religious beliefs have nothing to do with this, and this pathetic event called a crusade, has never been officially recognized by the Catholic Church, and even the Church's bishop denounces it." Reynald just sat down and smiled.

Even though the governor tried to calm things down, it was too late. The council was polarized on religious grounds. No matter what was said or argued about over the next hour the council would not reach a decision. Reynald had accomplished what he sought out to do.

22

THE SEA

William patting his nervous partner on the back as they stood out on the docks watching the loading. "It looks like we will fill all seven ships after all."

"I'll just be glad when we've lifted anchor and hoisted the sails," said Hugh. "I don't trust that vice-governor. He's been breathing down our necks for the past two days, and well, he may try to block us still."

"Hugh, you are like an old woman worrying all of the time. We've always succeeded in staying a step or two ahead of him and this time won't be any different. Besides, I've already received word from Reynald that the council is divided." William chuckled. "You'll never see the day when that pompous young politician will outwit me."

The docks were extremely busy as the dockworkers tried to load the ships provisions while the crusaders were boarding. "This is crazy," said one of the dockworkers as he lifted a box over the head of a young child.

"Why in the world didn't they let us get this stuff on before they started loading the kids?" complained one of the tuffs to his boss.

"Quit your yappin' and load," growled the dock boss. "And watch what your doin'. You might run down one of the little beggars." The boss didn't like the situation either, but he was getting paid a bonus if he could get everything on before sunrise the next morning.

"What now?" asked Antoine, thinking out loud. The small group of friends sat alone in a circle, staring at the sand. Madoc had regained his senses but sat in a daze with no emotion showing on his swollen face. Almost all of the other "rebels" had left by now. Most went on to the ships while others went to the city.

"I'm worried," said Anna finally.

"That's news," chuckled Louis sarcastically.

"No, I mean that I'm worried for Phillip."

"Phillip!" said Louis. "You mean our great and fearless leader. Why should you be worried for him? He has recanted and returned to favor."

"Something doesn't seem right," said Anna.

"That's what I say," said Antoine. "I've not found anybody that's seen him since yesterday."

"That's because he was the first one on board, remember" said Louis still with a sarcastic tone.

"I know what we heard," said Antoine, "but after all that we talked about; and the governor's promise to help us get back home, and everything. I just don't get it."

"I want to go too," said Madoc softly without changing expression. The others stopped and looked at him. "I want to go," he repeated. Anna scooted over and put her arm around him. "No, I mean it," said Madoc emphatically.

"You'll stay with me," said Anna gently. "We'll find our way back home somehow."

"I don't got no home," said Madoc. "And I don't like it here neither."

Anna put her hands on Madoc's shoulders and held him at arms length so that he could see her face. "Madoc, my home is your home. You'll always have a place with me." Madoc looked into Anna's eyes but his expression still didn't change.

"Come on Madoc," said Louis. "You can't be serious. You can't even walk." At that, Madoc stood up, walked a few yards, turned around, and walked back and sat down.

"To tell you the truth," began Antoine, "I was thinking about going on too."

"What!" shouted Louis jumping to his feet, "are you out of your mind? Antoine, wake up! You don't, for a minute, believe that this crusade is going to reach its destination do you?"

"I don't know what I believe, but I don't have anything to go back to either."

"What do you mean," said Louis. "We'll go back to the seminary, of course."

Antoine looked at his friend. "Don't you see how ridiculous that sounds now Louis? I don't think that they would let us back in, even if we wanted to get back in."

"Maybe you're right," Louis admitted, "but why go on with the crusade when you don't really believe in it?"

"Why not?"

Louis threw his hands up in the air. "Ahhhhhhh!" he screamed through gritted teeth. Then turning to Anna he asked, "And you. What are you going to do?"

"I'm going home," she said. "I don't know how, but I'm going home."

"Thanks be to God!" exclaimed Louis cupping his hands together. "In all of this insanity, someone is sane!"

With only about an hour of daylight left, Anna, Madoc, Louis, and Antoine found themselves on the docks saying good-bye. Tears filled Anna's eyes as she watched Antoine, with two bags thrown over his shoulder, helping Madoc walk around the few supplies that still had to be loaded and towards the ship's plank. Then Anna's eyes scanned the deck of the ship full of crusaders standing at the railing; hoping. "Good-bye, Phillip," she whispered.

"What?" asked Louis.

"Nothing," responded Anna. "Let's go."

As the two friends turned to walk away they were almost hit by two tired and impatient dockworkers. "Out of our way," said two big sweaty men trying to roll a barrel onto the plank that led to the last ship.

"How is it that this barrel got overlooked?" grunted the shorter man to his companion, as they kept moving.

"It didn't get overlooked," said the other. "I had specific orders to put this one on last."

"It sounds half hallow," said the shorter man as they finally reached the plank.

"Just don't dump it," said the other. "It's got something special in it. It's going straight to the Captain's quarters."

Late that night, after all of the crusaders found a spot to lay down below decks, and things were ready to set sail early the next morning, the captain arrived at his cabin exhausted. He was just about ready to take off his shoes when a noise a few feet away startled him. He looked at the barrel that stood beside his desk and grinned. "I hear that you have been quite valuable," he said to the wooden container. "Still, I don't know how I got the privilege of baby sitting you." The captain latched his shoes again and walked out.

A few minutes later the captain re-entered his cabin with a young sailor. "Open it boy," said the captain pointing to the barrel. "Mind you, be careful."

Not knowing what to expect, the sailor obeyed orders and began to carefully undo the top. The barrel again began to make strange noises. The sailor took a step back and looked at the grinning captain. "Don't worry boy, it won't bite you," he said. "Now go at it."

When the sailor finally got the top off he again stepped back. "Help me get 'em out," said the captain walking over to look down into the container. Finally the two had to dump the barrel over until the half drugged crusader spilled out.

The young sailor looked curiously over at his captain. The captain answered the inquiring look by smiling and saying, "Boy, I have a special assignment for you to help me with for the next few days." The two of them looked back down at Phillip who was struggling to get to a sitting position.

"Actually," said a young man to Antoine and Madoc who finally found a place in the middle of the wooden floor to lie down on, "you all are lucky. They say that the other ships are fuller than this one, and that a lot of the crusaders had to find a place on the decks to sleep."

Neither Antoine nor Madoc were much in the mood for talking. It had been a tiring day and after getting on board they were ordered about by, everybody, it seemed. "Go here. No, over here. Do this. No, do that. Move over." They were thankful, however, that one of the sailors was a sort of medic and had looked at the cuts and bruises of Madoc and had given him some ointment to help with the pain and speed up the healing.

They were told that the crusade would be setting sail at dawn the next morning and that they would need to go to sleep early. It was obvious that on a ship you are not asked to do anything. Everything was a command. However, the command to go to sleep was a welcome one.

Madoc lay awake for many hours even though he was exhausted. Even though the ship was docked and the sea was calm, the constant movement of the ship caused by the waves was something that he had never experienced. It wasn't a pleasant experience. The creaks and slight bangs didn't help the sleeping process either but finally Madoc dozed off.

As promised, the ships filled with the crusaders were up and ready to weigh anchor by the time the sun broke over the eastern horizon. The crusaders were told to stay below decks so that the sailors could do their jobs without the hindrance of curious children walking around and asking questions.

From the docks, William gave the lead ship the signal to up anchor. Hugh had decided to sleep in. He told his partner that he wasn't feeling good. William cursed his partner's weakness, but only to himself.

From a vantage point high up in the city there was another spectator. Rufus gritted his jaw as he watched the lateen-rigged ships begin to move out. The Italian designed vessels were made with two large triangular sails that allowed them to sail as easily into the wind as away from it. The wider merchant ships weren't as fast as the thinner war galleys, but they could hold up to 140 tons of cargo. This time, however, the cargo didn't cause the vessels to ride low in the water because of excess weight. Human cargo wasn't as heavy but was always more difficult to handle.

"Lord, you say that you are the avenger of the innocent," whispered Rufus in prayer. "Please set things right." The vice-governor then sat and watched for a while longer as the merchant ships carried their cargo towards the southeast, towards the Promised Land.

After three days at sea, Madoc's wounds were feeling better, but his stomach hadn't quite recovered.

Though the food wasn't in abundance, the crusaders were thankful just to have daily rations. The problem most were having was not with the food, but in keeping it down. Almost none of the children had seen the ocean before getting to Marseilles. Now they were riding on a ship for the first time in their lives. What seemed to be such and exciting adventure at first quickly became monotonous.

Just before the sun set, Madoc and Antoine took time with their group to go up on deck to breathe the fresh air and see if they could see anything but water. Antoine had found the sailors to be a little rough but friendly, so he set out to talk to one of them and get a little information. Coming up behind a middle aged sailor who was working to untie and refasten one of the ropes that helped keep tension on the main sail, Antoine began casually, "Looks like the breeze has changed a bit." The man didn't pay attention. Antoine tried again more directly, "I'll bet you really know this sea don't you?"

The sailor finished his task by whipping the end of the rope around into a knot that fastened onto the tie down peg and looked back at Antoine. The sailor looked a bit agitated at first, but turned his attention to the ragged Antoine and Madoc and then his hard gaze softened up. "Come 'ere lad," said the sailor motioning to Madoc. The sailor's face was dark and leathery from working in the sun too much. "Looks like you got the worst of it," he said, looking at Madoc's bruises. "Did the other 'un look as bad?"

Madoc didn't budge from Antoine's side. "It's all right, Boy. I got a boy 'bout your age. Haven't seen him in a while though." Madoc still didn't move. "Just as well," said the man straightening his hat. "To tell ya the truth, my boy don't like me neither." The sailor began to laugh out loud.

"It's not that," said Antoine. "He's just been through a lot lately, and he is kind of shy around new people."

"Who are you?" said the sailor, "the boy's mother?" Again the sailor slapped the knee of his tattered breeches and laughed out loud.

"Alexius," thundered a voice a few yards away. The sailor whipped around to attention at the sound of his name. It was the captain and he was pointing his stubby finger at the sailor that Antoine and Madoc were talking to. "Here the other men are working their butts off and you're making jokes. Now get those loose riggings tied down before this breeze turns into a blast."

Alexius returned immediately to his task but shot a glare at the captain after he'd turned away to bark out orders to the other sailors.

It wasn't much longer until the captain was standing on the main cargo door in the middle of the ship and telling all of the crusaders to go down below deck. "Down below," he kept saying. Then looking up at the darkening sky he cursed under his breath and barked out more orders to the crew.

Phillip had lost all since of time because he was kept below deck in the captain's room. The captain himself only spent short periods of time in his quarters and that was only to sleep. But who knew if the captain kept daytime hours or nighttime hours.

Phillip was constantly tied up and felt sick all of the time. He had assured himself that he was not dead or dreaming, even though he didn't have a clue as to what had happened to him or anybody else. Even though he'd never been on a sailing vessel before, he was quite sure, from the sounds, movements, and dress of the two men that he had contact with that he was on a ship going somewhere. The few times that he tried ask the captain something he was ignored or told to shut up or he'd be gagged.

Phillip tortured himself with awful thoughts about what might have happened to his friends on the shores of Marseilles, but then he would assure himself that nothing bad could have possibly happened to them. At least they had each other. He was the one that was alone.

He relived the events of that last night over and over in his mind. He had gone to talk to Father David and was taken outside of the camp to wait for him in private. He had gone to a building located beside the sea docks, given some tea and hard bread, and told to wait. He was sure now that it was the tea he was given that knocked him out, but how could he have expected to be drugged? He must have been set-up by one of the unscrupulous young men that worked with Father David and Stephen. But, "Why?" Every time that he thought he had figured it out, he came to a dead end. It just didn't make since. Why would he be drugged, loaded on a ship, and then held captive? "I've got to find out what's going on," he thought. "Maybe its not to late to get back to Marseilles."

Though the captain acted like Phillip didn't exist, there was a young sailor that attended him for his basic needs. The young sailor was just about Phillip's age and with the few opportunities that Phillip had to ask him questions, he seemed friendly but reluctant to speak. Phillip did discover that his shipmates called him Carver.

"Carver," said Phillip one time as the sailor came in with a tray of food, "somebody has to tell me something." Carver just looked over at him and smiled. "I figure that if you were going to kill me," said Phillip, "that you already had your chance."

"I figure that too," said Carver setting the tray beside Phillip and beginning to untie his hands.

"You don't have any idea what's going to happen to me do you?" asked Phillip.

"Nope," was the response.

When Phillip's hands were free he rubbed his sore wrists. Carver handed him a rag with some ointment on it. Phillip thanked him and wiped the rag gently over the burns. Carver pushed the food tray over to Phillip and sat on the floor against the far wall to watch.

"All right," said Phillip reaching for his food tray. "If you won't tell me anything about what's going on, or can't," Carver nodded and smiled at Phillip and then Phillip continued, "Maybe I can just tell you a little bit about myself and about the crusade."

"Go ahead," said Carver. The young sailor hadn't been told anything about the prisoner and the captain made it clear that no one else was to know about him. After a couple of days of taking attending him and avoiding all questions, his curiosity got the best of him.

Phillip ate slowly as he told his story. The other lad leaned forward and wrapped his arms around his legs as he listened with interest about Paris, St. Denis, and the beginning of the crusade. Soon Carver began to ask questions and after a while the two were discussing some of the events and people of the crusade. "Interesting," said Carver as Phillip told the tale. "Fascinating," he would interject. When he disagreed with something that was done he would sit back and ask, "Why in the world did they do that?" or simply say, "That's crazy."

Phillip was trying to make the story interesting for the young sailor by not just telling the basic facts. Phillip himself began to realize what a horrible but fascinating event the children's crusade actually was. And he was sure that the story wasn't finished yet. Not by a long shot.

Phillip was a bit disappointed when the interested young sailor picked up the rope and signaled him to put his hands behind his back again. "I got 'a go now," said Carver, "but when I come back, we'll talk more." He picked Phillip's plate and cup up, put it on the tray, and vanished out the door. Phillip heard the bolt lock the door shut from the outside and then just the normal sea noises and boat creaking.

For the next hours Phillip sat there thinking of how he might escape. He even began trying to work his ropes loose, until his wrists began to bleed a little. Then he shook his head and smiled at his stupidity. Where would he go, even if he did get free?

The more time he had to think, the more depressed he became. What a disaster the whole crusade had been for him. But then he would console himself with the thought that the governor of Marseilles was probably helping find a way to feed his friends and get them home to Paris.

Phillip thought about his life in Paris. How it had been. It seemed so fake. The more he thought about it the more he realized that he had nothing, really, to go back to, and no real reason either. He was going back to take Anna and the others back. That realization made his mind switch from the past to the future. What would his future be now? He couldn't even guess.

23

STORM

Another few hours passed before the bolt to the cabin door slid back, and the door opened and the captain appeared. He shot a glance over at Phillip but didn't say anything. He walked over to a wooden chest that he kept his clothes in, and began cursing as he dug down into it. He pulled out an old rain overcoat and slid the wooden chest back under the bed. The captain looked over at Phillip and shook the coat at him, "Be glad you're gonna be down under. We got a blow comin'. I'll bet it'd blow a skinny kid like you right over the rail, I'll bet."

Right as the captain was stepping in to the narrow corridor he met Carver coming with some bread and water for their captive. "No dallying," said the captain sternly to Carver, "I need you up top right away, hear me."

"Aye captain," retorted the young man. Carver entered and shut the door.

When the young sailor reached around to untie Phillip's bonds, he pulled back for a moment and looked Phillip in the face. "Whatcha tryin' to do? You can't escape."

"Sorry," said Phillip, "my arms ache."

"It's all right," said Carver working at the knot. "If it were me, I'd go nuts too." He got the knot loose and said, "Now eat up." He sat in his usual place against the far wall to watch.

"The captain said something about a blow," said Phillip, "what's that mean?"

"A bad storm, he thinks."

"Will we sink?"

"Heck no," chuckled Carver. "The captain's been through a hundred storms. He's more nervous than usual because we got a ship in front of us and a ship behind. He don't like to be crowded. When the wind blows you got to go with it a bit."

Phillip stared at Carver for a minute. "You mean that there are other ships?"

Carver realized that he had slipped. "Well yes, I guess so."

Phillip started to turn pale, "How many ships are there?"

Carver hesitated but thought that there couldn't be any harm in telling him. "There are seven," he said.

Phillip put his bread and cup of water down. "The crusade," he whispered to himself in unbelief.

Carver heard him. "You would have found out soon enough. Isn't that right?"

Phillip hesitated for a minute and then answered, "I suppose so." Now he couldn't help but ask a question. "Why am I here?"

"I told you," began Carver, "I don't know. When I first saw you on the ship, I figured you were here for a different reason. You know. Someone wanted you gone or something. When you told me that you had been part of the crusade, I was surprised. I mean all of those little beggars crawling all over the ship and you down here."

Just then a strong wind blew so hard that the ship tilted a bit. "Now hurry up and eat," said Carver.

While Phillip gulped down his last drink, Carver reached into his coat pocket and pulled something out and tossed to Phillip. Phillip picked it up. It was a wooden carving of a great bearded man. "It's Neptune," said Carver, "you know, the sea god. I made it."

Phillip looked it over. It was extremely detailed for such a small piece of wood. He then began to toss it back. "Wait," said Carver. "Keep it. It'll bring you luck." Phillip looked into the sincere eyes of his new friend and stuck it into his pocket.

Another stiff wind rocked the ship and Carver quickly gathered up the tray and left the room. Phillip heard the bolt slam shut on the other side. He reached into his pocket to look at his trinket and then looked up, surprised, at the shut door. Carver had forgotten to tie his hands. It wasn't like he could escape but at least he could move around a bit.

Antoine and Madoc had returned to their places down two flights of stairs. It was a struggle to keep from tumbling down. Many crusaders found sitting places against the walls or columns, but there were more children than wall space.

Antoine and Madoc struggled for a while to keep in their spot but the ship seemed to be tipping more and more each time and the two friends couldn't help but slide into the others. Finally they were invited to hang on to some others that were hanging on to ropes that ran along the wall.

Mixed in with the terrible creaking of the wooden ship as it was tossed about in the waves, were the spoken prayers of the children, and the crying of others.

A few attempts were made by some panic stricken youths to get out by going up the stairs. One boy that tried was sent tumbling back down as the ship hit a wave with such force that many of the children that had secured themselves were thrown out onto the floor.

Phillip was very thankful that Carver had left his hands untied so that he could keep his balance. As the ship began to rock with more force he decided to untie his feet and find a good place to hang onto. Everything in the cabin was nailed or bolted down so he crawled into the corner where the bed was and held himself tight between the bed and wall.

Soon Phillip began to hear the high-pitched screams of the children. The ship was like a woman being burned at the stake. She was twisting and turning and screaming out for mercy on a deaf sea. The storm went on at full force for hours and neither the captain nor Carver came in. Phillip closed his eyes and prayed.

The captain leaned against the rail in exhaustion. "Captain," yelled the first mate, "You got to get down below and rest a bit."

The captain looked to make sure there were two men on each of the rudders and then looked back at the mate and nodded. "All right Beti," he yelled, "give me two hours and then come and get me." He took a good look in the pitch dark and pouring rain all around. "I haven't seen nor heard another ship in a good while. That's good. But Beti, if you get a glance at one those other blasted ships or of one of those blasted islands that are supposed to be around here, get me immediately, hear?"

"Of course, Captain," yelled Beti while the rain poured on his face. The captain turned, opened the nearest hatch and then secured the hatch from the inside.

Phillip heard the cabin door open and the captain appeared, dripping wet, at the threshold. He looked in and just stared at Phillip for a few seconds. A tired smile appeared on his face. "You're a smart lad," he said pulling his knife out his belt. "Now you're just going to come out of there and lay yourself on the floor so that I can tie you back up." At that moment the ship tilted violently but the captain leaned slightly against the doorpost, absorbed the tilt with ease, and kept an eye on Phillip the whole time.

Phillip didn't even try to argue. He just rolled out of his place between the bed and wall and laid face down on the floor. In a way, he was glad to see the captain. It gave him the feeling that things weren't so bad as they seemed.

The captain was annoyed to have to mess with the youth, so he jerked him around roughly as he secured the ropes on his hands and feet. Phillip was soaking wet from the captain's clothes by the time he was done. The captain then labored to pull the heavy wet clothes off of his body and then threw them against the far wall. He stuck his large knife in the wall just above the bed and reached in to his clothes chest and quickly put on some dry ones. He then crawled into bed and went right to sleep.

The first big tilt that the ship made caused Phillip to fall to the floor. He lay in that position for what must have been an hour. The storm seemed to be letting up a bit when suddenly the captain woke up with a start. He sat straight up in bed and seemed to be straining to hear something. "Blast!" he screamed between his teeth. He slid his feet into his shoes, grabbed his coat, and ran out the door leaving it wide open.

Phillip looked up at the Captain's bed and saw that his knife was still stuck there. He crawled up to the bed and started to wiggle his way up onto it when he was violently thrown all the way against the opposite wall with a crash. Phillip shook his head clear. "They had hit something!" The ship screamed with terror!

This time the ship did not rock back to correct itself but stayed suspended at an angle of about 20 degrees. Phillip was helpless. He had to get to that knife. He struggled up the floor and finally reached the bed again. The ship tilted more in the same direction. Phillip twisted his way up onto the bed and began to rub the ropes that tied his feet against the blade of the knife, but he was too impatient and put too much force against the knife dislodging it from the wall. The knife tumbled off of the bed, onto the floor, and rolled down the slope to the other side where the door was.

Water began pouring into the room from the door and the knife disappeared in the flood. Phillip's heart sank.

Carver jumped through the opened door and the two sets of terror stricken eyes met each other. Taking a few giant leaps, Carver grabbed hold of the bedpost with one arm and took out a small carving knife with his free hand. The water began gushing through the opened door now.

"We hit something," yelled Carver sawing frantically at Phillip's bonds, "a rock I think. We're going down."

"What about the others?" asked Phillip, "the crusaders?" Carver cut through the ropes on Phillip's wrists and began on his feet.

"The other men are getting them out," he said, "but I don't know what good it'll do." The severed rope popped off. "Let's go!"

The cabin was already knee deep in water when the two young men started for the door. Phillip followed Carver through the narrow passageway to the stairs struggling against the water flowing in. Before they could reach the stairs they ran into a large group of panic-stricken children climbing over each other to get to the hatch. The water was not coming in from the deck so at least the crusaders were able to get out quickly. However, Carver wasn't sure if it would be quick enough.

"This way," said Carver grabbing Phillip, "we'll never get out this way in time." Carver led Phillip back into the darkening passageway. They came to a stairway that led down and Carver immediately began down them.

Phillip hesitated for a few seconds. It didn't make sense going down into a sinking ship.

Carver noticed that he wasn't following. "Hurry up before it fills up down here," he said.

Phillip obeyed and descended into the darkness with Carver. The water in the room was waist high and swirling but Carver pressed on with confidence. "Over here," he finally called out. "It's a smaller passage, but I don't think anybody will have come this way."

At the end of the room was another set of stairs. The two took no time in getting up the two flights of stairs that led to a small hatch. Carver thrusted his forearm at the hatch. "It's locked from the outside," he said looking around the dimly lit room below. "Let's get something that we can force it open with."

The two anxious young men leaped back down one flight of stairs into the little storage room that was filled with tools and a few barrels that hadn't been touched by water yet. "There should be something," yelled Carver pulling things over. "This is where most of the tools and extra weapons are kept."

Phillip struggled to pull down a long thin wooden crate that was stacked up high. When it came tumbling down, it smashed open on the floor and a handful of common swords tumbled out with a clank. Carver stopped rummaging when he heard the noise and leaped over to where Phillip was.

Both young men, now carrying swords, scurried up the stairs and started awkwardly hacking and stabbing at the hatch. Trying to jab up through the hatch to the solid wooden door proved to be quite a job. One sword was broken before the two finally cut a hole in the middle. Water poured in from the hole for a second and then let up. Carver stood back with his face completely wet. He then jabbed the sword back up to make the hole larger. Again a gush of water came through.

"Dang it!" exclaimed Carver. "The waves must already be coming over the top!"

"What now?!" screamed Phillip.

"We have no choice. We have to go through here." Fighting the water coming down into his face, Carver hacked more furiously than ever at the widening hole in the hatch door. The water came through with such force that Carver was knocked down the stairs. Phillip, holding the broken sword, climbed up to the hatch and started taking a turn at hacking.

The broken sword proved to be the very thing they needed. With a shorter blade the task went faster. A few times Phillip was almost knocked down by the incoming water, but somehow his grip on the top rail held. Now the water was coming in almost without stopping.

Carver yelled, "That's enough, let's go," but the rushing water made it impossible for Phillip to hear. Carver grabbed Phillip's arm, pulled him to one side, and started to force himself up into the water and through the hole. Phillip watched as Carver's feet went through and then his sailor friend was gone.

Phillip grabbed a hold of the jagged opening in the door, took a deep breath, and he also began the struggle to pull himself through. Phillip was out to his waist when something in the rushing water hit him on the shoulder with such force that it almost knocked him unconscious. Without thinking, Phillip grabbed on to the object that had run into him. It lifted him out of the hole and within a few seconds up to the surface.

Antoine had thought quickly and had saved himself and Madoc. As soon as the ship was wrecked, he grabbed Madoc and headed for the stairway. They got to the outside hatch before many of the children on the decks above where they had been had even figured out what happened.

The terrible screams that soon reached them from below as the lower decks began to fill up with water were like the screams of hell itself. Madoc covered his ears with his hands while Antoine pulled him along.

They got out quickly but once on deck didn't know what to do. The incline of the ship and wet deck made it difficult for them to walk. Madoc fell down constantly.

Antoine found a place against the rails to hold on and look around. The pouring rain was making it difficult to see anything. He thought he could see a half a dozen sailors working on something close to them. They were cutting at something with their knifes. Then he figured it out. The sailors had let down a lifeboat and were now cutting it loose.

"Let's go!" Antoine yelled at Madoc, grabbing him by the arm and pulling him along. They struggled up the deck for a few yards but finally reached the rail where the sailors had been. They had already jumped over.

Antoine grabbed Madoc up in his arms and lifted him over the rail. "Help!" he yelled down to the men in the boat. "Help us!" One sailor looked up and saw them. He stood up and extended his arms. Antoine dropped Madoc down into his arms. Then Antoine jumped down into the water beside the boat trying to grab the boat's edge but the crazy rocking of the little boat on the tormented sea made him miss. He only succeeded in scraping and bruising his arms as he bounced off the side. He went down into the water but had slowed his descent enough that he didn't go down very deep. Two strong sailors quickly pulled him into the boat.

The lifeboat was overflowing with children within minutes. Some sailors were pulling them in out of the treacherous water as fast as they could while the ones with oars were trying to keep the bow of the little boat turned toward the incoming waves. Finally the sailor in charge screamed out the orders to the other sailors to man the oars and start rowing away from the sinking ship.

Because of the thick storm clouds one could hardly tell that it was morning. However, when the lifeboat was far enough away they could see what had happened. The ship had struck some large rocks that lay mostly hidden beneath the water. Not too far away was land. The lifeboat headed out away from the rocks and then back towards the shore.

Madoc was almost buried in the middle of the boat by coughing shivering bodies, but Antoine, who had been helping in the rescue, stood to one edge looking back at the tragedy. The ship suddenly broke loose from the rocks that had dealt it the deathblow. Temporarily the ship was upright again. Soon however, the ship sank so low in the water that the deck was only a few feet away from being totally under water. It was sinking fast.

Antoine watched with horror as the vessel went down. It created such an undertow that everything floating close to it was pulled down in a swirling rush of water. Even the sailors who were rowing stopped and watched helplessly as hundreds of young lives were swallowed up by the sea.

Phillip was only conscious enough to know that he should hold on to the object that had at first hit him. He heard the crash of the waves as they smashed full force on the rocks in front of him but was too dreamy to even be afraid of what that meant. He just knew one thing—Hang on or die!

24

RESCUED FOR WHAT?

Before Antoine and Madoc's lifeboat found a beach in which they could land, the storm subsided. When the boat filled with the 37 exhausted survivors was finally pulled to shore everyone crawled out and collapsed on the wet sand. Within minutes, it seemed, the sun was shining and a great host of birds were singing and playing in the after breezes of the storm as if the great torment had only been a dream.

In shock and total exhaustion Antoine and Madoc laid motionless for hours taking in the warmth of the sun. The night's events replayed over and over in their minds.

Phillip woke up laying on the wet ground with the bright sun beating down on him. He sat up squinting his eyes and trying to remember what had happened. His left shoulder was throbbing with pain, but as he examined it with his right hand, he couldn't find any cuts or any broken bones.

He sat up straight and adjusted his eyes to look out at the sea. The shore was a full 50 feet away from him. It was fairly flat but was made up of mostly large boulders and sand. Phillip couldn't imagine how he could have gotten through the rocks that lay out in the ocean ahead of him or how he could have crawled over the boulders onto the shore in order to get to where he was now.

After resting for a little while longer Phillip's thirst drove him to get up and begin to walk inland. Maybe he could find some source of water. After finding water he would look for people.

Later in the morning Madoc and Antoine sat on the shore and watched as four lifeboats arrived on the shore. They were from a different ship. Soon some of the sailors from the lifeboats were passing out food and water to the survivors. Other sailors began walking up and down the shore looking for signs of other survivors and picking up anything that might be useful.

Only five ships set anchor off the shore of the little island. The news that they had received was that one of the ships had definitely sunk with almost complete loss of life while another was nowhere to be found.

"I don't care what they're screaming about," said Captain Pola of the lead ship to his first mate. "There is no room to let them all come up on deck right now. Besides we have to get this %$&·/& mess cleaned up." The Captain pointed his finger toward the ramshackle deck of his ship. The storm had torn everything loose, and ropes, riggings, barrels, and other things were littered from port to starboard.

The exhausted sailors moved as quickly as they could to get things in order. Finally the captain allowed the first group of crusaders to come up top.

The foul odor that rose from the opened portal was sickening. The poor crusaders had been forced to stay below deck during the entire storm and the vomit mixed with the loose sewage from the spilled toilette buckets made it unbearable. After only about a half hour on deck the crusaders were made to go back down, get buckets, and begin cleaning up the mess below. The entire day was a process of crusaders taking turns coming up and going back down again.

"Captain," began the first mate watching, "don't you think it would be a good idea to spend a couple of days here and shuttle passengers back and forth to shore?"

The captain was already shaking his head but before he had time to explain his reason to the first mate the sailor on lookout began to yell out, "Visitors comin' aboard." The captain and the first mate walked over to where they were letting down the ladder.

"May I come aboard, Captain?" asked the visiting sailor.

"Come aboard," said the captain. The captain and sailor walked around the ship for next twenty minutes as the sailor told his story of the shipwreck.

"Only one life boat?" asked the captain in unbelief after listening.

"I saw another life boat being let down Captain, but who knows what happened to it," said the sailor. "If they took the lifeboat towards those #!?# rocks, I'm sure they're lost. Nothing could survive the beating that those rocks would have given them."

"Captain," interrupted another sailor. Captain Pola turned and faced his sailor with an annoyed look on his face. "The priest demands to speak to you," he said timidly.

The red-faced captain pointed a finger in the sailor's face. "Tell that pest that I am working at getting this ship and all of the other ships moving again and I cannot be bothered right now." He then waved the sailor off.

Later that day Captain Pola had called the other four captains to his ship to discuss their next move. "This whole mess has forced me to play my hand early. We turn here. We'll get those survivors on board tomorrow morning and lock the whole lot of 'em up down below." Then a big grin came across his face, "and as far as our good priest David is concerned. He's been so eager to fulfill his destiny with God. Soon he will."

"What about the boy prophet?" asked one of the other captains, "won't he cause problems too?"

"The boy's only a tool," said Captain Pola. "I've watched 'em over the past days. When the priest is out of the way, the boy will be lost. Besides, why should we waste money? That boy will bring a good price in Algiers."

Later that night Captain Pola invited the agitated priest up on deck to speak with him. As Father David began his tirade of accusations aimed at the captain, two sailors quietly approached him from behind. "Maybe you have forgotten, Captain that I am in charge of this crusade," he began. The captain remained calm and silent. "Over the past few days your conduct has been intolerable. Not only will Monsieurs

William and Hugh have something to say to you, but God himself will judge you. This crusade is his precious army."

"Yes, Father, I know. I've been told that continuously every day since the moment you set foot on this ship," replied Captain Pola without emotion. Father David was about to continue with his accusations when the captain held up his right hand to silence him. His two awaiting men stepped forward. "Jon," said the captain looking straight at one of the men, "I do not wish to hear another word come from this idiot's mouth."

Father David shot a stunned look at Captain Pola. The other sailor raised a club and with one blow knocked the priest to the deck. The two sailors picked up the limp body and unceremoniously dumped it over the side of the ship. Captain Pola watched with satisfaction. "And so ends your precious crusade," said the captain whispering into the night air. "May God have pity on your miserable soul."

25

THE SARACENS

Anna stared down at the little cooking fire. "I wonder what's happening with the crusade?" A half dozen faces looked over at her without saying a word. It was a question that everyone was asking themselves. A week had passed since the ships had left carrying the crusade to its destiny and even though these particular young people had decided to abandon it, they couldn't help but think about it constantly.

The group of seven had found each other after the departure of the ships. Besides Anna and Louis, there were four other boys and a girl about Anna's age named Matty.

"I think maybe we should have gone too," said Matty solemnly.

"I admit that I've had my doubts," said Louis, "but I still can't help but think that we're right. I mean, we may be having it tough right now, but I can't imagine what the crusaders are going through."

The small group had spent the past days scrounging for boards, rocks, and whatever else they thought might be useful for building. They built their little shelter right against the large outer wall of a textile factory. The shelter consisted of just two rooms. There was only one small sleeping area for the two girls and one larger room for the boys, but after sleeping in the open air for three months the small group was content with the shelter.

On the fifth day after the departure of the ships, Louis had found a temporary job for him and the other boys loading two ships. They worked from dawn until dark with a group of rough men for two exhausting days. They arrived home each night and collapsed onto their bedding.

On the third day they went to pick up their pay. The man who hired them had hired them for half of what someone would have gotten in Paris for doing the same work. When they went to pick up their pay, the man only paid them half of what he had contracted them for. The boys argued until the man threatened to leave without paying them anything, so they grudgingly took what was offered.

When the five boys got back to their shelter with the money, they were very disappointed. However, the excitement that the girls showed in having real money cheered them up. Anna was glad just to be able to go to the market and she promised to show Matty how to shop. Before they left that morning to shop, Anna planned out exactly what they were going to buy.

The brief shopping trip, however, proved to be more educational for Anna than fun. The market area in Marseilles wasn't as orderly and clean as the market in Paris and the hard French summer meant that there was a lot less variety of food. Prices of the foods were higher than they were in Paris and Anna and Matty returned with less than they had hoped to buy.

That night the day's disappointments were lightened when the seven friends sat around and shared a good hearty meal.

"This is just the beginning, you know," said a boy named Josh. "With all of us workin' together we'll never go hungry."

"Wait just a minute," said Matty. "Just because our stomachs are full right now doesn't mean that in a couple of days we won't be missing meals again."

"She's right, you know," said Louis. "It's not going to be any easier finding work in this city tomorrow than it was yesterday. We're going to have to split up and began beating the bushes for work."

"What about the girls?" asked a boy named Timothy.

"We can work too," said Matty, "can't we?" She asked, looking over at Anna. Anna nodded. "Besides," said Matty, "lots of women are working outside of their homes in Paris. It can't be that different here."

For the next couple of hours they all sat around and talked about possible jobs that they would to find. They dreamed out loud about how they were going to make money and live well. Being hungry and miserable would only be bad memories that soon would be forgotten.

The seven friends also made a pact that if any one of them got work that they would split their wages. That night everyone went to bed with renewed hope.

The thoughts of the recent conversation among the friends uplifted Anna's spirit. She laid her head on her pillow with a smile on her face. Soon, however, her thoughts drifted, as they did every night. Her pillow became moist with tears as she thought about Madoc and Phillip on the crusade and her mother back home in Paris.

The thought that she would possibly never really be happy again filled her mind. Finally, after tormenting herself with these thoughts, she did the one thing that always brought her peace and hope. She prayed.

After an hour of searching, Phillip finally found a small stream that ran almost hidden through a group of tall trees. Quenching his thirst with the cold water he laid down in the shade and slept again.

When Phillip awoke, he noticed that the sun was only an hour or so from setting. For the first time since he found himself on the island, the fear of being alone gripped him. He didn't want to be by himself when the sun went down. He had to find someone, anyone.

Phillip walked briskly looking from side to side and then behind him. He explored the immediate area around him. If someone had been watching, it would have been difficult to decide if he was running from something or looking for something.

The sun finally did set and Phillip resigned himself to the fact that he was going to have to find a place for the night. He decided to go back down to the seashore and find a good-sized rock to rest against. At least there he would be protected on one side by the water. The steady pounding of the waves on the rocks helped him to not feel so alone.

Early the next morning Anna, Matty, Louis, and the others were up nibbling on some leftover bread and telling each other where they thought they would go to look for work. The boys felt that the obvious place for them was the port area. Surely they could find some work at the docks loading, unloading, or maybe cleaning up in one of the big warehouses.

A couple of days earlier Anna had passed a big textile factory and decided to see if she could talk to someone about work there. "I'll go with Anna," said Matty. "Maybe they can use someone to clean up or just do errands."

Without much more delay the determined young people were closing up their little house and heading down the city streets. They melted into the morning crowds that were busily going about their daily routines. "Maybe if we're lucky," they thought, "we'll return later with good news."

Antoine and Madoc were suddenly awakened by an anguished cry. Startled, they sat up to see what was happening. They looked over toward the opposite wall, but the darkness made it impossible to see anything. Soon the same boy who had cried out was sobbing uncontrollably, "No, no Lord...Pierre, you can't leave me." Even without being able to see, everyone knew what had happened. Death had become a common neighbor to all of the crusaders.

One older boy close by moved over to console the crying lad while another began a prayer of supplication for the soul of the dead one. Others joined in the prayer until almost everyone in the large crammed room was repeating it together. When the prayer ended, silence returned to the room and most of the crusaders returned back to their sleeping position.

One appointed young man rose up and climbed the ladder to knock on the hatch door above. Soon the square wooden hatch door opened to the room above them and the young man whispered, "Someone died." The boy that was attending the hatch above them relayed the message and within a few minutes a couple of men came down and got the body out.

"Maybe I'll die next," thought Madoc as he lay there next to Antoine. The idea didn't scare him. It even seemed like a pleasant possibility.

The next two days on the ship were miserable. The room that they were staying in smelled worse all of the time and the rotten air seemed to be making more and more people sick.

The captain had allowed them to come up on deck one time to get some fresh air and that was at night. On the next day the ship hit another storm, but even though it lasted a whole day, it was not very bad. However it did make things worse down below the deck.

"I don't think we'll ever make it to the Holy Land," said a boy that sat next to Antoine. "

Another boy chimed in, "Well then, where do you think we're going? We got to be going somewhere you know."

"Well, how come we ain't heard nothin' from Stephen since we left that island?" said another.

"Maybe he and Father David changed ships."

Antoine and Madoc sat there looking at each other in disgust as they tried not to listen. Those boys had had the same basic conversation for three days now and they were sick of hearing it. "What do you think?" one of them asked looking at Antoine.

"Don't know," said Antoine. "I figure we'll find out some time."

"Yeah, but I think we got a right to know," said the boy looking back at the others, "Don't we?" Then the boys fell back into the same discussion. Madoc and Antoine got up and walked around the room a bit.

The next day and night passed without an opportunity to go up on deck. Antoine and Madoc were on the second floor down and the children on the floor below them repeatedly asked when they were going to be allowed to come up. However, the crusaders on the second floor were pounding on the hatch above them asking the same question to those on the next floor. The reply that got passed down was, "Nobody's answering us and the hatch to the top deck is locked tight."

Rumors flew around the room until the children scared themselves into a panic. A small fight broke out at one end of the room that threatened to spread. Madoc squeezed between Antoine and the wall he was leaning up against.

Then, without warning, the ship banged against something. Antoine's heart fell. Madoc repeated out loud what he was thinking already—"Rocks!"

Everyone fell silent. Then all began to shout as they pushed their way to the locked hatch door. Below them there was a panicked banging on the hatch that led to the lower parts.

Antoine grabbed Madoc and started for the hatch but Madoc wouldn't budge. "No," he said. "This time I'm staying," and then sat down.

Suddenly the hatch opened and kids started fighting each other to get out. Antoine shouted down at Madoc, "Come on! It's open!"

Madoc just wrapped his arms tightly around his knees and didn't move. Not knowing what to do, finally Antoine's panic got the best of him and he left Madoc behind and started for the door.

The people on the deck below were frantically pounding on the hatch. "Please, let us out!" they shouted. Madoc crawled over on his hands and knees and unlocked the hatch. As soon as he unlocked it, the door flew opened and kids started bursting out. The stronger children came out first followed by the weak and sick. They all ran directly up the ladder to the next hatch door, while Madoc crawled back to his spot next to the wall.

Madoc sat there until everyone was gone. He prayed peacefully in the dark waiting for the flood of water to fill up the room, but it never came.

26

TO WHAT END?

Madoc listened as the panicked shuffle of feet on the deck above stopped. He figured that everyone had gotten out but then suddenly he heard cheering. Then he didn't hear anything for a while. Then he heard screaming and crying followed by another panicked shuffle of feet above him. He could tell that the deck above was being cleared now. His curiosity was piqued but he still couldn't muster up enough energy to get up and see what was happening.

He didn't know how much time had passed before he heard the heavy footsteps of someone coming down the ladder. He looked up in the dim light and watched as a man with a lantern made his descent. His eyes widened as the stranger reached the bottom of the stairs revealing him completely in the lantern's light. He was not a sailor.

Madoc had seen two men in Marseilles dressed like him and remembered what Phillip had said, "Look, that is what the pagans look like that live in and around the Holy Land." This pagan was dressed similar to the ones in Marseilles but his skin was black and tough instead of light; his beard was short and scraggly instead of full and shapely; and his clothes were old and dusty instead of delicate and rich.

When the roughly dressed man noticed Madoc, he walked cautiously towards him. Madoc was too afraid to move. A few feet away, the man stopped and leaned forward, looking closely at little ragged boy. When he was convinced that the boy was alive he stood up and grunted out some command to him motioning the lantern towards the hatch. Madoc was stiff. "What would he do?"

When Madoc didn't move, the pagan reached behind him with his free hand and pulled out a long curved knife. He smiled a toothless grin and again waved the lantern toward the hatch door. Madoc arose quickly and scooted along the wall keeping the man and his knife at a safe distance. He darted up the stairs through the hatch and then up the next flight of stairs without stopping.

Madoc emerged on the deck squinting his eyes for the bright sunlight, but before his eyes could adjust someone grabbed him firmly around the shoulders and pushed him forward. He caught himself from falling and stood up straight looking out over the side of the deck. He stood looking at a port full of ships and the strange looking city that was set on the hillsides all around it. "This must be it," he thought disappointedly, "the Holy Land." It wasn't at all what he had imagined.

A sailor from the ship came up from behind Madoc and put his arm around him. "Go along boy," he said gently pushing him toward the gangplank. Madoc took a few steps and then turned around looking at the Sailor.

"Is this the Holy City?" Madoc asked him. A few other sailors that stood nearby laughed out loud.

The first sailor waved at the others to stop laughing and bent down to Madoc's level. "Go on boy. Your friends are waiting for you," he said kindly. Madoc turned and walked down the plank.

He knew that something was wrong. He walked to the end of the dock where another pagan was impatiently motioning for him to hurry up.

Madoc picked up his pace a little until he got to the man at the end of the dock. The man waited until the boy passed him and then he reached down to grab hold of the boy's dirty tunic. Madoc's old instincts took over and by impulse he ducked under the man's hand and bolted away. The long robed pagan yelled out something, and he and three others began to chase after the boy.

Though Madoc should have been weak, the adrenaline pumping through his veins allowed him to jump, dodge, and sprint through the crowds until he was hidden safely behind a pile of rubble stacked up in a narrow alley. "Just like old times," he thought. "Just like Paris...except now there's no Hungry."

The whole day had been a series of hope, disappointment, and finally complete disaster. After the initial scare about the ship sinking the children were relieved to find out that the banging on the side was just the ship hitting against the heavy beams on the side of the dock. The children crammed themselves up on deck and the sailors all moved into different spots around the side. The gangplank was pulled up to the ship and the captain and another man rushed off.

Soon all of the children were talking and pointing at the strange surroundings. They could also see the other four ships docked at various places along the port area. Could this be it? Hope rose in them for the first time since the storm hit that sank two of the ships.

The crusaders began to call out, "Stephen!" It was time for the boy prophet to lead them on. Antoine looked around for Stephen, father David, and the others that usually accompanied them. There was a commotion close to the gangplank of the ship that caught everyone's attention. Two older boys were lifting someone up on their shoulders. It was Stephen! A cheer went up.

The boy prophet looked pail and thin. His eyes were sad and dark. Children all around became silent as they looked into the fallen face of the once confident leader. His expression didn't change.

One girl called out, "Speak to us. Tell us what to do." Still Stephen didn't change his expression.

Others pleaded, "Please, what do we do?" The boy prophet appeared to be deaf and mute. He stared straight ahead. No words came from his mouth.

No one had noticed that the captain had again come aboard. Captain Pola climbed half way up on the side rail by the plank only a few yards from where Stephen was. "All of you listen to me," he shouted out. Their heads turned to look at him. "You will all do what I ask. No one will be hurt." Captain Pola swept over the ship with a gaze that caught the attention of all of his sailors. They pulled out their knives and stood up straight.

"Stephen, what is going on?" shouted out one of the children.

Stephen finally came to life a bit. He looked over at the captain. "What are you doing?" he asked defiantly. "I demand that you let us off of this ship," he said in his high-pitched voice. Captain Pola only smiled a sinister smile.

Stephen tried again, "This is God's crus...ade." In the middle of the sentence Stephen's voice cracked, signaling that his boyhood was coming to an end.

Captain Pola paused a minute and then motioned to two men that stood by him to bring Stephen to him. The two men pulled Stephen from the shoulders of the boys that were holding him up and brought him over to the captain. The children began to fidget as they watched Captain Pola's men take Stephen roughly off of the ship and down onto the docks.

When they reached a point between where their ship and the next ship were docked, the captain stopped. He yelled out loudly enough for both shiploads of children to listen, "From now on, all of you will listen to me." He reached out his hand and the sailor next to him put a long knife into it. The two men held Stephen motionless. His eyes grew wide with fear. "Please, no!" he screamed. Captain Pola raised the knife high into the air and came down with all of his might striking the twelve-year-old boy fully in the chest.

Screams rose up from the ships as they watched Stephen drop to the dock and curl up in a ball. His blood painted the wooden planks underneath him. Antoine felt faint. His knees buckled and he had to grab onto two boys in front of him to keep from falling.

All watched helplessly as the boy prophet and the great crusade died together.

Immediately the sailors starting herding the children off the ships and onto the docks. When Antoine regained the strength in his legs, he remembered Madoc. He tried to go back toward the hatch door that led down to the lower parts of the ship but it was futile. The sailors were pushing everyone forward.

After being herded off the ships, the children were sorted into apparent age groups and sent to various different warehouses that lined the port. Antoine and the other older boys were moved into a well-built wooden building by an armed band of soldiers. Many of the soldiers watched the boys from inside the building standing at the doors and also by the one window that faced the sea.

The soldiers were intimidating in appearance, and escape wasn't even considered. The soldiers yelled out orders to each other and to the boys in their strange harsh language. Their feet were bare and callused. They wore baggy pants that were fastened at the waist by a large black belt, puffing out in the middle and tied tight just below the knee. Their shirts were of loose fitting white cotton with long sleeves.

Each of the men wore a full beard and an ornate earring in each ear. Large blue turbans sat high on each head. Deep dark eyes stared across the room but didn't seem to be looking at anything in particular. However, most intimidating of all were the large curved swords that the men held against their chests with both hands.

Antoine and the others were forced to stand in the middle of a large room for more than two hours, until Captain Pola and four other men came into the room. Two of the men stood at the door and counted the boys while the other two walked in amongst them and picked out any that were sick, crippled, or physically hurt. When they were finished they left with sixteen of the boys who were in bad condition.

Captain Pola waved to one of his sailors to come get the sick boys. "Take these to the warehouse there on the end," he said. "We will have to try to get them in better shape before we can present them to be sold." The men started off with the boys but Captain Pola called out to them, "And make sure that doctor knows that I want them healthy within the week.

Captain Pola talked to the men in Arabic as the small group walked on, "There had to be close to four hundred in there. Some good strong boys."

"Yes, but probably only a few of these will be needed by the governor Al-Kamil," said the shorter white bearded man who had been counting. "He told me himself that children older than 12 would be too difficult to train."

"They'll be good workers in the fields then," said Captain Pola.

"Perhaps Captain, but that does not concern us," said the man. "You can try your luck with them on the open market." Captain Pola did not looked pleased. He knew that the market for slaves was dangerous and unsure. He had to try to sell as many to the governor as possible in order to assure a good sale. His profit depended on it. Hugh and William had made that point very clear.

The small group walked to the next warehouse. Captain Pola stood at the door and announced, "Here are the adults and priests. There are not many of them but a number of them are well educated. I'm sure your governor will be pleased to buy some of these."

The small white bearded man held up his hand to him. "No, we do not need to see the adults and especially not the priests," he said.

Captain Pola looked stunned. "I thought the governor was looking for translators and scholars," he said. "These are already trained."

"We do not want European trained adults. We have found in the past that they are too difficult to retrain and can never be trusted," said the governor's man. "We will only take children. The younger the better."

"What am I to do with these?" he asked pointing to the door to the warehouse.

"I do not really know, Captain, but I'm sure that you will think of something. Maybe the military can use them in the iron mines to the South. They are constantly looking for replacements."

Captain Pola passed on to the next warehouse with the men. He was beginning to get the feeling that the whole business was going bad.

Before the day was over, Captain Pola and the Algerians had visited every warehouse. In the end the captain was pleased with the amount of children sold to the governor. They bought 123 of the 151 girls. Their ages didn't matter because a European girl was considered a great prize to win at any age. The only girls not bought by the governor's men were the ones with handicaps or obviously scarred.

The governor's men also bought 447 of the younger boys. "Now, Captain," said the white bearded man, "we will come tomorrow for these that we have picked out. The governor authorized me to choose up to 700 children, if I thought there would be that many worth buying." Captain Pola's eyes widened. It was the first time that he had heard that they were interested in so many.

The governor's man continued, "At our last count we had 598 in total. We are willing to buy some of the older children that are at least literate in French. If you can find some before tomorrow, then we will buy them also." The man then reiterated, "But no adults."

"Of course," said Captain Pola, happy to have the opportunity to sell off some of the older boys. "They will be ready tomorrow when you come."

Antoine and the other boys around him had been allowed to sit but still couldn't talk to each other. Antoine sat there with his legs crossed, resting against the back of another boy who was sitting behind him. His whole body ached.

Little by little Madoc moved farther away from the port area by working his way through alleys. He didn't have any idea where he was going but figured that the farther away from trouble the better. He was noticed by a number of people. Most of them just saw in him as another poor beggar boy while others noticed that there was something different in his appearance.

When Madoc finally reached the outer parts of the city he found the houses to be much poorer and also found that the streets twisted and turned without any apparent design. He was sure that he could hide here forever if he wanted. The only thing that might give him away would be his clothes.

He noticed that the other boys his age dressed a little differently. Most wore a long loose fitting shirt with pants that were made out of the same material. The most important thing, though, was their hat. All of them wore hats. Even the poorest beggar wore a hat of some sort. He decided that if he wanted to remain unnoticed he would have to get one also, but how?

The thought of stealing did not appeal to Madoc. He had rarely stolen before and even though the crusade didn't work out for him he had come to accept and trust God. No, God wouldn't want him to steal. He would have to find another way.

He looked down at his ragged clothes. There was nothing of value on him. He wore a simple robe with a thin worn out belt. From his belt hung a small leather pouch that he used to carry his valuables. It was empty. On his feet he wore some old worn out sandals that were too big for him. He remembered how often he was thankful to have sandals at all. Many of the kids on the crusade didn't even have any, and ended up with bruised and cut feet.

Madoc walked around for a while until he came upon a group of boys playing in a little humble market area. He sat down and watched them as they ran around chasing each other and running from each other. A couple of the women nearby were constantly yelling at them to calm down because they were kicking up too much dust. They would slow down for a few minutes, but then they would forget and start running again.

Madoc stood up and inched closer and closer to the group of boys. One of the boys stopped and noticed him standing there. He called the others over to look at the strange looking new boy standing there. They all made comments, laughed, and pointed. They pointed to his hatless head, his funny clothes, and then noticed his sandals.

When they began to point at his sandals and talk Madoc bent down and untied them. He took them off and held them up for the boys to see. One of the boys directed a question at Madoc. Madoc put one finger to his closed lips and shook his head from side to side, hoping to indicate to them that he couldn't speak. The boys chuckled a little but seemed to understand.

Then Madoc held out the sandals again and pointed to the hat of one of the boys. Immediately all of the boys took their hats off and offered Madoc a trade. It was obvious that the sandals were worth much more to them than their hats. Madoc pointed to the boy with the nicest hat and they traded. The boy took the pathetic looking sandals quickly and the others crowded around to look.

Madoc placed the hat on his head and started walking away. He looked back at the group of boys. They were busy watching the one boy trying to tie up his new sandals. A couple of them looked over at Madoc and laughed. He realized then that he probably could have gotten a lot more from the sandals in trade; maybe some food. Madoc then walked quickly for the shade of the nearest building because the hot dirt was beginning to burn his tender feet.

Madoc went back into hiding for the rest of the day. He had found a perfect place in an unattended stable. It was only big enough for a couple of horses but there were no horses in it now. It was kept surprisingly clean. Most importantly of all it was well hidden. Madoc knew that he was hungry but for some reason he couldn't feel it. That night he slept well. It was the first good sleep that he had since Marseilles. He never had been able to sleep well on the ships.

Captain Pola and a few of his sailors visited the warehouse that housed Antoine and the other boys of his age just after the sun went down. He called for their attention and told them that he was going to send his men in among them, so that they could read something written in French. Each man held a sheet of paper with writing on it in one hand and a lantern in the other. They went in among the group of boys and began to ask each one to read part of what was written.

When one of the men got to Antoine he lifted up the piece of paper and Antoine read the large print words quickly. He was told to go and stand at the warehouse door with a few of the others. To Captain Pola's disappointment, there were only about forty boys that could read what was written.

Captain Pola told his men to go in amongst the boys again and find some more, even if they could only recognize the letters. The men grumbled but obeyed.

A few hours later Antoine and seventy of the older boys were translated to another building. Finally they were allowed to lie down and rest, so Antoine took a place next to the back wall of the room to lie down. He fell asleep within a few minutes.

The soldiers got the prisoners up early the next morning but they just sat around. A little bit later some men came in with food and water. Antoine couldn't ever remember being so thankful for food before. Not even when they were starving in the middle of the hot French summer along side the Rhine River. Breakfast was only flat bread, but it tasted good and didn't upset the stomach.

Even though there were a dozen sword-carrying soldiers in the building with them, some of the boys got up enough courage to begin talking to each other. At first only a few talked in hushed tones but before long most of the boys were talking. The soldiers didn't try to keep them quiet.

It was soon obvious to Antoine that no one had any idea what was going on. They didn't have any idea where they were or what was to be done with them. Most agreed that they must be in the Holy Land somewhere but that instead of coming in victorious they were being made prisoners. Some boys believed that the Lord was going to rescue them at any moment but most, after witnessing the brutal death of Stephen, were sure that they had no hope of anything but a painful death.

Shortly after eating, a nicely dressed pagan came into the building where Antoine and the others were, and the soldiers immediately hushed up the boys. The man looked at them for a moment and then left again. Within just a few minutes the double doors were swung wide open and some more soldiers came in. The boys were prodded out of the building and into a large open area where they joined a large number of the other former crusaders.

The multitude was then marched carefully around the city. The citizens of the area all came out to watch the spectacle. Antoine studied the people and the city carefully.

The city was comprised of many houses built one right next to the other or, more accurately, one on top of the other. They were built of stone, wood, dirt, brick, and stucco and looked to be very old. The streets were usually narrow and filled with clutter. Thin ropes hung over the alleys and streets so that wet laundry could be dried.

The people were frightening. The men were normally dark skinned with very dark eyes and wore beards. They all seemed to wear different styles of clothing though. Some wore a baggy shirt and pants with a turban that just covered the tops of their heads. Others wore long robes with intricate colors. Still others wore durable looking, one-piece hooded cloaks.

Most of the women wore long sleeved dresses that flowed down to their bare feet. They wore a large shawl that covered their heads and drooped down over their shoulders. A lot of the women also wore a veil over their faces so that only their mysterious eyes could be seen.

Antoine and the others passed through the strange looking crowd without too much commotion. Some of the local children laughed and poked fun but most of the adults were very solemn and quiet. The soldiers had no trouble with the prisoners nor with the local citizens, and soon the large group stopped outside of the city where they joined up with a large caravan.

27

MAJOR ADJUSTMENTS

Hour after hour Phillip stared up at the stars. Only a quarter moon shone and so the twinkling night lights were clear and brilliant. Phillip breathed the cool summer air in slowly and deeply.

"God...where are you?" he moaned. Phillip waited for a response, half expecting, even hoping, that God would strike him down for impertinence. Again Phillip watched the stars and listened to the steady beating of the waves. Nothing. Nothing changed. Maybe nothing ever changed. Phillip breathed slowly and deeply but his heart was pounding.

The crusade was over for Phillip. Hope of going home was gone. Probably his life was over also. "So this is how it would end." His dreams had turned out to be worthless. There would be no Holy Land; no great faithful act; not even God was there for him in the end. He himself was nothing.

Madoc woke up the next morning with the sun. There was only one thought on his mind—food! No one had said anything when he helped himself to water at the public well, but food would not be so easy to come by. He had not seen anyone begging, so he wondered if they begged in this strange city.

Soon the starving boy was up wondering around trying to find a way to get what he needed. He walked by many little markets that sold different sorts of food and household wares but could not think of any way to get to the food without drawing attention to himself.

He eventually came upon a large busy street. It ran down toward the port area though.

A number of times he had thought about going back down to the port area to see about the crusade but he couldn't help but remember how fierce those men were that had chased him. Now after studying the large crowds that seemed to be heading in that direction, he thought about two things. The large crowds meant bigger markets and bigger markets meant a lot of food. He also knew that large crowds were easier to hide in. He stepped into the stream of people and started down the slight incline toward the port area.

It wasn't long before Madoc's initiative was rewarded, when he arrived at a huge market place. He found a small group of people that were shopping together and stayed close by them for cover. He studied the area meticulously as the small group walked from stand to stand. He also kept a lookout for the man that had chased him.

The large market gave Madoc hope. There were stands of food spilling over onto each other. There was a larger variety of food and more abundance of it than he had seen even in the markets in Paris or Marseilles.

There were a handful of beggars. There were the very old, the very young, and the crippled holding their hands out and pleading. Begging seemed to be the same in these pagan lands as it was in the Christian lands. "At least some things don't change," he thought gratefully.

Madoc found a place where an alley emptied into the market place to beg. There were food carts all around and if he saw trouble coming he would easily be able to dart into the alley for a quick getaway. He stood back a little and waited for prospects to pass by. In no time he was into his act as a poor homeless boy who couldn't hear or speak.

Madoc was older than the other little children that begged, but he was so thin and sickly that he looked more needy than any of the others. It was only a short time before a chubby little man looked into the eyes of the deaf mute beggar boy and dropped a perfectly ripened apple into his hand. The starving Madoc sat down in the dirt by the wheel of a wagon and tore into it. Before he had even finished, two other individuals, who happened to be watching, came over and gave him some fresh bread and a small melon.

The market closed down at early afternoon because of the heat and those with carts moved them off. Madoc decided to try to find his "home" again and take a good nap. He got lost a few times, but eventually arrived at the cluster of houses that marked the area. He looked around and when he was sure no one was watching, he slipped into the empty stall, curled up into a corner, and slept.

Madoc was awoken abruptly by someone standing over him. He had been dreaming about being back in Paris with his mother picnicking by the river on a beautiful spring day when he was jolted back to consciousness by a horrendous grunting noise. He sat up quickly but it was too late. He was trapped.

About six inches from his face was the head of a great beast. Madoc pulled his knees up to his chest and covered his face with his arms to avoid being bit. The thing moved in closer and loudly sniffed Madoc all over. Then it pulled its head back a little and let out such a big sneeze that it sprayed Madoc down completely with mucus and slobber.

A man's voice then interrupted. The man spoke a few curt words and flailed his hands around while speaking. Madoc only moved his arms enough to peer out.

The man was not speaking to him. He was speaking to the animal. The animal had some sort of rope around its neck that the man grabbed and tied to a nearby post.

Madoc finally got a good look at the animal. It was like nothing that he had ever seen before or heard of. Its head wasn't much different than that of a horse but it had a long neck and large awkward body. Its back was arched up into a large hump. Fear gripped Madoc with such force he froze.

After the man tied the beast up so that it couldn't get at Madoc, he came over, bent down, and gently talked to him. The man was covered completely in a long thin robe and wore a full turban that covered his head, neck, and shoulders.

Madoc pointed to his ear, then to his mouth, and finally shook his head from side to side. The man nodded and extended his hand out to Madoc. For some reason Madoc didn't try to run. He reached out to the man. The strong right hand of the man tenderly pulled him upright.

The man took a step back and got a good look at Madoc. His thick eyebrows dipped down into a frown. It was not a frown of anger, however. Madoc had made a living by reading people's faces and this man was not angry. He was concerned.

When the man motioned to Madoc to come out of the stall, Madoc wasn't sure about what to do. Sleeping here with the beast was better than nowhere. He motioned down at the spot where he had been sleeping and folded his hands together in a gesture of pleading. The man shook his head indicating that he would not allow it. Madoc pleaded again, but the man extended his right hand towards Madoc and motioned him to leave the stall. Reluctantly, Madoc obeyed.

Madoc walked around the beast and out of the stall. The man motioned for Madoc to walk with him. He put his hand on Madoc's shoulder stopping him. Madoc looked up at the man curiously. The man smiled and pointed over to one of the nearby homes. Madoc didn't move. Again the man pointed over at the house.

Madoc got the idea that the man wanted him to go to the house but he didn't like it. He had learned from his mother to never enter into the house of a stranger. No matter how kind the person was.

When Madoc shrugged his shoulder away from the man, the man did not try to restrain him. The man looked seriously at Madoc and motioned with his head over at the house. Madoc stood firm. Finally the man nodded at Madoc in understanding and started slowly walking away. Halfway to the house he stopped, turned, and looked over at Madoc again. Seemingly against his own will, Madoc took a step toward the man. The man smiled gently and motion over to the house once more.

Madoc walked at the same pace as the man but kept a good safe distance. When the man arrived at the door of the house he shouted something at it. Within seconds the door was opened and a woman stepped out to meet the man. They briefly embraced and then the man called the woman's attention to Madoc who was still standing about 20 feet away. The woman looked over at Madoc and smiled. She waved at him to come in. Again, Madoc obeyed without knowing why.

The woman walked into the kitchen while Madoc and the man stepped into the little entrance room. The man sat down on a small pillow and began to untie the thick leather sandals that he was wearing. Madoc just stood and watched. When the man had his sandals off, he stood up and stepped into a large shallow pottery bowl that was half filled with water. He then grabbed a nearby cloth and washed his feet and ankles. Then he stepped out onto another small cloth and dried his feet.

When the man turned to go into the main part of the house Madoc began to follow. Suddenly the man turned around and looked sternly at Madoc. Madoc froze in fear. Then the man looked down at the water container and then back at Madoc. Madoc got the message and imitated what he had just seen the man do. When he was done he looked up at the man and saw a smile on his face.

The woman joined the man and Madoc in the main room and offered them some dried fruit that she had in a bowl. The man smiled and took one piece out. Madoc took out three. He immediately put two into the leather pouch that hung to his side.

When they had all sat down the man removed his turban and set it down beside him. The lady put the bowl of fruit down at a table that only stood about 10 inches off of the floor and then sat down on a pillow beside her husband. For the next little while the couple watched Madoc eat and talked softly to each other.

"Who is he Jamal?" asked the lady to her husband.

"I don't know, Fadia. I found him just a few minutes ago sleeping in Cacha's stall," said the man.

"I wonder why he is dressed so oddly," began Fadia. "That funny looking robe he wears is so heavy but yet there are no sleeves to protect him from the sun and the cloth only goes down to his knees. He must be terribly uncomfortable."

"I am sure that the boy is an outcast," said Jamal. "He acts like an animal. He has no manners at all. Probably some family that couldn't stand the thought of living with a deaf mute threw him out years ago."

"How sad," said Fadia, "to think that someone would actually turn their own child out." The two sat there for a while longer watching Madoc. He was such a pathetic little creature.

Madoc took another piece of fruit from the bowl and stood up indicating that he wanted to leave. He was starting to get nervous. Fadia shook her head and motioned for him to sit back down. Madoc took a step toward the door. Fadia tried to make hand gestures about the sun being so hot, but Madoc just took another step toward the door. Jamal grunted, stood up, and escorted him out. He watched the strange little boy walk away down the street keeping to the shadows along side the buildings.

The caravan marched away from the city with Antoine and the other almost 700 ex-crusaders. They had marched only a few hours before they stopped and rested from the hot mid day sun. Antoine took the opportunity to look over the camp.

There were many things that Antoine had never seen before but the most interesting were the animals that were being used. There were a number of horses that either pulled carts or were being ridden by colorfully dressed men. There was also one small herd of goats. However, the most intriguing were the camels. Antoine had read about them and even seen drawings. The large beasts were like nothing that he could have imagined. They were tall and clumsy but strong. Each one was loaded down with a heavy burden.

As the camp rested from the heat, the burdens were taken off the animals and they were allowed to lie down. Antoine, who loved horses, was sure that he wanted nothing to do with these strange looking creatures.

The caravan seemed to be traveling west along a route that kept them close to the sea. The land was rolling hills covered by dried grass and numerous trees that were turning fall colors. There were many fields and groves along the way and many sheep and goats being herded. This was rich fertile land.

Before the caravan got moving again some soldiers came and divided the children into groups. Antoine and the older boys were moved to the front of the caravan, the girls were put in the middle, and the others were put at the rear.

It was obvious that the girls were getting the preferential treatment. They were all given a cloth and taught how to wrap it over their heads so as to protect them from the sun. Every time the caravan stopped to rest, some designated men put up temporary tarps so that their fair complexions could be protected from the direct sunlight.

Antoine found another boy his age that he had talked to a few times during the crusade and made friends with him. The two boys talked a lot about what had happened to them and guessed at what was about to happen to them. The slaves were treated well by their captures except for one time when one boy tried to run away at night. He was captured within a few hours and the next day publicly beaten with a thick heavy stick. He was hit numerous times on the back until he collapsed.

After nine days of traveling, the caravan stood on top of a tall hill looking out at an enormous city built by the sea. This city was many times larger than the one that they had left nine days earlier. The two most impressive features about the city were the huge port area and the large castle fortress that sat high upon a nearby hill. The rest of the city seemed to be built around those two landmarks.

The men of the caravan grew talkative and cheerful as they looked down at the beautiful modern city. This was their objective. The leader of the caravan rode his horse to the front and began to scream out orders. The men snapped into place. The guards tightened up their ranks around the newly bought slaves. After a few moments of last minute preparations the caravan marched down into the city.

Madoc could not believe how the people responded to him in the market place over the next days. After begging for only a few hours he would leave with his stomach and his pockets full. However, even though he had enough he made it a point to go by the house of Jamal and Fadia during midday.

In the early evenings Madoc would wonder back down to the port area hoping to find out information about the crusaders. He noticed that the ships that had carried the children stayed docked. He found it impossible to find out anything since he couldn't speak or understand what was being said.

After about a week, Madoc woke up late one morning and started toward the market area. A few blocks before he got to the open market he was held up behind a densely congested crowd. He wanted to see what was causing all of the commotion so he slowly began slipping through.

Finally Madoc got to a point where he could hear someone yelling out words but he couldn't see whom it was or why he was doing it. He climbed up the wooden spokes of a nearby cart and stood firmly on the hub so that he could get a better view.

What he saw shook him up so badly that he lost his footing and would have fallen off if it hadn't been for a man behind him that caught him and placed him back up on the hub. There was a large platform set up at the far end of the market where a well-dressed man was standing and yelling out to the crowd. On the platform with him were ten boys that Madoc immediately recognized as fellow crusaders. Directly behind the platform were standing another fifty boys who were surrounded by men with swords. It was an auction. The boys were being sold as slaves.

Madoc stood motionless for the next half-hour as he watched the former crusaders being auctioned off individually and in groups. Then from behind him Madoc felt a tug on his tunic. He looked down to see a man chattering something at him. The man was pulling at his tunic and pointing to the platform. It suddenly dawned on Madoc that the tunic that he wore identified him with the boys being sold. His heart sank.

The man saw the look in Madoc's face and knew that he was right. He grabbed the little escapee around the legs. Madoc knew that it would be useless to struggle against the man's strong grip so he threw himself onto the man with his full force knocking him off balance. Both of them fell into the thick crowd behind them. As they fell the man who had a hold of Madoc let him go. Madoc tumbled into the crowd and kept tumbling until he found himself at the feet of a few agitated spectators.

Without waiting, he jumped up and started slipping through the crowd again. The man who had recognized him did not give up easily. He tried pushing through the crowd and keeping an eye on Madoc but ran smack into a large farmer who wasn't at all happy about being pushed. The man found himself trying to appease the unhappy farmer and forgetting about the little boy.

28

A NEW MASTER

Phillip stayed close to the shore of the island for a few days thinking that he might see another ship pass by. He wasn't in too much of a hurry about finding a way off though. The days were beautiful and the nights peaceful. Over the next days a number of things washed up on to the shore from the shipwreck. He found a few useful things but most of it was useless rubble.

One day Phillip decided to go a little further down the beach in order to see if some more useful stuff had shone up. He picked up some broken pieces of wooden planks but not much more.

There wasn't any wildlife in sight with the exception of birds. There were lots of birds along the seashore.

Phillip spotted an area that seemed to have a larger concentration of birds than normal. He went down to check it out but when he got there what he saw horrified him. He spun around and looked the other way but it was too late. In a split second his mind had recorded every horrid detail of a human body half eaten by crabs and birds. A cold chill shook him, he fell to his knees, and threw up in the sand.

Phillip returned to his little campsite with the events of the shipwreck replaying themselves in his mind. Later he thought about going back and burying the body but he just couldn't bring himself to do it. He decided not to go exploring for a while.

Madoc ran all of the way to Jamal and Fadia's house. He pounded on the door but nobody answered. He had to hide. He felt sure that it wouldn't take anybody that got a good look at him very long before they reached the same conclusion as the man in the market place. He pounded more frantically on the door.

When nobody answered he ran to Cacha's stall. The beast was there but he was too afraid of being out in the open to care. He got the camel's attention and eased around her until he reached the far wall. Cacha bent down and sniffed him like she had done the first day. Madoc put his hand up and stroked her head. "Good girl," he said. He searched around in the stall and found a few pieces of food that had fallen into corners and gave it to her. Before long, the two were getting to know each other and getting along like old friends.

Before mid day Jamal arrived home and found Fadia who had just come in from doing the daily shopping. "Fadia," he said, "you remember the slave sale that they have been advertising for today?"

"Yes," she answered, "you had mentioned something about it to me. Why?"

"I went down to the market to watch," he said.

"Why would you do that?"

He looked a little sheepish. "I was curious," he said.

"Awe, curious," she began, "my father always said..."

"I know what your father always said," he cut her off smiling. "He always had something to say about everything. Anyway," he began again, "I saw the French children and they look just like the boy." Fadia knew what boy he was talking about.

"What do you mean?" she asked.

"He just looks like them; and you know those funny clothes that he wears. Those French children wore clothes just like them."

Fadia thought for a moment. "Don't be ridiculous Jamal," she said. Then she looked serious, "Do you think he really might be one of them?"

"He could be. He showed up at the same time that the slave ships came to the port. He doesn't talk and he pretends not to hear, but one time I thought I saw him turn his head and watch you come from the kitchen as if he heard your footsteps." Jamal sat down on a pillow.

"Fadia, I think the boy's a pagan."

Fadia chuckled, "He's not a pagan. He's a little boy."

"We'll see," said Jamal. "It's almost lunch time and the boy should be here soon."

Fadia, who was normally very submissive, stuck out a finger and shook it at Jamal. "If that little boy shows up here today we're going to treat him just like we have every other day. I don't want you doing anything to scare him off. Do you understand me?"

Jamal loved his wife and felt very fortunate to have found such a wonderful mate. She was smart and gentle but when she really felt strongly about something she wasn't afraid to speak her mind. Other men might have been insulted by such a woman, but he was thankful for her.

The couple had only had one child and that was a girl but they loved her deeply. It had been over two years ago that she died. It was so strange for one that was so strong and healthy, like her mother, to get suddenly ill. She suffered for two days and passed away. Fadia took it better than Jamal. She seemed to understand that the will of Allah was unquestionable and unchangeable but Jamal could never quite accept it that easily.

Now Jamal looked up at his wife standing over him with her finger held out and realized that the presence of the boy had been good for her. Maybe she missed mothering someone more than she had let on for the past years. Jamal looked up, smiled, and nodded in understanding. "Don't worry," he said, "I will behave myself."

Lunchtime came and went and the strange little boy never showed up. Jamal noticed the disappointment in his wife's face as she washed the lunch dishes and straightened up. When it was time for him to leave he went up behind her and gently kissed her on the back of the head. "I have to go now. I am going to take Cacha and work for Abdul this afternoon. He still has to clean off some of his land for next years crop."

When Jamal walked out Fadia stopped looking busy, went into the living area and sat down. She began remembering how much she enjoyed having Deborah follow her around the house "helping out" with the chores. It took her almost twice as long to do her housework with their little girl but it made life sweet. A tear was coming to her eye when she heard Jamal open the door. She jumped to her feet and wiped her eye with her sleeve.

"Come here Fadia," Jamal called out.

"What is it?" Fadia answered hurrying to the door. At first she was concerned but then she noticed that Jamal had a smile on his face. She repeated, "What is it?"

"Come and look in Cacha's stall." The two of them walked across the street to where the camel was kept and looked in. There sleeping against the far wall was Madoc.

Fadia smiled. "Well, don't just stand here," she said to her husband, "go and get him. He'll be much more comfortable in the house."

"I already tried," began Jamal, "but as soon as I walked into the stall, Cacha cut me off and wouldn't let me pass." Fadia looked at how Cacha had moved her body into position so that nobody could get to the boy. Just then Cacha turned, looked at Jamal and Fadia, and snorted at them. The two couldn't help but laugh.

"I'll wait here until the boy wakes up or until Cacha let's me by," said Jamal. "Fadia, you go and get a little lunch ready. I have a feeling that our little stranger will be hungry when he gets up." Fadia turned and walked bouncily back to the house.

Anna and Matty worked hard at their new job and received the pay for just one. It was Matty's idea but it got them the job. The man in charge said that he wasn't looking for any new employees but showed a little interest when Matty told him that Anna's parents were in the textile guild in Paris. After listening a little while longer to the two girls, the man shook his head and said, "There just isn't any need for you."

Matty then said. "What if we work for the pay of one?"

The man laughed, "The owners hardly pay enough for one person to survive on." Anna stood silent.

Again Matty spoke up. "Whatever it is, it will be more than we're getting right now. Give us a chance."

The man laughed again. He then looked at the two girls seriously. "Be here tomorrow morning just after sunrise. You'll arrive here before everyone else and get things ready for the other ladies. You'll work all day and when everyone else leaves you'll clean up." Both girls smiled and thanked the man.

After a month of hard work, the boss began to ease up on the girls a little. When there wasn't a lot for the girls to do he even showed them how the spinning wheels were used, the dyes applied, and the looms worked.

The boss was hard on them but he grew to like them. Not only did they do everything he wanted, but they also were practically slaves to the other ladies. Yet they went about their work with a smile and never complained. Most of the other ladies warmed up to them in time also.

One day a lady ripped her dress on one of the looms. She told the boss, "Mark, I have to go home and change my dress."

Mark was not happy. "I've got to get this material off of the loom today. Can't you just pin it up and keep working?"

"I guess so," she said pitifully, "but it's ripped all the way up to the waist."

"I can sew it up for you while you work," said a voice coming from behind Mark. Heads turned to see Anna standing there with a broom in her hand.

The lady on the loom smiled, "No, that's all right sweetheart. I'll just pin it up and fix it when I get home."

Mark looked back at Anna. "Can you do it right?" he asked.

She nodded, "It's not difficult. I've been sewing since I was a little girl."

The lady at the loom looked over at her boss, "Mark, I only have two work dresses. I can't afford to have one ruined. I'll just wait until I get home." Anna turned to go back to her chores.

"Wait," said Mark smiling. "Aleen, I'll bet Anna can do it. Let her work on your dress while you're working. If it doesn't turn out right, I'll pay for you to get it fixed."

"You're crazy Mark," Aleen said, "but you're on." Everybody went back to work and Anna went to get a needle, some thread, pins, and little piece of chalk. Within a half-hour the dress was done.

From that day on, many of the ladies asked Anna to work on little rips and tears in their clothes. Mark finally had to put a stop to it when some of the ladies began bringing clothes from home for Anna to work on. "Not on my time," he told them. "If you want Anna to work on your clothes, she'll have to do it when she's not here."

Some of the ladies gave Anna garments to take home and mend. She worked on them at lunchtime and also a little on Sunday afternoons. The ladies would give her food and other things as payment. She started to get quite a nice pile of cloth, needles, thread, and trinkets to put with her other things at the little house.

Louis and the other boys worked on-and-off. They sometimes went a whole week without work, but there was always enough food because of the girls.

Huge crowds of people mobbed the caravan as it walked into the grand city with its 700 Christian children slaves being brought in. When the Al Kamil heard that his prize had arrived he sent out another 60 guards to make the entrance even more impressive. People watched with wide eyes and talked loudly as the group walked into the city and started up the hill toward the guarded citadel called the Kasbah.

Once inside the fortified area Antoine and the other boys his age were taken to a large barracks. The barracks consisted of one large room with a stone floor and mats lay out on the ground. The boys were marched in and made to stand. A few minutes passed and a man dressed a light blue flowing robe walked in and stood facing the boys. The man had a delicate white turban on his head. He had a long black beard that was flawlessly combed down to rest on his chest.

"I am Beni Saf," announced the man with a thick accent. "You are now property of the Al Kamil and you will serve him for the rest of your lives." He paused and looked into the faces of every boy. "This is a great privilege. You will be treated very well and those of you who show promise will receive a very good education and lead very comfortable lives."

"All of you have been specially chosen by Allah. You are not here by accident. It is the will of Allah and you will learn to appreciate this."

The man held his hands to his side and spoke without any facial expression. "It is, however, the wish of the Al Kamil that you not be forced to accept the teachings of Mohammed at this time."

"You will be given the opportunity to learn. You will be instructed in the culture of Algeria and in the Arab language daily." At this, many of the boys turned and looked at friends. It was the first time that they had learned where they were. Antoine had heard of the country of Algeria but could not remember exactly where it was located. It was a Moslem country and that was all he knew.

Antoine's heart pumped quickly as he stood and listened to Beni Saf talk. He had imagined the possibility of death many times while on the crusade but what he was hearing now were things that he could never have imagined.

Beni Saf talked for almost ten minutes straight before he stopped. "Now," he said, "you will all pick a bed as your own. You will take the clothes that are laid out on them and carry them with you out to the bath." Nobody moved. "Now!" repeated Beni Saf. The boys quickly picked out a mat and removed the clothes that were laid out on it.

Ten guards led the boys out to a large outside bath. It had a constant stream of water running into it and then out of the other end and was big enough for ten or fifteen to wash up at the same time. After an hour of scrubbing with soap and water the boys put on their new clothes and stood for inspection. Beni Saf looked them over and smiled. "A definite improvement," he said. "There may be a few scholars among you heathens after all."

Later that night Antoine was lying on his comfortable clean mat staring out of a high window at the stars. He tried to remember his life in Paris, the crusade, Andres, Phillip, Madoc...his entire past life. He barely remembered what the places and people looked like. It all seemed like an unreal dream. "God," he whispered, "help me to never forget."

29

ANY JUSTICE?

One night after a long hard day, the girls arrived home to find the boys already there with the little fire lit. Anna and Matty walked in and immediately sensed that something was wrong. The boys were all sitting quietly around the fire and the flickering light showed saddened faces.

"What is it?" asked Matty. "What's wrong with you guys?"

Louis looked up and looked at the girls seriously. "The ships arrived back in port today."

"What ships?" asked Anna. "What's wrong?"

"The crusade ships," said Eloy. The two girls froze. They didn't dare ask what happened.

Louis finally told them, "We heard some of the sailors talking this afternoon." He looked directly at Anna. "The crusaders were shipped to Northern Africa and sold to the Saracens as slaves." Both girls gasped at the same time. "Not only that," continued Louis, "but two of the ships sank in a storm with almost complete loss of life before they even got to Africa." The girls sat down and cried. They didn't even question if what the boys were telling them were true or not.

That night the youth didn't feel like eating supper and went to bed early. Eloy and Martin decided to leave and just walk around. Everyone needed some time to think and mourn.

Vice-governor Rufus was waiting in the governor's office when he arrived. Rufus stood in respect for his superior as usual but the governor noticed right away the stern look on the face of his younger friend. He stopped before even sitting down and asked, "Rufus, what is it? You look like you're about to eat someone."

Rufus ground his teeth before opening his mouth to speak. "Monsieur," he began, "those two devils in merchants clothing have outdone themselves this time."

"You mean your old friends William and Hugh?" asked the governor smiling.

"Please don't call those beasts my friends even in jesting, Monsieur, but yes, that is who I am talking about."

"What is it, Rufus? What has happened?" The governor sat down. Rufus told him about the rumors of selling the crusaders to the Saracens as slaves and then assured him that he had enough witness to confirm the reports. The governor sat stunned as he listened.

"I'll call the counsel together immediately," said the governor.

"No monsieur, please don't do that. This has gone beyond politics or opinions. This is a criminal case. If we let those scoundrels have one day more, they will either buy their way out of this or they will escape and live like kings anywhere in the world," said the vice-governor.

The older statesman looked up at Rufus and saw the furry in his eyes. He sat back and sighed, "What is that you suggest we do then?"

"I say that we go get them now. Right now! We don't wait another moment." He paused and took a step back. "If we're lucky, we might just catch them napping."

"On what grounds are you going to charge them?" asked the governor. "You have to have a good reason to arrest them without notice."

"What stronger ground can there be than treason?"

"Treason?" asked the governor.

"Monsieur, is it not a treasonous act to sell French children, our own flesh and blood, to the Saracens so that they can do, God knows what, with them?"

For the first time in the whole conversation the governor let the truth sink in. He was so used to making everything political that he had been weighing the positives and negatives instead of seeing the horror it. He stood up. "Rufus, send for the constable."

Again Rufus sighed, "Monsieur, may I suggest that we send a military guard instead."

"Why?" asked the governor.

"William and Hugh are very powerful and very rich, monsieur. They have a web of informers that you wouldn't believe. I have been trying to catch them at their game for a long time but they are always a step or two ahead of me. I'm afraid that if we go through the conventional methods of arresting them, they will be long gone before the constable ever arrives."

Rufus moved in a little closer to the governor, "Monsieur, if they get out of this one, I fear God himself will reach down and hit us with more plaques than Moses ever saw in Egypt. Who knows, He may anyway." He paused to catch his composure. "Please let me do it my way this time, Monsieur. I swear to you that I will not dishonor you or this office."

"They are, as you said, powerful citizens of this country," the governor reminded him. "If this turns ugly, you may pay a high price." He looked again at his resolute friend. "All right, but you will lead the guard yourself to get them."

Rufus smiled and stood up straight. "It would be my pleasure, monsieur. I wouldn't miss getting to see their faces when the captain of the guard accuses them of treason, ties their hands, and leads them through the streets in humiliation."

That day at work Anna broke down a few times weeping as she went about her regular duties. When Mark and the other textile workers found out what the problem was, they kept quiet. The place was full of the noise of machines whirring and tapping but there was a kind of silence that went beyond sound. Even at lunchtime no one spoke. Most of the ladies were mothers and the thought of what had occurred to the children on the crusade made everyone of them feel the loss.

Louis and the other boys went out to the docks looking for work. Some of the men who knew that they had been part of the crusade made comments to them as they wondered around. "Its sure a good thing you boys got out of that crazy crusade when you did," said one man. Somehow, that day, the boys weren't able to rejoice in their decision.

It seemed that everyone was talking about it. Some of the men were openly angry about it while others said that the children got what they deserved.

At one of the docks Louis was asking a man that he had worked with before if there was any work, when a drunken sailor came up to them both and looked Louis over. Louis took a step back. It was unusual to see even a sailor drunk at this time of the day. The sailor shook his finger at Louis and said, "I hear you're one of those stupid little crusader slaves." He staggered back a little and laughed. Louis didn't respond. He tried to walk away but the man caught him by the shoulder.

"I didn't say you could leave, crusader slave," the man said in Louis' face. Louis took the man's hand off of his shoulder and turned to leave again. The man followed him. "I'll bet we could have gotten another 20 pieces of silver for you," he said to the back of Louis head. Louis stopped, turned around, and glared at the sailor.

"Oh my goodness!" said the sailor putting both of his hands up to his mouth in mock surprise. "It seems like the little crusader slave is angry." Louis kept staring at the man. "Funny," said the drunken sailor out loud, "all of the rest of your little crusader slave friends went to the auction block without so much as a mean look." By this time many of the workers around stopped working and drew closer to watch.

"That's right," said the sailor loudly, "it was the easiest money I ever made." He reached down into a pocket and pulled out a good-sized money pouch so that the others could see. Then he shook it at Louis and repeated, "Easy money."

The warehouse manager finally spoke up, "Mike, that's enough." The sailor ignored him.

Louis' furry peaked. He reached over and knocked the money pouch from the sailor's hand. The sailor just laughed and looked over to where the pouch lay. Right then Martin, who had been asking about work next door, came in and saw his friend in trouble. He walked quickly to Louis' side.

"What's going on Louis?" asked Martin.

Before Louis had a chance to respond, the drunken sailor looked at Martin and said, "Oh no! Don't tell me it's another crusader slave boy. Well, #####? if we didn't forget a whole #####? of the little beggars." Just then the sailor grabbed Martin by the back of the head and shoved him to the ground beside his pouch of money.

Louis took a step forward and slugged the man square in the mouth with a right hook, but the sailor barely flinched. He looked over at Louis and smiled a bloody smile. "What's wrong boy? I just wanted to give him a taste of what his other slave friends are going through right now."

The sailor turned his head to one side and spit out a little blood, "Now I'm going to give you a taste." He pulled his arm back and stepped toward Louis, but just then he froze in mid motion. A short, stocky, middle-aged warehouse worker caught the sailor's arm from behind and whipped him around. Before the surprised sailor knew what happen the warehouse worker brought down three crushing blows to his face, pounding him unconscious into the dirt floor.

Another one of the warehouse workers picked up the man's money pouch and stuck it in the unconscious man's pants pocket. The stocky worker, who had intervened, called over a friend, "Come on Walt. Let's carry the bum out into the middle of the street. If he's lucky enough to not get run over by a horse cart, the police will pick him up." The two men disappeared with the sailor's limp body.

Louis and Martin were about to leave when the warehouse manager called out to them. "Hey boys, I got some work for you to do." The two young men looked back at him. "Well," said the manager, "you want it or what?"

"I say we get out of here now," said Hugh to his portly friend who was sitting back in his chair with his feet propped up on his ornate desk. William just sat there without answering. "Don't just sit there like that," said Hugh. "Haven't you heard what I've been telling you? Everybody knows now. We have to get out of here."

William looked up at his nervous friend who was hovering over his desk. "When will you learn Hugh? I have this city under control. I know what the governor's thinking even before he thinks it. I have people everywhere. Nothing happens without me knowing it." William sat up and put his feet on the floor. "Nobody's doing anything. This whole thing will blow over in a few weeks and nothing will ever be said again."

"Well, I've heard that the people are angry. I've heard that . . . . ." started Hugh before he was interrupted.

"You've heard. You've heard," said William mocking. "You've heard from who? You've heard from sailors, prostitutes, and nobodies. Let 'em talk. They don't count." Hugh stepped back and sighed.

William stood up. "Those nobodies can't and won't do a thing. They talk a lot but they don't really give a #####! There's only one person who really concerns me."

"You mean the bishop," offered Hugh.

"No, you fool. When will you learn to tell the difference between a lion and a lamb? The bishop will be one of the first to dismiss the whole thing as 'the hand of God's providence'; or some such thing. I'm talking about that #####? Vice-governor Rufus." William sat down again.

"What will we do about him?" asked Hugh.

"We wait and watch. That's what we do. We wait and watch very carefully." William said. "Do you have the "Landora" loaded and ready to go?"

"Of course. Just as planned."

"I'm still betting that the whole thing blows over like a bad storm, and when it does, not only will we recuperate the loss of our ships but we'll live higher than ever right here in good old Marseilles." William sat back in his plush chair and kicked his feet up onto his desk again.

Just then, the two merchants heard heavy rapid footsteps in the little hall that lead to their office. The clerk dispensed with the usual formality of knocking and burst into the room with a look of terror on his face. "Soldiers coming," he said "They're about a block away." William and Hugh looked at each other. The clerk then said something that made their hearts sink, "and the vice-governor is with them." Nothing more needed to be said. The two partners ran for the door. In a matter of a few more seconds they were out the front door of their offices and were jogging down the street toward the nearby docks.

The two men gained hope as the Landora came into view. The plank was down and ready to receive them but as they stepped into the open dock area four soldiers stepped in front of the plank cutting them off from their get-away vessel. William and Hugh stopped and looked around. More soldiers stepped out of waiting places as they spotted the men.

When William saw that they were trapped, he headed toward the "Landora" once again. "Let us through!" he demanded to the guards.

"No monsieur, we can't do that," answered one of the men as he drew his sword and held it against his chest. The others then imitated him.

William and Hugh turned around again to see if there was any way out, but what they saw was the captain of the guard, the vice-governor, and six more soldiers coming directly at them. News traveled like lightning and a tremendous crowd arrived at the scene at about the same time as the captain of the guard.

"William the Pig and Hugh the Iron?" the captain said loudly enough so that all could hear, "you are hereby formally charged by the French government with supporting the Saracens against the French King and against the Christian world. You are charged with selling French citizens as slaves to the enemy. These charges constitute treason to France and blasphemy to God." William looked over at Rufus who was standing beside the captain with a very intense look on his face.

"William the Pig and Hugh the Iron you are hereby prisoners of King Phillip Agustus of France." A great cheer arose from the crowd that stood around, and soon many more people were rushing in to see what was going on. "Sergeant," said the captain to a soldier next to him, "detain these men." An even greater cheer rose up as the sergeant tied the two traitor's hands behind their backs.

The soldiers had a difficult time pushing their way through the dense crowd with the prisoners. As the people of the city heard what was going on, the streets flooded with onlookers who spat and cursed at the two traitors passing through them.

30

FOR THE SAKE OF CHRIST?

Madoc spent several days avoiding being seen in public and living only on what Jamal and Fadia gave him everyday at lunchtime. He spent his nights sleeping in Cacha's stall. With the great beast looking over him at night he slept soundly.

One day as Madoc sat at lunch in Jamal's house Fadia left the table for a minute and then reappeared holding out a shirt and pants for Madoc. The little orphan looked over at Jamal who was motioning him to take it. He stood and felt the nice soft cloth of the shirt. Fadia took the clothes into a connecting room and motioned for Madoc to follow. Once inside the room, Fadia put the clothes down on an empty cot and walked out. She latched the curtain that acted as a door so that Madoc could have some privacy.

In a few minutes Madoc unlatched the curtain and stepped out looking every bit the son of a humble Berber city dweller. Jamal and Fadia both grinned from ear to ear.

That day after lunch, Jamal motioned for Madoc to follow him to the stall. He hitched up Cacha with her work harness as Madoc watched. Then he motioned him to go with him. Madoc had no idea what to expect and a few times almost bolted and ran. He wasn't used to following people and had decided that he could not trust anyone. However, he couldn't help but trust Jamal and he was also curious as to what he and Cacha did every day.

After leaving the city walking down an old dusty road for about twenty minutes Jamal came to the edge of a large vineyard where he tied Cacha up underneath a tree and made her to lie down. He began going through the large satchel that he had placed on her back and soon pulled out a light coverall cloak, which he put on. It was stained but clean.

Jamal pointed to Madoc and motioned him to stay with the camel. Jamal picked up a large basket that was laid at the corner of the vineyard and pulled out a small hooked knife from a pouch that he wore on the outside of his coveralls. Soon Jamal joined a handful of workers that were already working in the vineyards, cutting off the bunches of ripe grapes quickly and putting them in the basket.

Madoc watched for a while underneath the tree with Cacha but got bored watching and so decided to try to help work. He noticed that there were other children his age or even younger working. He found Jamal and made the motions trying to explain to him that he could help too. Jamal shook his head and pointed at Madoc's new clothes. Madoc understood and went back to stay with Catcha.

Madoc had never been to a vineyard before and found the whole picking process very interesting. He paid attention to how carefully the workers looked through the grapes only cutting out the ripe ones. They would fill their baskets and then go to a large cart where a man was waiting. As the basket was emptied into the cart the man in charge marked it down in his book, gave the person a wooden token, and then the worker went back to the vineyard with the emptied basket.

Madoc watched Jamal work quickly. He noticed that everyone worked at a different pace and Jamal was one of the fastest. He made a game out of watching Jamal go back and forth to the cart by seeing if he could fill up his basket faster than the others. In the end, there was only one young man that was able to work faster than Jamal.

Madoc began to daydream a little and soon he found his mind wander back to the events on the crusade. He thought back through all of the incredible events and shook his head.

He thought of Hungry a lot but also thought about Anna. Madoc thought about how much Anna trusted the Lord and how much she liked to pray. He had learned how to pray from her.

It suddenly dawned on Madoc that he hadn't prayed in a long time. He knew why. He didn't feel like it. He could hear Anna saying, "Sometimes you won't feel like praying Madoc; especially when things aren't going well. But . . ." she would say, "that's when you need to pray the most."

Madoc looked out and watched Jamal work relentlessly. He looked over at Cacha. She seemed content enough.

Madoc slightly bowed his head and closed his eyes. "Lord..." he didn't know what else to say. He began again, "Lord..." He still didn't know what to pray.

He kept his head bowed for a minute in thought and then suddenly, like a rush, all of the events of the crusade came flooding back to him. This time they came with emotion. He couldn't help but grimace and cry. Fearful that someone might notice he opened up his eyes, lifted up his head, and looked around. Nobody was looking over at him or was even close enough to notice him.

Madoc bowed his head once more and, with tears in his eyes, he asked in anguish, "Why Lord? Why did all of those bad things happen? We did it FOR you Lord."

Madoc remembered that when he prayed with Anna he often felt as if God were answering their prayers even as they prayed. He did not expect, however, to hear such a definite answer come to his heart. "Madoc, I still love you and I always will. I have never abandoned you and never will. Be strong in faith."

Madoc's heart felt completely at peace as all anguish was immediately gone. He continued to listen, "Madoc, you must learn to ask, listen, and follow my direction."

Madoc finally lifted up his head, opened his eyes, and looked around. Still nobody had paid him any attention. He sat there appearing outwardly just as he had before, but there was something different...inside.

When the day was almost done the workers began leaving at will. Jamal was one of the last to leave the vineyard. He turned in his tokens and was paid for his day's work. He came over to where Madoc and Cacha were. The first thing he did was to take off his coverall cloak. He pulled out a leather pouch filled with water; not the same water that he drank, and washed his hands. Madoc noticed for the first time how callous and discolored Jamal's strong hands were.

The three walked home together and got to Cacha's stall just before sun down. Jamal took his camel's harness off and hung it over the gate. He opened up a little shed and got some hay for her and then gave Madoc a bucket and pointed to the well down the street. Madoc went and got the water. He had poured the water into Cacha's trough and was about to put the bucket down when Jamal looked at him and held up three fingers. Madoc went back two more times.

Jamal put Cacha's harness away and took one step toward the house before he stopped. Madoc was already climbing over the gate to get into Cacha's stall when Jamal whistled. Madoc stopped and turned to look. Jamal met his eyes with a powerful stare. The two of them stared at each other for what seemed to Madoc a long time. Then Jamal motioned for Madoc to come to the house. Jamal put his hands together and placed them on the side of his face making the gesture of someone sleeping.

Madoc understood, but was scared. He was perfectly content sleeping with Cacha. He also understood that this meant much more than just being invited to sleep in the house for the night.

Anna went home with Matty after work and found the boys already eating. The two girls stayed later than normal and so the sun had set an hour earlier.

Anna forced herself to greet the others. Without eating, she went straight to the back room where she and Matty slept. She couldn't stand for another minute. The others watched her go by and didn't attempt to stop her or even try to offer her supper. She had been almost inconsolable over the past days.

Anna collapsed on her bedding and buried her face in her pillow. All day she tried to pray but just couldn't. Her mind was spinning with thoughts and memories.

Finally she forced herself to start a prayer, "Lord..." Just the mention of His name cleared her mind. "Lord, please help us. Please help

Phillip and Madoc." She started crying as she thought of them.

"Lord, I am so lost and confused. Help me remember and pray for my friends; all of them." Anna prayed on and on. She prayed for hours. Her mind became so keen that she remembered many of the children from the crusade that she hadn't thought about in a long time.

When Anna was very much at peace she breathed in deeply and asked a question that she had avoided asking for weeks, "Lord, why have you allowed all of this to happen?" She paused for a few seconds. "We wanted to do it FOR you."

Unexpectedly an answer sprang into her mind, "I never asked you to."

Anna sat stunned. The truth of the answer was painful. She had asked the Lord about almost every little thing concerning the crusade but she had never really asked the Lord directly whether or not He wanted her to go. "How could I have done that Lord?" She was still in unbelief at her foolishness. She had nobody to blame but herself. She had convinced herself that she wanted to go; she needed to go; she should go; but she had not asked God for final directions.

A few more moments of stunned silence followed before Anna was able to recapture her attitude of prayer. "Lord, forgive me. Please lead me from now on in every decision." She paused one more time, " . . . and Lord, if You will, please find a way to lead me home."

Each day for Phillip was exactly the same. He got up with the sun. He looked around a little for food and combed the beach. After mid-day he would return to his camp and do nothing but lay in the sand and sulk.

Fortunately there was plenty of food around for Phillip to eat. The few months that he had spent with the crusade had taught him how to fish, trap, and test if plants, roots, and berries were eatable. He also learned the very important art of how to start a fire. There was a fresh stream of water just five minutes walk from where he had set up his little shelter. From it he was able to drink, prepare food, and wash.

The next week found Phillip more than content with the simplicity of his new life. One day, however, Phillip woke up to gloomy clouds hanging overhead and soon he would begin to change his opinion. It began raining at mid-day and didn't stop until late into the night. It was then as he shivered in the cold that Phillip realized that his comfortable little shelter was inadequate.

Two weeks had passed since Phillip had been ship wrecked and left on the island but after the rain he decided that it was time to explore again. He kept to the shoreline and walked out in the open. He figured that from the beach he would be able to see anything that might be on the sea. The Island didn't seem to be very large at first but after walking for an hour or so Phillip realized that it was bigger than he had originally thought.

Phillip spotted a good sized hill in the distance and after more walking, he realized that the hill was quite tall and that if he could get to the top of it he would be able to see much more and walk a lot less. He left the beach and entered into the brush toward the hill. Many times birds and small animals startled Phillip as he fought his way through the thick bushes and tall grass. Towards the top of the hill there was a nice rocky clearing where Phillip stopped and took a break.

"I wish that I'd brought a little water," he thought breathing heavily. "And maybe a little food too. Oh well," he said standing up again, "on we go."

Soon Phillip was on top of the hill trying to get to a place where he could look over the thick bushes. He spotted a large boulder and climbed up. The view was great. He quickly scanned the island in all directions.

It was a good-sized island and Phillip could see a lot of the shoreline from his new vantage point. The island would not be large enough for many people to live on for very long. There weren't many of the natural resources for people to use for building and the land would be hard to work for crops. Then Phillip looked at the horizon in all directions to see if he could spot land. "There!" he said out loud pointing. There was land. Probably another island but it looked much bigger than this one. However, it was easily thirty miles, or more, away. "It might as well be 100 miles away," thought Phillip.

He looked over the island again trying to study all of the important landmarks. He noticed a cove on a part of the island that he had not been to yet. "That would probably be a better place to live," he thought. There were even a number of small trees close to it. "I'll go down there tomorrow and see if there is a stream or something with fresh water in it," he told himself.

As Phillip studied the area around the cove something caught his eye. There was something moving down there and it was big enough to see from the hill. Phillip squinted and looked more intensely. There was a small clearing close to the brush line on the cove and something was definitely stirring.

After his new discovery, Phillip decided to forget about waiting until the next day to explore the area. He trotted down the hill toward the other side of the island. He got lost in the tall brush so decided to cut straight toward the coast and then follow it until he got to the cove.

In about a half hour Phillip could see the area where the coastline dipped inward to create the little cove. When he arrived, he noticed how the waves were much smaller and the beach longer and sandier. It was quite different from the place that he had been staying for the past few weeks. He looked around only briefly. He was more interested in finding whatever it was that he had seen from the hill.

As he walked toward the brush line, his eye picked up a trail. He stood and stared at it for a minute trying to decide what it meant. He followed the trail for a short way and came into a small clearing. Phillip lifted up his eyes, he stopped, and then his heart jumped with hope. There were two little shacks built beside each other.

Even though the shacks were in bad repair and one of them stood with its door open, Phillip still was glad to see something that told him humans were here, or at least had been here. He called out, "Hello there. Is anybody home?" He heard something moving inside one of the shacks. He took a step back and waited for a response...but no one came out.

"Hello," he called out again. He took a few cautious steps toward the shack, "Anybody in there?" No response. He stood up on his toes trying to peer through the little open window that faced him but, since the house was raised up off of the ground, it was no use. He moved up to the little steps that led to the door.

Phillip climbed the steps to reach the door and was about to enter when a large animal jumped at him. "Ahh!" Phillip screamed. He was knocked back as the animal brushed by him. Phillip half jumped, half fell off of the steps onto the ground. He quickly rolled and looked to see if the animal would attack. Instead, he saw the backside of a goat scurrying away down a path that lead into the thicket. "A goat!" he said to himself in disgust. "Just a stinking goat!"

Phillip picked himself up and climbed the steps to the shack again. He stuck his head in the door and took a quick look around. There weren't any more goats and the place was a mess. It was obvious that no one had lived there for quite a while. He went to the other shack and found that the door was jammed shut. He easily worked it open and went in.

The second shack was in much better shape than the first but the thick covering of dust that covered everything confirmed his disappointment. Nobody was at home. There were a few crudely made stools, a small table against the wall, and a larger table in the middle of the room. Phillip stamped hard on the wooden floor and found it to be pretty solid. This would be a much better place for him to stay.

Phillip explored a little more and then decided that he would sleep at his newfound home that night. That afternoon he discovered that there were many goats roaming around.

On one occasion an older goat heard him coming and ran directly at him. Phillip froze on the trail as he saw the animal trotting towards him. The female goat didn't appear to have any hostile intentions toward him so he stayed until the friendly goat arrived. The goat nuzzled up to Phillip and he stroked the wiry hair on its head. It was obvious that the goat had been domesticated. Phillip broke off some tall grass and offered it to the goat. The goat sniffed it, nibbled on it a little, and then turned and walked away.

The next day Phillip was following the beach line around the island to his old place in order to gather some of his belongings when he happened upon some more wreckage washed up on the shore. He stopped and watched from a distance as broken planks, ropes, and masting gently moved in and out on the tide.

Phillip's curiosity finally got the best of him and he picked up a long stick that he could use to poke at the wreckage without having to actually touch it. After sifting through some boards and looking under some of the cloth that had made up the sails of the ship, Phillip began to drag useful items up on the shore.

He was untangling some rope from one large piece of water soaked cloth when he noticed that the cloth had a red strip on it. When he finally untangled the cloth and held it up, there was the unmistakable shape of the red cross sown on to a solid white background. It had been a banner for the crusade.

That night Phillip built an unusually large fire about 20 feet from the shack he was using as his new home. He took down the crusade banner from where he had hung it to dry in the sun and placed it on the long stick that he had used earlier. He held the banner over the flame and watched intently as it slowly caught fire. The banner smoked profusely as it was being consumed. Even as the smoke began to choke Phillip and burn his eyes he stood erect holding on to it.

Phillip imagined that he saw figures and faces from the past looking at him in the smoke. There was Father Timothy from St. Denis shaking his head in disappointment; Bernard the Jew looked up at him with condemnation through a bloodstained and beaten face; He saw the body of Andre lying motionless on top of a fresh grave; Splendidly dressed Michelle was holding her hand out to him invitingly but then her figure moved slowly farther and farther away until she was gone; finally Phillip saw Anna kneeling and praying.

Tears were streaming down his smoke filled eyes now. Phillip closed his burning eyes for a moment for relief. He suddenly snapped back into reality as the stick that he was holding was in flames and beginning to burn his hands. He dropped the stick into the fire, took a step backward, and kneeled down.

"Oh God, how could you let this happened to us?! We wanted to do it FOR you," cried Phillip.

EPILOGUE

A chapter in the lives of Phillip, Anna, Madoc and the others has closed. However, their lives will go on until the story of their time on Earth is completely written and God shuts the book.

The crusade wasn't their life. It was part of their life. God wasn't finished with them yet.

We might look at the incredible events of the Children's Crusade as a dreadful time of history. However, history has continually proven to be unpredictable and often beyond our imaginations. God never works in the ways that we think, "He should."

Like the crusaders, we will experience doubts, fears, faith, friendship, and even disaster. Some will experience life with God and others will experience life alone. But . . . we will all experience life.

In our own lives, when one chapter is done, we must go on to the next. Phillip, Anna, Madoc and the others finished the chapter of the children's crusade in their lives but they still had more experiences, more adventures to live. But those adventures are another story to be told.

APPENDIX

Appendix A:

Personal Questions Raised by the book:

1. What are some possible explanations to the story of Stephen of Cloyes? What might have been an explanation for the testimony of Stephen and the letter that he presented?

2. How could you avoid being caught up in something as spectacular and disastrous as the crusade?

3. Who was to blame for the children's crusade?

4. Do you believe that Anna, Madoc, and Phillip had a personal relationship with Jesus Christ?

Appendix B:

What does God's Word say about who really has a saving personal relationship with Jesus Christ?

1. The Bible says that all people in the world are imperfect before God.
   As it is written, There is none righteous (in perfect standing), no, not one (Romans 3:10).

2. The Bible says that when people disobey what God says it is "sin."

   For all have sinned, and come short of the glory of God (Romans 3:23).

3.   The Bible says that God is a holy (pure an perfect) God. The Bible says that because of His holiness God will have to judge all people. Because of the sinfulness of all people, none have a chance of being acquitted (pronounced innocent).

For the wages (payment) of sin is death; . . ." However . . . .(Romans 6:23a).

4.   God has made a way for every person to be acquitted (pronounced innocent). That way is through the person of Jesus Christ.

. . . but the gift of God is eternal life through Jesus Christ our Lord (Romans 6:23b).

For God so loved the world that he gave his only begotten Son,   that whosoever believes in him will not perish, but have everlasting life (John 3:16).

For by grace are you saved through faith; and that not of yourselves: it is the gift of God: Not of works, lest any man should boast (Ephesians 2:8-9).

5.   The Bible says that a person must want to acknowledge Jesus Christ as Lord (one who has all rights to our lives) and as Savior (one who can and will rescue him from sin's penalty of death). A person must "accept" Christ as personal Savior.

But as many as received him, to them gave he power to become the sons of God, even to them that believe on his name (John 1:12).
That if you will confess with your mouth the Lord Jesus, and will believe in your heart that God has raised him from the dead, you will be saved. For with the heart man believes unto righteousness and with the mouth confession is made unto salvation (Romans 10:9-10).

6.   God promises that a person who calls on Jesus to save him "will be saved."

For whoever will call on the name of the Lord will be saved (Romans 10:13).

These things have I written unto you that believe on the name of the Son of God; that you know that you have eternal life, and that you may believe on the name of the Son of God (1 John 5:13).

Appendix C: Historical Account of the Children's Crusade (Henry Treece)

King Phillip of France was at St. Denis when a twelve-year-old shepherd boy, Stephen of Cloyes, near Orleans, came to him with a letter which the peasant lad sad had come from Christ himself, bidding him organize a crusade to march on Jerusalem.

King Phillip ordered the boy back to his Father's house. Stephen disobeyed the king, announcing that in a vision, Christ had promised that the sea would dry up and allow Stephen, and his followers, to walk dry shod to Jerusalem.

Most clerics were appalled and thought the idea blasphemous.

Pope Innocent III announced that the lad's zealousness "the very children put us to shame," he said.

Children from many parts of France flocked to the boy who had great power of persuasion. They carried banners with signs of the "Ori flamme."

In June 1212 at Vendome an estimated 30,000 young people assembled for the march. They didn't have maps or food supplies.

It is not known why the parents let them go. Maybe the children defied: maybe the parents were afraid of the Popes statement. A lot of fathers were away at war.

Many adult hangers-on joined in, and also some priests.

They marched through Tours and Lyon down to Marseilles, finding food and shelter where they could.

The summer of 1212 had been unusually hot and grain crops failed and food and water scarce (drought).

Many children died by the wayside, while others turned back and tried to find their way home.

After a few days at the Port (the sea not parting), two unscrupulous merchants later to be hanged for attempting to kidnap Emperor Fredrick on behalf of the Saracens, named Hugh the Iron and William the Pig, offered transport to the children in seven ships free of charge.

Steven saw it as the hand of God and accepted. Some days out, the fleet hit a great storm. Two of the transport ships were wrecked on the island of San Pietro, off Sardinia, with almost total loss of life

When the storm abated, the remaining five ships sailed southward to the Saracen port of Bougie, in Algeria, where the French children were sold into slavery.

Some were sent to Egypt where Frankish slaves fetched a good price. About 700 of them were bought by governor Al-Kamil, who used the children as interpreters and secretaries. They probably led nice lives. Al-Kamil made no attempt to make them Islam.

In Bagdad it was reported that eighteen children were beheaded for not converting to Islam.

Note: The very next year a German boy named Nicholas preached a very similar message in Germany. He also mentioned that the Mediterranean Sea would open up for them.

He set off with 20,000 followers towards the Alps. While trying to cross the Alps they were sadly depleted by death and desertions.

They did, however, finally reach Genoa. At Genoa the governor turned away the "hungry sickly rabble."

The crusade shuffled southward but found little pity among the Italians, who could barely feed their own. Some children were halted by the Bishop of Brindisi who fed them and ordered them home over the snow-covered Alps.

A pathetic few reached Rome, where they begged the Pope to release them from their vow until they got older. It is estimated that only 2,000 of the 20,000 ever reached their home again.